Studies in Renaissance Literature

Volume 14

A PLEASING SINNE

DRINK AND CONVIVIALITY IN SEVENTEENTH-CENTURY ENGLAND

Studies in Renaissance Literature

ISSN 1465–6310

General Editors
David Colclough
Raphael Lyne
Graham Parry

Studies in Renaissance Literature offers investigations of topics in English literature focussed in the sixteenth and seventeenth centuries; its scope extends from early Tudor writing, including works reflecting medieval concerns, to the Restoration period. Studies exploring the interplay between the literature of the English Renaissance and its cultural history are particularly welcomed.

Proposals or queries should be sent in the first instance to the publisher at the address below; all submissions receive prompt and informed consideration.

Boydell & Brewer Ltd, PO Box 9, Woodbridge, Suffolk IP12 3DF, UK

A PLEASING SINNE

DRINK AND CONVIVIALITY IN SEVENTEENTH-CENTURY ENGLAND

Edited by
Adam Smyth

D. S. BREWER

First published 2004
D. S. Brewer, Cambridge

ISBN 1 84384 009 X

D. S. Brewer is an imprint of Boydell & Brewer Ltd
PO Box 9, Woodbridge, Suffolk IP12 3DF, UK
and of Boydell & Brewer Inc.
668 Mt Hope Avenue, Rochester, NY 14620, USA
website: www.boydellandbrewer.com

A catalogue record for this title is available
from the British Library

Library of Congress Cataloging-in-Publication Data
A pleasing sinne : drink and conviviality in seventeenth-century England
/ edited by Adam Smyth.
    p. cm. – (Studies in renaissance literature, ISSN 1465–6310 ; v. 14)
Includes bibliographical references and index.
    ISBN 1–84384–009–X (hardback : alk. paper)
    1. Drinking of alcoholic beverages – England – History – 17th century.
2. Drinking customs – England – History – 17th century.   3. Drinking
of alcoholic beverages in literature.   4. Alcoholism in literature.
5. England – Social life and customs – 17th century.   I. Title: Drink and
conviviality in seventeenth-century England.   II. Smyth, Adam, 1972–
III. Series: Studies in Renaissance literature (Woodbridge, Suffolk,
England) ; v. 14.
HV5449.E5P54 2004
394.1'3'094209032 – dc22   2003025516

This publication is printed on acid-free paper

Typeset by Pru Harrison, Woodbridge, Suffolk
Printed in Great Britain by
Cromwell Press Trowbridge Wiltshire

CONTENTS

Contents

CONTRIBUTORS

Stella Achilleos completed her Ph.D. in English Literature at the University of Reading in 2002 and is currently a Lecturer in English at Frederick Institute of Technology, Cyprus. Her research interests focus on the early modern period, particularly on the social, cultural and political contextualisation of literary products and the dissemination of texts to different audiences.

Karen Britland is a Lecturer in Renaissance Literature at Keele University. She works predominantly on Queen Henrietta Maria's court drama, and has published articles on the Queen's French connections and politics. She is also interested in the dramatic representation of women in the Renaissance, and is starting to work on a new project about the relationship of women to tragedy.

Cedric C. Brown is Professor of English, formerly Head of Department, and now Dean of the Faculty of Arts and Humanities at the University of Reading. His publications mostly concern seventeenth-century literature, particularly in relation to its social and political contexts, and include *John Milton: a literary life* (1995) and the co-edited collection *Texts and Cultural Change, 1520–1700* (1997). His current work concerns the social transmission of poetry texts, especially into rural societies. He is also Co-Director of the Renaissance Texts Research Centre in the university and General Editor of the book series *Early Modern Literature in History*.

Tanya M. Cassidy is a cultural historical sociologist employed in the Department of Sociology at the University of Windsor in Canada. She has published widely on issues of drinking, Ireland, national identity and the sociology of ambivalence.

Louise Hill Curth lectures in Early Modern social history at the University of Exeter. Her publications include a number of essays on early modern medical beliefs and practices, vernacular medical books and almanacs. She is editor of *From Physick to Pharmacology: Five Hundred Years of British Drug Retailing* (2004), and author of *Almanacs, astrology and the popular press, 1550–1700* (2004).

Vittoria Di Palma is Assistant Professor of Art History at Rice University, Houston, Texas. After gaining a Ph.D. in Architectural History at Columbia

University, New York, she taught Architectural History and Theory at the Architectural Association, London, from 1999 to 2003. She is currently completing a book on natural history, landscape aesthetics and architecture, entitled *Fragmented Landscapes.*

Marika Keblusek is Professor of Book History at the University of Amsterdam and research fellow at Leiden University, where she leads the research project 'Double Agents: Political and Cultural Brokerage in Early Modern Europe'. She has published several books, and has co-edited *Princely Display at the Court of Frederik Hendrik and Amalia van Solms* (1997). She curated exhibitions at the Hague Historical Museum and the Royal Library, The Hague, and is currently finishing *The Exile Experience,* a study of the intellectual life and book culture of royalist exiles in the Low Countries (1642–1660).

Charles C. Ludington recently completed his dissertation at Columbia University on 'Politics and the Taste for Wine in England and Scotland, 1660–1860'. This study examines the relationship between politics, the taste for wine, the construction of British national identity, and conceptions of English, Scottish and British masculinity. He has published articles on British and Irish intellectual history, the history of the Huguenots in Ireland and the history of the Huguenot diaspora. He is currently working on turning his dissertation into a book and is a lecturer in history at the University of North Carolina at Greensboro and North Carolina State University.

Charlotte McBride completed her Ph.D. in English Literature at Cardiff University in 2001. Her research interests lie in Renaissance drama, sixteenth- and seventeenth-century medical treatises, modern drama and Shakespeare performance history and practice.

Angela McShane Jones lectures in Early Modern History at Warwick University. She has published a number of articles on political ballads, and is broadly interested in the culture of popular politics in early modern Britain and Europe.

Michelle O'Callaghan is a Senior Lecturer in English at Oxford Brookes University. She is the author of *The 'shepheards nation': Jacobean Spenserians and early Stuart political culture* (2000), and is currently working on early seventeenth-century print communities.

Susan J. Owen is Reader in English Literature at the University of Sheffield. She is the author of *Restoration Theatre and Crisis* (1996) and *Perspectives on Restoration Drama* (2002), as well as numerous articles on Restoration writing. She is editor of *A Babel of Bottles: Drink, Drinkers and Drinking Places in*

Literature (2000) and *The Blackwell Companion to Restoration Drama* (2001). Her new research area is working-class writing post-1900.

Adam Smyth is a Lecturer in English at the University of Reading. He is the author of *Profit and Delight: Printed Miscellanies in England, 1640–1682* (2004), as well as a number of articles on early modern poetry, textual transmission, and reading. He is currently working on seventeenth-century diaries.

ACKNOWLEDGEMENTS

This book has its origins in a two-day conference on Drink and Conviviality in Early Modern England, held at the University of Reading in July 2001: seven of the twelve chapters collected here began as papers at this event. Thanks to all the delegates, and to those at Reading who helped the conference run smoothly: in particular, Stella Achilleos, Cedric Brown, Jan Cox, James Daybell, Andrew Gurr, Christopher Hardman, Elizabeth Heale, Ralph Houlbrooke, and Christopher Wilson.

INTRODUCTION

On 8 February 1660, Samuel Pepys recorded a day of heavy, but not atypical, drinking. After a 'little practice on my flagelette, and afterwards walking in my yard to see my stock of pigeons', Pepys

> was called on by Mr. Fossan, my fellow-pupil at Cambridge, and I took him to the Swan in the Palace-yard and drank together our morning draught . . . [then] I met with Captain Lidcott, and so we three went together and drank there . . . and thence to the Renish wine-house, and in our way met with Mr Hoole, where I paid for my Cosen Rogr. Pepys his wine . . . At home, my wife's brother brought her a pretty black dog which I liked very well, and went away again . . . and thence to my father's . . . and I went down to his kitchen, and there we eat and drank; and about 9 a-clock I went away homewards, and . . . to bed with my head not well, by my too much drinking today. And I had a boyle under my chin which troubled me cruelly.[1]

In the course of his diary, Pepys records a great range of drinks that he consumed, including ale, cider, beer, brandy, buttermilk, chocolate, gruel, elder spirits, julep, mead, metheglin, water, milk, coffee, orange juice,[2] posset, tea, strong waters, whey, and many varieties of wine – Rhenish, Muscadine, English; sack, Bristol milk, canary, claret, hippocras, Malaga, Navarre.[3]

This litany of drink induces a familiar Pepysian swing between delight and guilty regret. Pepys proudly and competitively records the extent of his wine collection, describing his bottles as 'a condition it hath pleased God to bring me':

> at this time I have two tierces of claret – two quarter-cask of canary, and a smaller vessel of sack – a vessel of tent [red Spanish wine], another of Malaga, and another of white wine, all in my wine-cellar together – which I believe none of my friends now alive ever had of his own at one time.[4]

---

1   *The Diary of Samuel Pepys*, ed. Robert Latham and William Matthews (London: Bell and Hyman, 1970), vol. 1, pp. 45–6.
2   *Diary*, 9 March 1669, vol. 9, p. 477: 'to my Cosen Stradwicks . . . and here, which I never did before, I drank a glass, of a pint I believe, at one draught, of the juice of Oranges of whose peel they make comfits; and here they drink the juice as wine, with sugar, and it is a very fine drink; but it being new, I was doubtful whether it might not do me hurt'.
3   For a brief but highly entertaining survey of drink in Pepys's *Diary*, see Oscar A. Mendelsohn, *Drinking with Pepys* (London & New York: Macmillan, 1963).
4   *Diary*, 7 July 1665, vol. 6, p. 151. For further thoughts on this quotation, see Charles C.

But Pepys also notes in detail the physical ailments he suffered after drinking: 'I could not sleep . . . being overheated with drink . . . [and] quite out of order';[5] 'my brains somewhat troubled with so much wine';[6] 'About the middle of the night I was very ill, I think with eating and drinking too much . . . and vomited in the bason.'[7] These physical ailments seem to stand, for Pepys, as markers of his moral transgression. When Pepys realised he was developing a reputation as a heavy drinker, he was 'much troubled', and lamented how 'my late little drinking of wine is taken notice of by envious men to my disadvantage'.[8] Certainly Pepys regarded the sober Samuel as an improved self, both morally, and physically: 'since my leaving drinking of wine, I do find myself much better and to mind my business better and to spend less money, and less time lost in idle company'.[9] Consequently, resolutions to leave off alcohol – 'to drink no strong drink this week'[10] – echo throughout his diary. On 18 January 1661 Pepys notes a visit with

> Mr [Thomas] Hollier [the surgeon who operated on Pepys for the stone in 1658] to the Greyhound – where he did advise me above all things both as to the Stone and the decay of my memory (of which I now complain to him), to avoyd drinking often; which I am resolved, if I can, to leave off.[11]

Pepys's *Diary* does more than simply suggest the centrality of alcohol to the life of one early modern Londoner, and I would like – as a beginning to this volume – to extract three particular significances of the consumption of drink for Pepys and the culture he occupied. The moral ambiguity of alcohol is perhaps most vividly articulated. Pepys's account, I have noted, oscillates between celebration and regret. In part this reflects the writer's particular way of engaging with the world: his whole-hearted plunges at life, and his subsequent doubts and misgivings. But this oscillation also signals a larger cultural ambivalence about alcohol that is, to this day, unresolved. Was alcohol a source of health, or illness? A force for social bonding, or a catalyst for disorder and rebellion? A marker of social grace, or a sign of debasement? Just as Pepys wrestled with contradictory impulses – pride, guilt, delight, regret – so the great wealth of texts that reflected and shaped seventeenth-century culture contested the moral, social, and political significances of alcohol.

In addition to this sense of profound equivocation, Pepys's notes suggest a

---

Ludington's chapter in this volume, ' "Be sometimes to your country true": The Politics of Wine in England, 1660–1714'.

5 *Diary*, 9 March 1660, vol. 1, p. 84.
6 *Diary*, 1 December 1660, vol. 1, p. 307.
7 *Diary*, 27 December 1660, vol. 1, p. 323.
8 *Diary*, 27 September 1665, vol. 6, p. 243.
9 *Diary*, 26 January 1662, vol. 3, p. 18.
10 *Diary*, 9 March 1660, vol. 1, p. 84.
11 *Diary*, vol. 1, p. 17. As Louise Hill Curth and Tanya M. Cassidy note in their chapter in this volume, Pepys frequently renounced wine, but not ale or beer.

recurring connection between alcohol and sociability. Again, partly this is Pepys, with his compulsive conviviality, and his boundless curiosity for new people, ideas, experiences. But it is also more than this, and other texts that meditate on drink, whether encomiums or censures, overwhelmingly draw a similar connection. Indeed, the solitary drinker was (and is) a powerfully transgressive figure:[12] the courtier poet William Habington criticises the man who 'can in his closet drinke, / Drunke even alone, and thus made wise create / As dangerous plots as the Low Countery state',[13] and when Pepys records his drinking alone, he is careful to emphasise the medicinal function – to temper, or justify the act: 'I did all alone, *for health's sake*, drink half a pint of Rhenish wine at the Stillyard, mixed with beere.'[14] Thus to consider seventeenth-century drinking is also to consider friendship, community, conviviality.

Habington's alignment of solitary drinking with seditious plotting intro-duces a third connotation of alcohol suggested in Pepys's *Diary*: the potential connection between drink and politics. Drinking could be a highly politicised act, as Pepys frequently indicates, as both observer, and participant.

> Today I hear they were very merry at Deale, setting up the Kings flag upon one of their Maypoles and drinking his health upon their knees in the streets and firing the guns.[15]

> Two guns given to every man while he was drinking the King's health, and so likewise to the Dukes healths.[16]

Pepys also recalls a scene in Axe Yard where

> there was three great bonefyres and a great many great gallants, men and women; and they laid hold of us and would have us drink the King's health upon our knee, kneeling upon a fagott; which we all did, they drinking to us one after another.[17]

Pepys describes this scene as 'a strange Frolique', and his expression of surprised interest – his sense of the novelty of the scene – registers the degree to which drink could function differently, at different moments: the political significances of alcohol were shifting, even across the relatively narrow confines of Pepys's account.

Among many other things, this book investigates these three central issues:

---

[12] Susanna Barrows and Robin Room (eds), *Drinking Behavior and Belief in Modern History* (Los Angeles: University of California Press, 1991), p. 7.

[13] Quoted in Joshua Scodel, *Excess and the Mean in Early Modern English Literature* (Princeton & Oxford: Princeton University Press, 2002), pp. 215–16. Habington's lines come from his 'To a Friend, Inviting him to a meeting upon promise'.

[14] *Diary*, 21 October 1663, vol. 4, p. 343. My italics.

[15] *Diary*, 1 May 1660, vol. 1, p. 121.

[16] *Diary*, 22 May 1660, vol. 1, p. 152.

[17] *Diary*, 23 April 1661, vol. 2, p. 87.

the cultural ambiguity of drink; the connection between drink and sociability; and the changing political resonances of alcohol. And I stress alcohol: there are unfortunately not pages enough, here, to offer more than passing comment on other kinds of consumption (particularly coffee, tea, chocolate and tobacco), their seventeenth-century significance, and their relation to varieties of alcohol.[18]

While Pepys's account is enormously suggestive, it remains a single account, and it is worth finding space for some more general categories and definitions about early modern drinking: what was drunk; how much was consumed; and where drinking took place. These definitions – and the significance of these definitions – will, in the course of the volume, be nuanced and complicated, but they provide at least a point of origin.

In early modern England, there was a fundamental distinction between ale and beer, on the one hand, and wine, on the other. Ale (fermented malt, water, spices) and beer (fermented malt, water, and, crucially, hops) were cheaper, more widely available, and often (but not always) associated with health – hence Pepys's morning draught.[19] These drinks provided a cleaner alternative to water and were drunk by just about everyone, including children.[20] Across the sixteenth and seventeenth centuries, there was a broad shift in popular taste from ale to beer. For about the same price as ale, beer offered a stronger, clearer, brighter flavour, and could be preserved and transported with fewer detrimental consequences to its quality.[21] Initially confined to the south and

---

[18] For work in this area, see the forthcoming book by Marcy Norton, *American Offerings: A History of Tobacco and Chocolate, 1492–1700.* Among seventeenth-century texts, two are worthy of particular note. John Chamberlain's *The Manner of Making of Coffee, Tea, and Chocolate. As it is used In most parts of Europe, Asia, Africa, and America. With their Vertues. Newly doen out of French and Spanish* (1685) records that these drinks are (like alcohol) subject to contesting interpretations, and makes a vehement case for coffee as a drink with apparently endless benefits to the drinker's health. Coffee, 'being drunk dries up all the cold and moist humours, disperses the wind, fortifies the Liver, eases the dropsie by its purifying quality, 'tis a Sovereign medicine against the itch, and corruptions of the blood, refreshes the heart, and the vital beating thereof, it relieves those that have pains in their Stomach, and cannot eat: It is good also against the indispositions of the brain, cold, moist, and heavy, the steam which rises out of it is good against the *Rheums* of the eyes, and drumming in the ears . . . [/] It is an extraordinary ease against the Worms' (pp. 11–12). *The Character of a Coffee-House* (1675) is interesting for its application of established alcohol-connotations to coffee and coffee drinkers, and for its lament that while a literature celebrating alcohol exists, no fit language for coffee celebrations is available: 'All these [kinds of alcohol] have had their pens to raise / Them *Monuments* of lasting praise, / Onely poor *Coffee* seems to me / No subject fit for *Poetry*' (p. 10). This latter text suggests representations of taverns, inns and alehouses informed understandings of later coffee houses: another area that requires investigation.

[19] For notes on ale, see Mendelsohn, *Drinking*, pp. 28–39. As Louise Hill Curth and Tanya M. Cassidy note, below, wine was also sometimes associated with health.

[20] Judith M. Bennett, *Ale, Beer, and Brewsters in England: Women's Work in a Changing World, 1300–1600* (New York & Oxford: Oxford University Press, 1996), pp. 8–9.

[21] Ibid., p. 9.

east, and to Dutch or Flemish immigrants, the beer brewing industry gradually spread across England and ale was increasingly confined to rural areas.[22]

Wine was generally less common and more expensive,[23] and so tended to generate connotations of exclusivity.[24] In his 1587 survey of England and, in particular, in his account 'Of the Food and Diet of the English', William Harrison records the great variety of wines that were regularly consumed by his countrymen:

> small [weak] wines . . . as claret, white, red, French, etc., which amount to about fifty-six sorts, according to the number of regions from whence they come, but also of the thirty kinds of Italian, Grecian, Spanish [including the oft-mentioned sack, a sweet wine, rather like an unfortified sherry], Canarian, etc., whereof vernage [a strong, sweet Italian wine], cut [or cute or cuit; new wine boiled down to produce a thicker, sweet drink], piment [wine mixed with honey and spices], raspis [a strong, sweet wine], muscatel [or Muskadine or muscadel; from the Muscadine grape]; rumeny [or rumney or romney; a resinated wine from Greece], bastard [from the Bastardo grape], tyre [a strong, sweet wine, made in Calabria, Sicily], osey [or ossey; a Portuguese wine], caprike [a sweet wine], clary [a spiced wine, like hippocras], and malmsey [from the Malvasia grape, grown in Italy, Spain and southern Greece] are not least of all accounted of, because of their strength and valure. For, as I have said in meat, the stronger the wine is, the more it is desired.[25]

Harrison's account not only records diversity; it also suggests a discourse of wine that is alert to variations, distinctions, hierarchies. As the chapters that follow will show, this sensitivity is an important feature of seventeenth-century writing about drink.

Also consumed were spirits, sometimes known as 'strong waters', such as brandy, and aqua vitae (or 'burning water') – the latter generally a medicinal drink, distilled from wine, with herbs and spices and sometimes gold, and taken a spoonful at a time.[26] Composite drinks were popular, too, like Pepys's 'half a pint of Rhenish wine . . . mixed with beere'.[27] Among these drinks, most

---

22 Peter Clark, 'The Alehouse and the Alternative Society', in *Puritans and Revolutionaries. Essays in Seventeenth-Century History presented to Christopher Hill*, ed. by Donald Pennington and Keith Thomas (Oxford: Clarendon Press, 1978), pp. 47–72, p. 51.

23 For an estimate of the prices of drinks, see Stuart Peachey, *The Tipler's Guide To Drink and Drinking in the early 17th Century* (Bristol: Stuart Press, 1992), p. 9.

24 Notions of exclusivity did not always surround wine: as Louise Hill Curth and Tanya M. Cassidy discuss, below, in ' "Health, Strength and Happiness": Medical Constructions of Wine and Beer in Early Modern England', cheap wine was often available. Note, too, Angela McShane Jones, 'Roaring Royalists and Ranting Brewers: The Politicisation of Drink and Drunkenness in Political Broadside Ballads from 1640 to 1689', below, which also suggests that wine might have been more widely available.

25 William Harrison, *The Description of England*, ed. by Georges Edelen (Washington, DC & New York: The Folger Shakespeare Library and Dover Publications, 1994), p. 130.

26 Peachey, *Drink*, p. 35.

27 *Diary*, vol. 3, p. 343.

common were braggett (fermented ale and honey, often flavoured with spices); caudle (a warm and supposedly healthy mix of wine or ale with eggs, bread, sugar and spices);[28] buttered beer (a hot spiced mix of eggs, beer and butter); hippocras (or hypocras or ipocras; a hot sweet-spiced wine, filtered through a woollen bag known as 'Hippocrates' Sleeve');[29] and possetts and syllabubs – somewhere between a food and a drink, composed of a mix of ale or sack (or, later in the seventeenth century, cider) with milk or cream and often bread.[30]

Different drinks found particular favour in different regions. Perry, or pear cider, for instance, was popular in the West Marches, while cider was most frequently consumed in the West Country. Metheglin (a kind of mead – that is, wine and honey – with cloves, ginger, rosemary, hyssop and thyme) was considered a Welsh drink.[31]

By most modern expectations, early modern consumption of alcohol was strikingly high. Pepys's writings attest to this, but so too do many other sources. Stuart Peachey's analysis of the account books of the Berkshire farmer Robert Loder between 1611 and 1618 provides a quantitative indication of consumption levels for one particular household.[32] Loder's farm was large, with between 8 and 11 individuals working his 300 acres, and Loder's accounts suggest the household was making on average one gallon of first brew (a stronger beer) and half a gallon of small (weaker) beer, per head, per day. This means that on average between 6 and 8 pints of beer were consumed per person, each day. What seems like a strikingly high figure is partly explained by the fact that beer was the standard drink for those involved in manual labour, and a replacement for water. Nonetheless, the levels are remarkable from a modern perspective. William Harrison, author of the *Description of England*, notes that he had 200 gallons brewed every month in his household, for a cost of only 20 shillings a time. The size of Harrison's household is not known, but clearly consumption was significant, and production cheap.[33] Perhaps conscious of these levels, Harrison displaced the cause of English thirst on to geography:

> The situation of our region, lying near unto the north, doth cause the heat of our stomachs to be of somewhat greater force; therefore our bodies do crave a little more ample nourishment than the inhabitants of the hotter regions are accustomed withal . . . it is no marvel therefore that our tables are oftentimes more plentifully garnished than those of other nations.[34]

Harrison and Loder were brewing and drinking privately, but as Pepys's

---

28 Mendelsohn, *Drinking*, p. 58.
29 Ibid., pp. 51–2.
30 Peachey, *Drink*, pp. 57–66; Mendelsohn, *Drinking*, pp. 57–8.
31 Clark, 'Alehouse', p. 51; Mendelsohn, *Drinking*, pp. 54–5.
32 Stuart Peachey, *The Yeoman's Food* (Bristol: Stuart Press, 2000), p. 7.
33 Keith Thomas, *Religion and the Decline of Magic* (London: Penguin, 1973), p. 21.
34 Harrison, *Description*, pp. 123–4.

account suggests, alcohol and sociability were linked and drinking sites were often public. The principal public spaces for consuming alcohol were the alehouse, inn, and tavern.[35] There is some slippage between these terms, but there were also connotations surrounding each site, and a clear sense of a hierarchy between the venues. Alehouses (or 'tipling houses', or, after about 1660, 'public houses'[36]) were the most common drinking venue, and were perceived, at least by the middle and upper classes, as establishments run by the poor, for the poor.[37] Peter Clark lists the visitors to one particular unlicensed alehouse at New Romney in 1606, run by a Samuel Wood, and records a Jonsonian range of types: an itinerant baker; a Fulham butcher, unemployed and looking for 'work in haying'; a shoemaker; and a Dover rippier called 'Jack the Pouch'.[38] Alehouses were often contained within the normal house of the keepers – they might constitute a cellar, or a curtained-off area in a large room: poor households often set up as alehouses to supplement their income, with the wife playing a central role in the running of the alehouse.[39] Ale and beer (frequently brewed on site) were the drinks generally consumed; basic food might also be available, including cakes, buns and cheese, and there was often a room available to travellers.

The law dictated that the proper function of alehouses was either 'for the receit, release, and lodging of Wayfairing people travelling from place to place about their necessary bussinesse', or 'for the necessary supply of the wants of such poore persons as are not able by greater quantities to make their provision of victuals'. Alehouses were not 'ment for the entertainment or harbouring of lewd or idle people, to spend or consume their money or time there'.[40] Inevitably, despite these official declarations, different kinds of functions emerged.

---

35 The most important sources here are two works by Peter Clark: *The English Alehouse: A Social History 1200–1830* (London: Longman, 1983), and 'Alehouse'. Also valuable are Beat Kümin and B. Ann Tlusty (eds), *The World of the Tavern* (Aldershot: Ashgate, 2002), in particular Judith Hunter, 'English Inns, Taverns, Alehouses and Brandy Shops: The Legislative Framework, 1495–1797', pp. 65–82 (for a more detailed version of this account, see Judith Hunter, 'Legislation, Royal Proclamations and other National Directives affecting Inns, Taverns, Alehouses, Brandy Shops and Punch Houses, 1552–1757', Ph.D., University of Reading (1994)); Alan Everitt, 'The English Urban Inn, 1560–1760', in his *Perspectives in English Urban History* (London: Macmillan, 1973); David W. Conroy, 'Puritans in Taverns: Law and Popular Culture in Colonial Massachusetts, 1630–1720', in Barrows and Room, *Drinking*, pp. 29–60; and Peachey, *Drink*.

36 Steven Earnshaw, *The Pub in Literature: England's altered state* (Manchester & New York: Manchester University Press, 2000), p. 5.

37 Clark, 'Alehouse', p. 53. On the question of who attended drinking establishments, see Beat Kümin, 'Public Houses and their Patrons in Early Modern Europe', in Kümin and Tlusty (eds), *Tavern*, pp. 44–62.

38 Clark, 'Alehouse', p. 54.

39 See Bennett, *Brewsters*.

40 Michael Dalton, *The Countrey Justice*, quoted in Peachey, *Drink*, p. 5. The first edition of Dalton's text (1618) is available in a recent facsimile (Walter J. Johnson & Theatrum Orbis Terrarum: Amsterdam and New Jersey, 1975).

Indoor games were commonly played in the alehouse – shove-groat, slide-thrist, tyck-tack, guile-bones or ten-bones, rifling, skittles, and nine-holes – and gambling, previously a largely upper-class phenomenon, became a popular alehouse pursuit.[41] The sixteenth century saw a huge expansion in the number of alehouses: by 1577 there were 14,000 alehouses in 27 counties, and numbers grew particularly quickly in urban areas.[42] Numbers continued to increase in the seventeenth century: one 1630s report cites 30,000 alehouses in England and Wales.[43] Despite attempts by government to exert control over the alehouses – statutory licensing was introduced in 1552; a 1621 proclamation offered a detailed list of prohibitions; and 1635 drinking laws attempted to regulate who could drink in establishments, costs, and the licensing of sites – laws were laxly enforced, and unlicensed alehouses were common.[44] As a result, alehouses became a source of anxiety for ruling classes – spaces associated with potential disorder and disloyalty. In a 1616 speech to Star Chamber, James I declared the 'abundance of alehouses' to be a major concern and linked alehouses with thieves by declaring that alehouses were places of 'receipt' for 'Stealers of my deer' and of horses, oxen, and sheep from the country at large: 'There would be no thieves, if they had not their receipts, and these Alehouses as their dennes.'[45] While Peter Clark has argued that alehouses never in fact became sites of serious social or political disorder, anxieties about their potential as disruptive influences were persistent.

The inn was, generally, a larger drinking site than the alehouse, with rooms that were furnished more grandly, perhaps with paintings and panelling. Inns catered for a more socially eminent clientele. Wine and distilled liquors were sold; a wider range of food was on offer (including hot food); and accommodation was available. Inns often occupied a central location, and might have extensive stables, and warehouses. As Peter Clark has noted, inns became increasingly important as locations for meetings between town merchants, county justices, and landowners, and, as a result, were often associated with a social and political elite. The 1577 survey of 27 counties listed about 2,000 inns, mostly in larger towns: far fewer than the number of alehouses at that time.[46]

The third drinking site, the tavern, is a space considered in several chapters, below. The tavern was positioned somewhere between the alehouse and the inn in terms of its facilities and the social position of its customers – although, as Michelle O'Callaghan makes clear, the tavern might play a crucial role, in the manner just described for inns, in fostering sociability among an urban elite. The term 'tavern' generally referred to a site selling wine[47] – indeed a

---

41 Clark, 'Alehouse', p. 63.
42 Ibid., p. 50.
43 Barrows and Room, *Drinking*, p. 36.
44 See Hunter, 'Legislative Framework', especially pp. 66–7.
45 Quoted in Barrows and Room, *Drinking*, p. 35.
46 Clark, 'Alehouse', pp. 48–50.
47 Hunter, 'Legislative Framework', p. 70.

tavern could be a sub-section of an inn, where wine was served – and the site was generally an urban establishment, in some ways, socially, prefiguring later coffee houses. Some food might be sold, but accommodation was generally not available.

Of course these terms of definition, simplistically distilled in this brief introduction, were subject to contestations and reworkings. (Michelle O'Callaghan's chapter, in particular, thickens and complicates my summary of the tavern.) In fact the notion that across the seventeenth century drinking and conviviality were practised in different ways, at different moments, and that they were subject to varying forms of textual representation and interpretation, is a fundamental point from which all of the following chapters begin.

Cedric C. Brown opens the book by juxtaposing two poets both speaking from rural locations – one famous, the other virtually unknown – for whom alcohol was a central subject. In 'Sons of Beer and Sons of Ben: Drink as a Social Marker in Seventeenth-Century England', Brown examines the social functions of alcohol by exploring rituals of friendship, civility, and conviviality in the work of his two poets. In Robert Herrick's epigram collection *Hesperides*, drink has a dual significance: it signifies a prosperous, unified society, but it is also socially gradated. Superior wine, resonant with notions of exclusivity, is consistently contrasted with common ale and beer. In the manuscript writings of the Derbyshire yeoman and poet Leonard Wheatcroft ('variously tailor, tree and hedge planter, alehouse keeper, church clerk . . . petty school master, militia man, self-styled "recorder" of his parish and country, and The Black Poet'), alcohol functions as a means to and a sign of social inclusivity, and Wheatcroft's habitual drink is ale or beer, not wine. He was what the essentially urbane discourse of Herrick, following Ben Jonson, sought to deny as a valuable category, a poet of ale and not a poet of wine.

Stella Achilleos sustains this interest in representations of wine and conviviality in poetry by considering the translation and dissemination of the *Anacreontea* – that collection of short Greek lyrics celebrating the pleasures of love and wine, ascribed, in the early modern period, to the Greek lyric poet Anacreon. In 'The *Anacreontea* and a Tradition of Refined Male Sociability', Achilleos demonstrates how the anacreontic was associated with male sociability and, in particular, a tradition of elite male clubbing, including the convivial drinking sessions of Ben Jonson and his 'sons' in the late 1620s and early 1630s. Achilleos then traces how, in later periods, the anacreontic genre became more widely reproduced in the vernacular, and became a more popular mode, informing a less exclusive, male leisure culture.

Drink and community is also the theme at the heart of Chapter 3. In 'Tavern Societies, the Inns of Court, and the Culture of Conviviality in Early Seventeenth-Century London', Michelle O'Callaghan's focus is the space of the London tavern and its role in fostering forms of sociability and identity among members of the urban elite. O'Callaghan considers in particular the 'right Worshipfull Fraternitie of Sireniacal Gentlemen', a group of writers, politicians, lawyers, courtiers, and business men who met at the Mermaid tavern in the early seventeenth century. This Sireniacal fraternity was a kind of mutual society, functioning to further the personal, business, and professional interests of its members; it provided a space for political discussion; and it served as a site for members to fashion and demonstrate their civility. Through this discussion, O'Callaghan shows how there were close relationships between London taverns, the Inns of Court, and the House of Commons.

Chapters 4, 5 and 6 consider the various and shifting ways in which drinking was imbued with particular political significances. In 'Wine for Comfort: Drinking and the Royalist Exile Experience, 1642–1660', Marika Keblusek's subject is the use of drink, and writings about drink, by royalists in exile in the Netherlands. Keblusek demonstrates that particular drinks articulated particular political allegiances, and she explores the dichotomy between wine, resonant with royalist connotations, and beer, often read (particularly by royalists) as parliamentarian. Keblusek considers royalist celebrations of wine, and the use of wine as a signal of defiant royalist identity; a means to mock puritan critiques; and a mechanism for driving off melancholy amid political hardship. Keblusek also argues that parliamentarians contested these interpretations, representing the drinking royalist as drunk and debauched: more lewd than loyal. Keblusek then explores the gap between royalist celebrations of wine in poetry, and the records of lived royalist experience – where drink, a unifier in verse, might function in practice as a source of division, discord and violence.

Shifting from elite to popular texts, Angela McShane Jones examines broadside ballads produced between 1640 and 1689, and in 'Roaring Royalists and Ranting Brewers', she considers the complex and changing political constructions of drink and drunkenness. Perhaps of most importance is McShane Jones's argument that earlier constructions of drink and drunkenness were picked up and developed in later political circumstances. The royalist–parliamentarian dichotomy of the 1650s – explored by Marika Keblusek – evolved, in the 1670s, into an opposition between drinking Tories (who claimed to be merry and loyal), and sober Whigs. McShane Jones also shows how particular political leaders were depicted in terms of drink and drunkenness – most famously Oliver Cromwell, but also, later, Anthony Ashley Cooper, Earl of Shaftesbury, whose colostemic tap enabled accusations that he had an ale tap in his side, and was a cask, personified.

Exploring some of the associations set out by McShane Jones, Charles C. Ludington pushes the chronology further and traces changing consumption patterns, and changing political connotations, of wine. In ' "Be sometimes to your country true": The Politics of Wine in England, 1660–1714', Ludington considers a profound shift in English drinking habits, as popular preference for wine altered dramatically from claret to port in the later seventeenth century. Ludington argues, first, that this change was a consequence of high politics, and, in particular, of England's largely hostile relationship with France; and second, that claret and port came to stand for particular kinds of political allegiance: as a French wine, claret symbolised the Tories and their desire for a *rapprochement* with France, while port, its supposed Portuguese equivalent, became associated with the Whig party and its anti-Gallicanism.

While Pepys's *Diary* is generally quiet about female drinkers, other early modern writers present a very different picture: commenting on drinking sites in London in 1599, Thomas Platter remarked that 'what is particularly curious is that the women as well as the men, in fact more than they, will frequent the taverns or alehouses for enjoyment'.[48] Recent work, including Angela McShane Jones's chapter in this collection, has argued that females were heavily involved in drinking cultures – as producers, sellers, and consumers of alcohol (and in particular of ale or beer).[49] Two chapters in this present volume consider representations of women and drink in dramatic texts. In 'Circe's Cup: Wine and Women in Early Modern Drama', Karen Britland investigates ways in which conviviality is represented in a selection of early modern tragedies, and considers how the convivial relates to ideas of the feminine. Through a discussion of Shakespeare's *Troilus and Cressida* and *Antony and Cleopatra*, and John Marston's *The Wonder of Women, or The Tragedie of Sophonisba*, Britland argues that woman is that upon which conviviality depends, and yet, at the same time, is that which conviviality attempts to exclude. Early modern dramatic representations of woman, Britland argues, suggest a paradox: 'Woman . . . is at once essential to the well-being and growth of a community, and yet her presence seems to threaten its integrity; she, like a Helen, a Cleopatra, or a Circe, can divert a man from his proper public role as a soldier and leader, and carry him into chaos.'

Susan J. Owen's 'Drink, Sex and Power in Restoration Comedy' considers two later seventeenth-century plays – William Wycherley's *The Country Wife*, and Aphra Behn's *The Rover* – and argues that drink was of central importance to these texts. In Aphra Behn's *The Rover*, Owen suggests that the treatment of drink reveals a profound ambiguity about libertinism: libertines are 'predatory but also desirable; powerful, but always in danger of becoming the disempowered objects of desire . . . of becoming the mocked rather than the mocker'. Owen then reads William Wycherley's *The Country Wife*, and argues that drinking – in particular, women drinking – has a vital role to play in

---

[48] *Thomas Platter's Travels in England*, translated by Clare Williams (London: Cape, 1937), p. 171. Quoted in Pamela Allen Brown, *Better a Shrew than a Sheep: Women, Drama, and the Culture of Jest in Early Modern England* (Ithaca & London: Cornell University Press, 2003), p. 73.

[49] For a study of the link between women and the brewing industry, see Bennett, *Brewsters*. For a discussion of women and alehouse culture that disputes depictions of the alehouse as an over-whelmingly male environment, see Brown, *Women, Drama, and the Culture of Jest*, chapter 2, 'Ale and Female: Gossips as Players, Alehouse as Theater', pp. 56–82.

altering the balance of power between the sexes, and in reflecting and inducing female agency.

In ' "Health, Strength and Happiness": Medical Constructions of Wine and Beer in Early Modern England', Louise Hill Curth and Tanya M. Cassidy survey the many early modern medicinal benefits ascribed to wine, beer, and ale. Through an examination of vernacular medical books, Curth and Cassidy argue that the controlled drinking of alcohol was considered an easily accessible means of maintaining health that individuals could self-administer, without recourse to a doctor. Such healthy prescriptions, however, were always susceptible to misuse, and Curth and Cassidy consider the fine line between alcohol as a force for health, on the one hand, and sickness, on the other. Both excessive and insufficient consumption of alcohol were regarded as causes of illness.

In 'Drinking Cider in Paradise: Science, Improvement, and the Politics of Fruit Trees', Vittoria Di Palma turns from wine, beer and ale, to cider – an unambiguously English drink, made from the fruit growing plentifully in Kentish and Herefordshire orchards. Di Palma examines the promotion of fruit tree cultivation and cider production by members of early scientific communities in England – including Samuel Hartlib, John Evelyn, and John Beale – and discusses the patriotic, religious, and scientific discourses embedded in their efforts to improve national husbandry. Crucially, the concept of improvement was used to liken the planting of an orchard to the cultivation of the soul: husbandry was presented as an activity leading to personal salvation, and the improvement of England through agriculture was made equivalent to the transformation of the wilderness into the Garden of Eden.

If medicinal guides, and writers such as Hartlib, prescribed an association between drinking, moderation, health and improvement, many other texts connected alcohol with a drunken excess that was vividly described, often lamented, and sometimes celebrated. Charlotte McBride considers the way in which perceived patterns of consumption – including ideas of extreme drinking – shaped notions of English national identity. In 'A Natural Drink for an English Man: National Stereotyping in Early Modern Culture', McBride argues that drunkenness, and drunken conviviality, were understood as particularly English conditions. Drunkenness was also considered a threat to the well-being of the nation state, and in order to control and stigmatise excessive drinking, drunkenness was often linked to madness.

My own chapter – ' "It were far better be a *Toad*, or a *Serpant*, then a Drunkard": Writing About Drunkenness' – presents, initially, a survey of the transformations that seventeenth-century texts suggest drunkards underwent. Drinkers were afflicted with a loss of reason, and of language, and of autonomy, and were converted from men into beasts. But I suggest that these writings about drink consistently exhibit two complicating anxieties: first, the narrator's expertise suggests a compromising familiarity with the world of drink being condemned; and second, in order to convince readers of the seductive dangers of alcohol, anti-drinking texts assert drink's seductive power, and so come precariously close to celebrating alcohol. Censure and encomium blur. I then consider one particular text, which sought to celebrate and indeed encourage heavy drinking, and investigate the ways in which this particular book engaged with and attempted to defuse the common criticisms made of drunkenness.

Drink and Conviviality in Seventeenth-Century England is the work of literary scholars, historians, and a sociologist, and while the chapters are united in their focus on early modern accounts of drink and conviviality, there is – as this brief overview suggests – a diversity of interests and methodologies. In their pursuit of textual representations of drinking, contributors turn to a great variety of sources: ballads; import records; drinking guides; drama by Behn, Jonson, Shakespeare, Wycherley, Fletcher, Marston, and others; parliamentary legislation; diaries; gardening and husbandry treatises; sermons; foreign treaties; verse collections; guides to medicine and healthy living; letters; statutes; popular pamphlets; and many other sorts of writing. On 10 December 1660, Pepys recorded an evening visit 'to the Coffee House in Cornhill, the first time that ever I was there, and I found much pleasure in it, through the diversity of company and discourse'.[50] I hope the present range of contributions is similarly inducive to interest and excitement, and I hope that the book suggests and begins to open up many large cultural issues still waiting to be fully explored.

---

[50] *Diary*, vol. 3, p. 315.

Identity and Community

1

Sons of Beer and Sons of Ben: Drink as a Social Marker in Seventeenth-Century England

CEDRIC C. BROWN

THERE is a huge, under-investigated connection between the cultures of drink and conviviality and the formations of literary texts in the early modern period. In the face of a bewildering number of choices across many literary forms, I want to identify some social encoding by concentrating on poetry texts by just two practitioners who between them span much of the seventeenth century. One of my exemplars is familiar: Robert Herrick in his collection of short, often epigrammatic poems, *Hesperides*.[1] Though probably assembled by 1647, this collection was published in 1649 in a post-Civil War context and from the perspective of his Devonshire benefice. However, as one scholar has put it, the very act of publication is, like one of the poems, 'His returne to London',[2] and the book contains many traces of his earlier poetic practice in social circles in London from the 1620s. The other is not canonical at all, and never could be, though his texts have a lot to tell us about the popularity and distribution of poems and songs in his provincial community. The poems of Leonard Wheatcroft of Ashover, Derbyshire, variously tailor, tree and hedge planter, alehouse keeper, church clerk (and 'register' and sexton), occasionally petty schoolmaster, militia man, self-styled 'recorder' of his parish and country, and The Black Poet, have miraculously survived, along with an autobiography and other manuscript books for which he and his son

---

[1] References are to *The Poetical Works of Robert Herrick*, ed. L.C. Martin (Oxford: Clarendon Press, 1956). For a recent discussion of Herrick's drinking poetry, see Joshua Scodel, *Excess and the Mean in Early Modern Literature* (Princeton & Oxford: Princeton University Press, 2002), chapter 7: 'Drinking and the Politics of Poetic Identity from Jonson to Herrick', pp. 199–224.

[2] James Loxley, *Royalism and Poetry in the English Civil War: The Drawn Sword* (Basingstoke & London: Macmillan; NY: St Martin's Press, 1997), p. 230.

Titus were responsible.[3] (Titus, the youngest son, was in effect his father's editor, and the chief agent in the formation of a book collection.) Wheatcroft's occasional poems come from the second half of the seventeenth century. I set these two bodies of work against each other, because the literary identities fashioned in them are much bound up with the social uses of wine and beer, and because I can create dialogue between them in a rather diagrammatic way. In fact, each body of work both supports and embarrasses the other. This dialogue in turn may suggest some wider patterns of definition.

To begin with, why choose Herrick's *Hesperides*? Because it furnishes a fascinating if problematical example of social encoding, as well as of accomplished genre writing, and many have remarked on the centrality in it of issues of friendship and drink. These in turn are associated with the production of lyric poetry. Herrick often records the enlivening of the imagination by drink, though he also conventionally contrasts the uncontrolled with the moderate. What is particularly sought and remembered in his texts in fact are rituals of civility, also providing the context for literary exchange. But drink is not simply to be explained as the precondition of poetry, without further distinctions. Let us start with material differences by classifying the drink, and I begin my stratification with ale and beer. Although there will be mention of different and special versions of both of these, and of wine, I leave to others in this volume a closer examination of the range and precise make-up of drinks in circulation at the time.[4] My concerns are with broader cultural definitions, and

---

[3] The poetry collection (hereafter 'Come you gallants') is Derbys RO, D.253A/PZ 5/1. For the autobiography (Derbys RO, D.2079) I quote from the printed edition: 'The Autobiography of Leonard Wheatcroft of Ashover, 1627–1706', ed. Dorothy Riden, *Transactions of the Derbyshire Record Society*, vol. XX (1993), 'A Seventeenth-Century Scarsdale Miscellany', pp. 71–117 (hereafter, *Autobiography*). Associated manuscript books, from Titus, are: PZ 5/2 in D.253, D577/1 (formerly Derby Library MS 3366) and D577/2 (formerly Derby Library MS 3367). For recent work on the Wheatcrofts, see Cedric C. Brown, 'The Two Pilgrimages of the Laureate of Ashover, Leonard Wheatcroft' in *Betraying Our Selves: Forms of Self-Representation in Early Modern English Texts*, ed. Henk Dragstra, Sheila Ottway and Helen Wilcox (Basingstoke & London: Macmillan Press, and New York: St Martin's Press, 2000), pp. 120–35; Cedric C. Brown, 'The Black Poet of Ashover, Leonard Wheatcroft', *English Manuscript Studies, 1100–1700*, 11 (2002), 181–202; Maureen Bell, 'Reading in Seventeenth-Century Derbyshire: the Wheatcrofts and their books' in *The Moving Market*, ed. P. Isaac and B. McKay (Oak Knoll, 2001), pp. 161–8. Earlier scholarship is reported in these.

[4] See this book's Introduction. Also, note S.K. Roberts, 'Alehouses, brewing and government under the early Stuarts', *Southern History*, 2 (1980), 45–71; Keith Wrightson, 'Alehouses, order and reformation in rural England, 1590–1660' in *Popular Culture and Class Conflict, 1590–1914*, eds E. and S. Yeo (Brighton: Harvester, 1981); Peter Clark, *The English Alehouse: A Social History, 1200–1830* (London & NY: Longman, 1983; hereafter, Clark); Judith Hunter, 'Legislation, Royal Proclamations and other National Directives affecting Inns, Taverns, Alehouses, Brandy Shops and Punch Houses, 1552–1757', Ph.D., University of Reading (1994) (hereafter, Hunter); David W. Conroy, *In Public Houses: Drink and the Revolution of Authority in Colonial Massachusetts* (Williamsburg: University of North Carolina Press, 1995); and Judith M. Bennett, *Ale, Beer, and Brewsters in England: Women's Work in a Changing World, 1300–1600* (New York & Oxford: Oxford University Press, 1996; hereafter, Bennett).

I shall be pointing to the often contradictory working of codes of social inclusion and exclusion, for we are dealing with an unstable mixture of prescription and practice.

Given the royalist character of *Hesperides* and the frequency of exhortations from the royal administration and supporting writers about the social benefits of maintaining traditional festivities, it is no surprise to find a cluster of poems in Herrick's book celebrating the winter festive season. This element in the programme is announced at the beginning in '*The Argument of his Book*' (p. 5), where as in the collection itself a full range of mainly seasonal festivities is given: maypoles, hock carts, wassails, wakes, and bridal cakes. Herrick's classic poem of celebration of rural festivity is '*The Hock-cart*' (p. 101), which affords a picture of complete social inclusivity. Lord and tenant are seen to be united, all go to the feast at the big house at the 'Lords Hearth' (l. 26), and 'we' become for the time 'Lords of Wine and Oil' (l. 2). The greatest symbol of unity of minds is the health, here offered to lord, plough, and the commonwealth. That here, as elsewhere, we have a mechanism of social control, as modern analysis quickly divines, is admitted in the poem: the effect of the large festive ritual organised by the big house is to encourage more work by labourers in the new agricultural cycle.[5] In other poems about rustic festivity, also, the patrician perspective is apparent: in '*The Wake*' (p. 255) the festivities are said to be for 'the Tribes' (l. 5), 'Drenched in ale or drowned in beer / Happy Rusticks . . .' (ll. 20–1), while in '*The May-pole*' (p. 239) there are healths drunk to the garlands and the girls, but the girls are said, patronisingly, to fantasise about marrying lords.

The greatest concentration of festive occasions comes however in the midwinter festive season, where similar pictures of inclusiveness are afforded. As usual, generous and ordered provision in the Christmas season becomes a main measure of the good household. So, in '*Ceremonies for Christmasse*' (p. 263), 'my good Dame' provides entertainment for all, with the expected log and strong beer, while in '*The Wassaile*' (pp. 178–9) the opposite is shown. Here in an unkempt and not nobly generous house, the healthful, inclusive ritual is frustrated. More positively, the supposed social and political benefits of inclusive generous festivity are rehearsed again in '*Twelfe night, or* King *and* Queene' (p. 317), centred on the winter hearth, where even in tipsiness ale and wassail lead to loyal healths to King and Queen.

If we look at the sequence of three poems celebrating the rituals of Christmas, beginning with '*Ceremonies for Christmasse*', we encounter a

---

5   Such readings have become commonplace especially since Leah Marcus, *The Politics of Mirth: Jonson, Herrick, Milton, Marvell and the Defense of Old Holiday Pastimes* (Chicago: Chicago University Press, 1986). For other politics readings, see Thomas N. Corns, *Uncloistered Virtue: English Political Literature 1640–1660* (Oxford: Clarendon Press, 1992), esp. chap. 4, pp. 64–128, and the references gathered there. However, the social codes are rather more widespread than suggested by the political (royalist/puritan) axis alone.

litany of the objects and practices: a band of musicians (a 'noise'), the bringing in of the great Christmas log, and a welcome in drink by the dame of the house:

> Come, bring with a noise,
> My merrie, merrie boyes,
> The Christmas Log to the firing;
> While my good Dame, she
> Bids ye all be free;
> And drink to your hearts desiring.
>
> . . . .
>
> Drink now the strong Beere,
> Cut the white loafe here,
> The while the meat is a shredding
> For the rare Mince-Pie;
> And the Plums stand by
> To fill the Paste that's a kneading.

The binding of all the ceremonies is, then, by the liberal distribution of the strong beer, leading into almost religious-sounding rituals, and the big winter feast. The next poem, '*Christmasse-Eve, another Ceremonie*', is a humorous text about setting up a guard over the precious Christmas Pie. The third, '*Another to the Maids*', is dedicated to the maids of the house and spiced with mischievous superstition, because there are rites and special responsibilities. So the country priest prescribes domestic rituals for his flock and defies the Puritan resistance of Christmas and its ancient rites, and in all this the inclusive festive drink is a special kind of beer.

In '*The Wassaile*', to which I have already referred, it is the lack of this kind of drink that is most lamented:

> Give way, give way ye Gates, and win
> An easie blessing to your Bin,
> And Basket, by our entring in.
>
> . . . .
>
> Alas! We blesse, but see none here,
> That brings us either Ale or Beere;
> *In a drie house all things are neere.*

This poem is a lament for past plenty, an elegy for the hospitality and house-keeping of former times, presumably before the war or the increased Puritan influence. (There are always earlier golden times, in conservative constructions.) The ritual welcome, creating the feeling of fellowship, is in drink; and since this is for the whole community, the whole household, the drink is beer. Just how much Herrick wrote prescriptively, rather than descriptively, is very hard to say.

Drink, then, is a sign and precondition of a prosperous, unified society, but it is also socially gradated. So far we have had mainly the ales and beers of the generality in special festivity,[6] but what of the wines of the master classes? For example, in '*The Welcome to Sack*' (p. 77), the answer poem to the earlier '*His fare-well to Sack*' (p. 45), the speaker gets so excited by his reconciliation to canary wine that at the inebriated close he unguardedly reveals a superior attitude:

> Swell up my nerves with spirit; let my blood
> Run through my veines, like to a hasty flood.
> Fill each part full of fire, active to doe
> What thy commanding soule shall put it to.
> And till I turne Apostate to thy love,
> Which here I vow to serve, doe not remove
> Thy Fiers from me; but *Apollo*'s curse
> Blast these-like actions, or a thing that's worse;
> When these Circumstants shall but live to see
> The time that I prevaricate from thee.
> Call me *The sonne of Beere*, and then confine
> Me to the Tap, the Tost, the Turfe; Let Wine
> N'er shine upon me; May my Numbers all
> Run to a sudden Death, and Funerall.
> And last, when thee (deare Spouse) I disavow,
> Ne'er may Prophetique *Daphne* crown my Brow. (ll. 77–92)

So here we have it in a contrived frank moment in a poem that plays, like others, with affectations of superiority. The refined drink is a kind of wine, and only wine supports the Muse. Both poetry and wine are signs of an exclusive society, and Sons of Beer can have no pretensions to refined understanding. (This is a perspective that we shall see contradicted in my second major set of examples.)

So, too, in '*A Hymne to* Bacchus' (p. 259), where social boundaries are dangerously crossed:

> I sing thy praise *Iacchus*,
> Who with thy *Thyrse* doth thwack us:
> And yet thou so dost back us

---

[6] One should of course distinguish between the traditional un-hopped, often spiced ales and hopped beers, made according to continental recipes, which had been progressively spreading from towns into the country. See for example this formula in a pamphlet of 1630:

> WINE: I, generous wine, am for the Court
> BEER: The City calls for Beer.
> ALE: But ale, bonny ale, like a lord of the soil in the Country
>   shall domineer.

John Grove, *Wine, beer, ale, and tobacco contending for superiority*, 2nd edn (London, 1630), quoted in Bennett, p. 81. This pamphlet is also quoted in earlier books on beer, e.g. H.S. Corran, *A History of Brewing* (Newton Abbot: David & Charles, 1975), p. 83. In general, old-fashioned spiced ales lingered longer in the North, but poor brews could be thick and murky (see Clark, chap. 5, 'The Drink Trade, 1500–1660', pp. 94–122).

> With boldness that we feare
> No *Brutus* entring here;
> Nor *Cato* the severe.
> What though the *Lictors* threat us,
> We know they dare not beate us [.]

In this solidarity against the precise, killjoy authorities, there are however some comic effects:

> When we thy *Orgies* sing,
> Each Cobler is a King;
> Nor dreads he any thing [.]

In fact, these cobbler types get quite out of their station:

> Yet he'le be thought or seen,
> So good as *George-a Green*;
> And calls his Blouze, his Queene;
> And speaks in language keene [.]

Wine, the sparkling inspiration of the refined, could be dangerous if somehow it got too far down the social scale. The poem mischievously mixes references from the ancient world – Iacchus, the thyrse, Brutus, Cato, the Lictors, orgies, and so on, which only gentleman are supposed to know about – with the less exalted vernacular of 'dangling breeches' and with romping triplets and quadruplets and obtrusive double rhymes. Technically, Herrick excels at playing ironically with social and stylistic registers.

A full set of examples in *Hesperides* confirming the main social divide between wine and beer is afforded by the comic mock epitaphs distributed throughout the book. With this very widespread minor genre, often mixed disconcertingly in seventeenth-century printed and manuscript collections with real elegies and epitaphs,[7] Herrick was particularly inventive, presenting a gallery of characters lacking civility and ruining their lives with beer-alcoholism. The indolent Buggins (p. 311) is drunk by night and asleep by day, Chub (p. 327) is so improvident that he can afford no beer for the Christmas festivities, the paunchy Punchin (p. 273) has a waistline spread by beer and ale, Blinks' pimply, glowing nose will 'light him home, i'th' dark' (p. 273), Prig is so habitually drunk that he lacks gentility in one poem and has to steal shoes in another (pp. 71 and 143), Guesse's pretensions to (wine-induced) gout are demythologised as trouble caused by beer (p. 98), Spunge's macho beer-swilling is mocked (with a side reference to Germans; p. 171), and Tap has so far lost his sense of duty and piety that he 'Sold his old Mothers Spectacles for Beere' (p. 272). To these morally defined examples we may add some other

---

7   Obvious mid-seventeenth-century print miscellanies to mention in this connection are *Wits Recreations* (editions beginning in 1640) and *Wits Interpreter* (editions beginning in 1655).

poems caricaturing tradesmen (again, as often in other seventeenth-century collections). In '*The Coblers Catch*' (p. 219) these artisans sit by the fire with cheeks ale-dyed and noses tanned with beer, and in '*The Tinkers Song*' (p. 320) we have a clear social differentiation – these men quaff from bowls of beer, are 'frolick' for very little cost, and never call for canary.

If the social demarcation is blatant with these beer swillers, who like Gryll seem unconscious of better things, then it can be much subtler in other poems dealing with kinds of aspiration, at different levels of society. Already noted is the case of 'The May-pole', in which the superior poet has the girls dreaming of socially advantageous matches, and I have quoted '*A Hymn to* Bacchus' in which each cobbler 'calls his Blouze, his Queene' (presumably in ignorance of that word's range of meanings). In '*To Phillis to love, and live with him*' (p. 192), Herrick's loose imitation of Marlowe's 'Passionate Shepherd', the girl is invited to think above her station, as is usual in such poems, and this is clearly marked in drink: 'Thou shalt have Possets, Wassails fine, / Not made of Ale, but spiced Wine'. A parallel device is used in '*To the Maids to walke abroad*' (p. 215). Here country discourse is set against educated discourse, and the girls are invited to aspire to wedding rituals and, again, possets and spiced wine. The tendency of intoxication to connect with pipe-dreams and social fantasies is nicely extended to the poet himself, as in '*How he would drinke his Wine*' (p. 187) he reveals a double affectation for unmixed wine in a crystal glass, proclaiming bravely, 'Fill me my Wine in Christall; thus, and thus / I see't in's *puris naturalibus*: / Unmixt . . .' (The Latin helps the affectation.) But two poems later, sadly, in '*The broken Cristall*', the maid breaks 'the purer Glasse', that delicate object: 'Then smil'd, and sweetly chid her speed; / So with a blush, beshrew'd the deed.' Our servants, bless them, being perhaps impure vessels themselves, do not understand! The viewpoint appears to offer an inclusivity, but is actually one of social superiority.

Wine is to be understood as the mark of social refinement. The celebration of wine in this regard is as clear, at the top end of the scale, as the evidence of ale is at the bottom. The sharing of wine in particular helps to mark out Herrick's 'fit audience'. Among the celebrated opening poems of Herrick's book, full of definitions of readers, is '*When he would have his verses read*' (p. 7), a piece that looks like a good-humoured manifesto:

> In sober mornings, doe not thou reherse
> The holy incantation of a verse;
> But when that men have both well drunke, and fed,
> Let my Enchantments then be sung, or read.
> When Laurell spirts i'the fire, and when the Hearth
> Smiles to it selfe, and guilds the roofe with mirth;
> When up the *Thyrse* is rais'd, and when the sound
> Of sacred *Orgies* flyes, A round, A round.
> When the *Rose* raignes, and locks with ointments shine,
> Let rigid *Cato* read these Lines of mine.

9

Commonsense might observe that the verses may not be used very often. The text displays a notable mixture of assertiveness – his verses have a magic effect, they are an enchantment, and should be thought of as holy incantations – with nervousness as to whether the right conditions will ever apply. Sober mornings may undo them, there are spoilsport moralists about who are never likely to read such stuff anyway, oiled with drink or not, and when exactly are the Roman preconditions ever going to obtain – the Bacchanalian rites, the rose, the ointments, the tipsy flirtation, the symposiastic gathering? Inclusively, the invitation is to the togetherness of mirthful gathering round the fire, but it is hedged about with exclusive definition. The society is choice and idealised, it grounds itself in literary know-how, and its evocation of ancient models is an exclusive sign. It is wine being drunk, as the laurel spirts in the fire and the thyrsus is raised. There are many similar gestures in *Hesperides*, and they have an exclusiveness akin to that of Ben Jonson, who is frequently mentioned. Such society looks unlikely in Devon as a general rule.

The short '*A Lyrick to Mirth*' (p. 39) has many of the same co-ordinates. This sort of Mirth is the cultivated Mirth promoted by Milton in his 'L'Allegro', and it shares with that poem the seven-line verse measure, a common English equivalent to the Anacreontic:[8]

> While the milder Fates consent,
> Let's enjoy our merriment:
> Drink, and dance, and pipe, and play;
> Kiss our *Dollies* night and day:
> Crown'd with clusters of the Vine;
> Let us sit, and quaffe our wine.
> Call on *Bacchus*; chaunt his praise;
> Shake the *Thyrse*, and bite the *Bayes*:
> Rouze *Anacreon* from the dead;
> And return him drunk to bed:
> Sing o're *Horace*; for ere long
> Death will come and mar the song:
> Then shall *Wilson* and *Gotiere*
> Never sing, or play more here.

Despite the beguilingly colloquial 'dollies' and the deceptively rustic 'pipe, and play', this depicts an educated male social group having a good time over drinks by exercising their knowledge of ancient lyric poetry accompanied by the best musicians for songs. It is an evocation of tavern scenes such as Herrick knew in his native London.[9] It suggests a club or some gathering of cultured

8   The Anacreontic persona is an important one for Herrick. For the most comprehensive account of Anacreontics in early modern England, see Stella Achilleos, 'The Anacreontic in Early Modern British Culture', Ph.D., University of Reading, 2002. In this present volume, see Stella Achilleos, 'The *Anacreontea* and a Tradition of Refined Male Sociability'.

9   See below, Michelle O'Callaghan, 'Tavern Societies, the Inns of Court, and the Culture of Conviviality in early seventeenth-century London'.

friends, in an earlier happy time. This kind of evocation happens quite often in *Hesperides*, in particular in the various Bacchanalian verses – whenever 'we thy *Orgies* sing' there would seem to be a reference to such societies.

There are also poems that judge wealth and social position through the disposition of drink. Two poems to his friend in the country, Mr John Wickes, are particularly good in this regard. '*To his peculiar friend, M. Jo; Wicks*' (p. 321), a reversed invitation poem in which the poet invites himself to the modest house of his gentleman friend, realistically marks the entertainment not in wine but beer. (This can be contrasted with Herrick's big house hospitality poem in Jonsonian mode, '*A Panegerick to Sir* Lewis Pemberton' (p. 146), where all kinds of drink are included in the large household, and the poems to Sir Clipsbie Crew (pp. 161, 182, 198, 217), also on a somewhat grander social scale.) In '*His age, dedicated to his peculiar friend, M.* John Wickes, *under the name of* Posthumus' (p. 132), however, a key poem of self-definition written at the Christmas festive season, the literary exchange between the two old gentlemen is marked in poetic convention with crowns of roses, but the poem ends with the sharing of the special range of drinks: spiced ale, brave Burgundian wine, and wassail. Their 'Holiday' is a remembering of the good old times. There is a celebration of the style of their 'middling' status and wealth, as they sit by the fire and recite verses about youth, allowing a recollection of the times back in London when he says he was respected for his poetry. Thus, despite the odd protestation about the deprivations of rustication to Devon, as in '*The departure of the good* Dæmon' (p. 132), there are in *Hesperides* poems that have a way of expressing reconciliation to the life of middling status in the country, in which some of the 'Roman' style is connected to the realities on the ground. This is seen beautifully in '*A Hymne, to the* Lares' (p. 234), where, again in winter, they sit by the fire in the hearth and have a wassail bowl filled with Northdown ale: 'I'll eat and drink up all here.' So the Roman gods, those markers of style, are happy to preside over the *local* style of cheer. Even in the apparently depressed '*His Lachrimae or Mirth, turn'd to mourning*' (p. 144), where he laments how he used to have mirth in society before his rustication, with 'The musick of a Feast' and the rehearsing of good lyric verses, he actually frames a lyric in his lamentation, and thus partly disproves the deprivation.

Like Herrick, Wheatcroft also has standard notions of social inclusivity for certain kinds of festive and sportive occasion. For example, when he tries the self-advertising trick of writing presentation poems for the birthdays of two local grandees, Samuel Pierpoint at Oldcotes, near Chesterfield, and the Earl of Rutland at Haddon (both six or seven miles away, but in opposite directions), he imagines such bountiful festivity to friends of all kinds as to go down in historical record. In the more practical economy of his own resources, his words to each are almost the same:

> Then Blest be god you may both sing & say
> Amongst your friends, this is your Joyfull day
> That you are pleas'd to sport, reioyce & sing,

> In Maskes, & carrols, and rich Banquiting
> Shewing your Bounty to all that com heare,
> In Sacke, & Claret, and rare Bottle-beare,
> That after Ages may have caus to say,
> A Noble Knight (was Borne) as on this day. . . .[10]

In such exemplary, inclusive festivity at the big house, the drinks are made up of wines and beers, though one has to say that Wheatcroft's keenness for mentioning bottle ale or beer may reflect one of the trades at home, shared with his wife Elizabeth, that of alehouse keeper at 'The Hand and Shears'.[11] Some retailed bottle beers were in fact quite expensive.

There is another celebratory socially inclusive poem marking a similar inclusivity with the same range of drinks. This is Wheatcroft's extraordinary celebration of the coronation of William and Mary on 11 April 1689. The elaborate title clearly shows how he seeks to invest his poem with both local and national significance:

> Upon the crounation of their Maiestyes, King William / and Queene Mary, and also vpon the admirable bonefier / which was made vpon a hey Mountaine in Derby=Shire / (vpon the .11ᵗʰ.day of Aprill. 1689) called by the name / of Ashouer hill, about .4. miles from Chesterfeild, / vpon which hill you may perfectly behould .6. seuerall / Countyes, York=Shire, Lincolne minster, Nottingam=Shere, / Leister=Shere, Stafford=Shere, and Derby=Shere, all thes[e] / ought not only to be taken notis of, but seuerall more / passages which are here expressed in these verses followin[ng] / By me Leonard: Wheatcroft de Ashouer, / the tune of the Soulgers departur[e,] / or Mummorths farewell.[12]

---

10 'Come you gallants', no page number but after the end of the first pagination. The quotation is from the Pierrepoint poem. The Manners poem (also no page number, twelve pages further on) is identical for these lines, except for accidentals and 'noble Earle' instead of 'Noble Knight' in the last line quoted. The presentation of the Manners poem is recorded in the *Autobiography*, pp. 97–8: 'My next jorney was to the Earle of Rutlands the[y] hearing of my poetry there desired that I would com to Haddon of my lordes birth-day and with all give his Honour sum verses upon the same which I did, it being May 29 1696 his age being then 58 . . . his honnour being no little pleased with them, and all the nobility besides gave us rare entertainment and sumthing besides.' The Pierrepoint presentation is recorded shortly before: 'and upon May 29 [1690] I went to his honours Parpoynts wher I presented to him verses of his birthday who veri well rewarded me' (p. 96).

11 Although Wheatcroft applied for the licence, his wife Elizabeth did the bulk of the work for the alehouse. In his impecunious years of exile in Bolsover (1664 to 1668 or 1669), Leonard undertook some work as a maltster (*Autobiography*, p. 84). However, when the family was back in Ashover, it is clear that his wife ran the ale business: 'there [at a house rented from John Farnworth in 1669] did my wife begin to sell alle, and so did continew many years after' (p. 85) and [in 1675] 'My wife continued all this while abrewing' (p. 90). Leonard however bought a large quantity of malt at Chesterfield fare in 1671, 52 quarters (p. 89). On the predominance of women in this work, see Bennett. The Wheatcrofts were short of money for long periods, and alehouse-keeping was one of the necessities of financial survival. Clark (p. 75) notes that tailoring was one of the poor trades, often requiring supplementation of income.

12 'Come ye gallants', pp. 143–7, first pagination. I have also made brief use of this poem in 'Black Poet', pp. 181–2.

In this proud celebration of 'country' and self, Wheatcroft offers anti-Catholic solidarity on behalf of his whole community. What is further 'to be taken notis of' is his assumption of the role of prophet as well as master of ceremonies. Ashover Hill, above the village, is aggrandised as a place of special vision and named as *his* hill:[13]

> Besides I can se six braue Countyes
> When on my hill I'am mounted hey.
> There did my glorious Bonefire glisten.
> Flaming vp into the Skey.
> That all these Countyes might behould it.
> O what a pleasant hill have I.   (stanza 4)

On this spot, where he and his friends built the coronation bonfire, Wheatcroft says he will build 'a fabrick' (stanza 5), to serve as a visual reminder for all his parish and probably as an example to neighbour communities: 'There I'le buld me vp a fabrick / to behould each pleasant day.' On this construction he undertakes to build a bonfire on each succeeding 11 April, thus leading a continuing act of loyalty to the Protestant king. That act of loyalty in 1689, like succeeding acts, will be sealed by communal drinking, according to Wheatcroft's inclusive threefold formula:

> And there I'le haue another rare trick
> For gallants for to sport and play
> I'le have suger sack and Claret
> Besides all sortes of bottle=beare,
> That will make your Toungs to rattle
> If you euer enter there [.]

The bonding of those drinks, in a gathering seemingly including local gentry (note the expensive bottle beer, again), is matched by communal commitment of a religious kind. Wheatcroft's memorial construction on the hill above the village has some characteristics attributed to it in the poem that seem to be allegorical. It is built in the form of an oval, and at its height, afforded by the elevation of the hill, 'It far in height exceeds our steeple, / tho it be .50. yardes and more' (that is, even if the steeple were more than one hundred and fifty feet high). Closeness to heaven seems to be the point, suggested also by a

---

[13] This is not the only occasion on which Wheatcroft used the vision from a hill for a major poem. In 'Black Poet' I feature a poem ('An elegy upon the death of all the greatest gentry...') surveying the decayed state of all the great houses above and below Matlock in Darley Dale, where the vantage point is Oaker Hill. In this poem the perambulation comes back to Ashover and Leonard's own hill, Ashover Hill, at the end of the poem: 'I will return unto my hill again'. Oaker Hill thus afforded a survey of great houses in the nearby 'country', and Ashover Hill, while also affording wide views, was specifically associated with Wheatcroft's own parish, where he had some position and command. The original of 'An elegy' is in 'Come you gallants', second pagination, pp. 126–8.

paradox: 'it cannot moue one Inch at all, / all=tho it do not touch the ground.'
It is steadfast, on good foundations, but looks heavenward rather than earth-ward. What is more, there is only one route to salvation – 'in it there is but one doore' – and all those who enter it on future coronation anniversaries 'they shall be welcom I'le declare it / the[y]'st neuer worke, nor card, nor spin' (stanza 8). In other words, the loyal innocent drinking community on Ashover Hill subscribe to the true Protestant faith, uniting against 'the Whore of Babells traine' (stanza 10), and without that religious commitment neither individual nor nation can be saved. Under the command of its convivial, alehouse-keeping church clerk, leading the singing whether in church or on hill, Ashover becomes a beacon to all the neighbouring counties.

As for the significance of the drink, binding the whole community together with wines and beers, the idealism of that social cohesion slips in the poem itself. When he imagines future gatherings at the place, he forgets the wines mentioned earlier:

> Then for the honour of King William
> I will sing a merry toane.
> When all is out I will cry fill-um
> And for that I'le neuer groane.
> And euery eleuenth day whilst I live
> I will make a Bone=fire there,
> Oth top of all my little fabrick
> Besides a good hogs=head of beere.
> Then com braue blades, and lets be merry . . .   (stanzas 9 & 10)

The fact is that ales or beers were pivotal to Wheatcroft's social practices, and despite his many attempts to connect with local big houses, wines could hardly be a main part of his experience.

Occasionally, there is an opportunity for the regular customers at such as 'The Hand and Shears' to reach out to the upper classes, as at a 'famous Hunting' at New Year, 1694:

> They traild him [the fox] to Asher w^t whop & w^t hallow
> And brauly they Beagls did after them follow
> Unto an Alle=hous where merrily wee,
> Did drinke of our Glasses, and sung merilee
> To Earles and to Lords, and Gentellmen ny,
> Wishing them all health, I'am sure tis no ly.   (p. 143, first pagination)

But it was only on special occasions like this that the mainly labouring customers at local alehouses could be in contact with the landowners, so that for the most part Wheatcroft's texts of conviviality are based, implicitly or explicitly, upon the consumption of ale.

In celebrating a horse race at Ashover in 1692, for example, when horses from four counties were put into competition, he imagines another event in the social calendar at which there would be a broad gathering, in this case consuming ale or beer, and tobacco. Many local brewers would have done a big trade at meetings like this, and tobacco was often sold through alehouses:

> There was seuerall sortes of gallupers
> Which there you might behould
> Each one a rider on his back
> With silver and with gould,
> Besides all sortes of femall kinds
> Rare Buties for to see
> Which some will never out of mind
> O Asher race for mee.
>
> Brewers & backers euery one
> You are all welcom thither.
> I hope we shall meet twice a yeare
> To drinke a glasse to gather ...   (p. 149, first pagination)

Whereas Herrick, following his more elite social coding, tends to deny best civility, and certainly the true muse, to beer, Wheatcroft develops a poetic practice that has ale at its heart.[14] Appropriately, in 'The Ale=drapers piticion to the Honorable Bench at Chasterfeild. Ap-rill.20.1677 for my Licence' – the poem seems to present a versified application for the annual licence – there is even an assumption that god Bacchus is present to enliven spirits in the house:

> For all that coms, pay but a peney a can,
> Rare bottell=ale, if aney Soule doe mind it[15]
> At hand & shears, in Asher you may find it
> With seuerall sortes of Inglish naping Lickuer,
> T'will make the dull=est sperits to seeme quicker.
> Then Backus like, each man with glasses fettell,
> Hectorian like, shewing your selues braue mettel[l]...
>   (pp. 111–12, first pagination)

Poetry enters this world through popular song. It is obvious that Wheatcroft, with his strong voice for leading the singing, took to providing new texts for familiar tunes. The manuscript book furnishes scores of examples. Even the early poems in his collection, copied from popular printed sources or picked up at fairs, are presented as by a ballad-monger as things for social amusement and communal singing, hence the running title of the

---

14 A brother alehouse-keeping poet for Wheatcroft is of course John Taylor of London, the celebrated 'Water Poet', but he is an urban phenomenon, and in that sense part of another narrative than this.

15 Note the range of customers indicated in the text: the cheap ale is for the labourers, husbandmen and artisans of very modest means, while the 'rare' bottle ale (probably retail) provides a more up-market option. Retailed bottle ales and beers, spreading since the invention of strong dark bottle glass in the 1630s, were quite expensive (see Clark, p. 210).

manuscript book: 'Com you gallants looke & by / Here is mirth and Melody.'[16] In fact, as a young man Wheatcroft seems to have presented a perfect example of the target market for the cheap print trade, ballads at a penny or chapbooks at up to four pence: 'The traditional chapbooks may by the end of our period have been aimed at a rural youth market.'[17] We know, too, that alehouses were popular places for various kinds of communal entertainment, including singing, and that ballads were often displayed or distributed there.[18] His company is generally of 'gallants' or 'blades', whether fellow militia men, horse racegoers, bellringers, or drinking companions in the alehouse or on Ashover Hill. In this sort of context drink and song always went together, and one of Wheatcroft's entrepreneurial roles was to furnish material for this communal activity.

Among the texts he writes for 'healths', the archetypal binding ritual, universally noted as popular in alehouse society (Clark, p. 156) is one for hunting, another 'to my love', and 'Another of the Muses':

> The wise men the[y] were seuen,
> Nere more shall be for me,
> The vertues the[y] were Twelue,
> And three the greater bee,
>
> The Muses were but nine,
> The worthyes is times. 3,
> The Cesers the[y] were .12.
> And the fatall sisters .3 [.]   (unpaginated, end of first pagination)

The featuring of the nine Muses in this drinking song justifies the telling of another Wheatcroft story, which has been told before but which shows fascinating evidence of social encoding through drink.[19] Wheatcroft's taking upon himself of the leadership of his community in connection with the Protestant accession, and the pretentiousness of his acts of construction and commemoration on the hill above the village, seem not surprisingly to have drawn wry comment. Someone evidently thought to puncture his presumption, but Wheatcroft tells the story in his autobiography as one of triumph over the dangers of humiliation:

---

[16] On the importance of fairs in print distribution, see most recently John Barnard and Maureen Bell, 'The English Provinces' in *The Cambridge History of the Book in Britain*, IV (1557–1695), ed. John Barnard and D.F. McKenzie (Cambridge: Cambridge University Press, 2002), pp. 665–86, esp. pp. 666–7, and the references collected there.

[17] R.C. Simmons, 'ABCs, almanacs, ballads, chapbooks, popular piety and textbooks' in *CHBB*, p. 513.

[18] Clark, pp. 138, 155, 229. Simmons (p. 510) reports that ballads' 'purchasers pasted them up in homes, alehouses and other public places'. See Natasha Würzbach, *The Rise of the English Street Ballad, 1550–1650* (Cambridge: Cambridge University Press, 1990), pp. 253–84.

[19] In 'Black Poet', p. 182, and 'Laureate', p. 122. Also in Bell, 'Reading', p. 162.

In the intrim I was desired of sum jentellmen to cum to Tupton [a village about seven miles away] to discours with one Ouldham who profesed himselfe to be a poet, and was one who had writ severall verses, not only against me but in derision of the frabricke [sic] which I had Bulded upon the top of Ashover hill, so according to their desirs we met, where great companey gathered togather, there did I challeng him to whake with me to Parnishus Hill, but we both mising our way, we chanced to light of an all-hous, and after we had drunk awhile we fell into discors concerning the 9 Muses which he could not name, naithe could he tell from whence the[y] came, or what the[y] had done, or what the[y] might doe, so I in the audienc of all the companey gave them their right names and all their right titles, where upon the[y] decked my head round with lorill branches to the great vexation of my antagonist, Ouldham. So ever since I am called the Black Poet. (*Autobiography*, p. 97)

So he says he gained special recognition in his community. But, for the purposes of this chapter, we have seen that grounds for challenging Wheatcroft's social self-placement are present in the instability of the text of his notorious coronation poem, in which the provisions to the gallants of sack, claret and bottle beer in the fifth stanza had collapsed to a good hogshead of beer by the ninth. Yet what he had proved against upstart poet Oldham of Tupton was superiority in another field of social demarcation. Village poets, who had only attended petty school, might not be supposed to know about the Muses in the way that some Latin-educated gentlemen should know. But Wheatcroft had read books of popular instruction and self-improvement, and he liked to parade a few classical and romance names in his verses. In brave tipsiness he proved his point against his less liberally educated opponent. Herrick had reserved poetry for the select company of wine-drinkers, both the wine and the poetry being symbols of a more refined style authorised by antiquity. Wheatcroft, it is true, occasionally reached out to the wine-drinkers, in the mode of client to patron, but his muse had its easier home in the company of gallants whose singing was primed by ale, and it was fittingly in an alehouse that he received his laurels as The Black Poet.

This chapter has used an extreme selectivity, in juxtaposing two sets of texts, those of the gentleman-priest in Devon and the yeoman or artisan church clerk of Derbyshire, of the rusticated poet and the rustic poet, as their self-definitions were informed by the cultures of drink. But even such a selective comparison already opens up a great range of definition available through the meanings of drink in the cultural practices of the period. With our two poets, drinking cultures and poetic cultures are teasingly entwined.

In point of fact, there is much in common between Herrick and Wheatcroft in terms of prescribed, conventional social value. Both subscribe to common patterns of belief celebrating the benefits of festivity and sport, and both celebrate special moments of communal ritual in festivity in their societies, sealed by drink. Both are conscious upholders of antiquity and tradition, guardian-historians in their different spheres. Nevertheless, their different stations and their different educational experiences produce, inevitably, sets of paradoxical oppositions, which are likely to be symptomatic of more general attitudes in the society around them. According to the cultural influences on Herrick, it was impossible to be both a Son of Ben and a Son of Beer; according to the experiences of Wheatcroft, would-be instructor and master of ceremonies in his parish, it was often the companionship of ale or beer that led to the occasions, even sometimes gave the inspiration, for verse.

And in this difference lies also the greatest similarity: that both conceive of poetry predominantly as a medium of social fellowship and exchange. One reason that the narrative of drink seems to run parallel to the narrative of poetry must be that the texts of both men use both drink and poetry as means of self-definition, constructing and recording a social identity and a role. As far as the subject matter of this volume is concerned, it may be enough to note that the ideals of communality and social inclusiveness that are prescribed for major seasonal festivals and similar events in rural society are nevertheless based on attitudes of exclusivity, marked by drink in many places in their texts. For our two poets, it is as much by their drink as by their verses that ye shall know them.

That thought might provoke a last brief comparison with a stage play, with London rather than provincial society, and with Ben Jonson, whom Herrick acknowledges as cultural master (and some of whose poems Wheatcroft would probably have read in popular print). In *Bartholomew Fair* (Act 1, beginning) a 'Littlewit' resents the elite canary-drinking poets of The Three Cranes, The Mitre and The Mermaid and supports a more popular set of writers eased by beer. So he writes a new play for the puppet theatre at the fair, a wonderfully bathetic reduction of the Marlowe/Musaeus Hero and Leander story adapted to Thames-side life. The puppet master, 'Lanthorn' Leatherhead, also complains that playwrights 'put too much learning in their things now o'days' (Act 5, opening). The potential audience for the play, gathering at the fair, also gets primed by beer, at Ursula's tent, to the point of excess. The climax of the comedy is therefore presented by an absurd, injudicious, if triumphant, performance of a 'beer' play to a 'beer' audience, in which something like social cohesion is achieved by the defeat of the common enemy, the anti-theatrical, anti-fair puritan Zeal-of-the-Land-Busy.

The learned, canary-drinking set is of course that of Ben Jonson himself, the ultimate puppeteer of the apparent triumphs of *Bartholomew Fair* (1614). As Stella Achilleos has described later in this book, when Herrick showed models for his feasts of wit, it was those select London tavern gatherings in 'The Sun', 'The Dog' or 'The Triple Tun' to which he referred, as in 'An Ode for him' (p. 289): 'Ah *Ben*! / Say how, or when / Shall we your Guests / Meet at those *Lyrick* Feasts, / . . .' There one can find wine, only wine, for inspiration: 'Where we such clusters had, / As made us noble wild, not mad; / And yet each verse of thine / Out-did the meate, out-did the frolick wine.' In this frame of things, Wheatcroft, who loved going to fairs and there accessed numerous popular

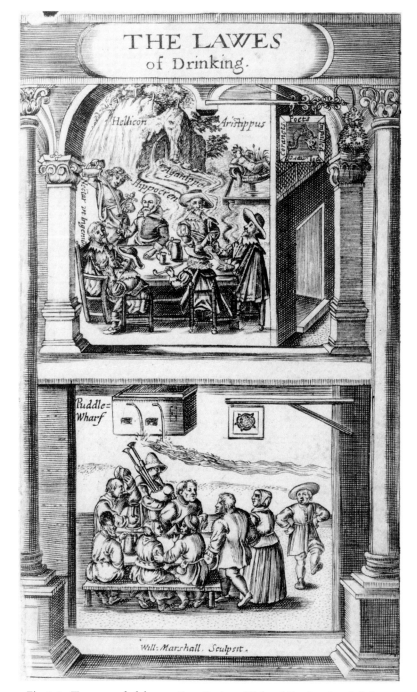

Fig. 1.1: Tavern and alehouse. Frontispiece, Richard Brathwaite, *A Solemn Ioviall Disputation* (1617). By permission of the British Library, C.40.b.20.

sources for songs, is a rustic Littlewit, and a Son of Beer and not a Son of Ben. Yet he evidently achieved something of a laureate status in his local community, much as Ben Jonson sought to achieve in his, and probably more than the rusticated Herrick could achieve in his (though his eyes may have been back on London). If we recognise that these poets define their identities and their social roles through their disposition of drinks and verses, then we also have to recognise that each could only validate his success upon the actual constituency around him, and that 'beer' audiences were probably a good deal larger than 'wine' ones.

One might think the same in reaction to a mischievous picture entitled 'The Lawes of Drinking' in Richard Brathwaite's *A Solemne Ioviall Disputation* of 1617 (Fig. 1.1). This again takes the definitions into the city rather than the country, and in that sense lies beyond the boundaries of this study, but the contrast between the tavern of the gentry and the alehouse of the humbler citizens is exactly along the discriminatory lines I have been sketching. The terms of reference are set in the tavern scene in the upper part of the illustration, where the claims to distinction are made largely by the associations claimed with poetry. The tavern sign bears the inscription 'Poets Impalled wth Lawrell Coranets', and the pouring of wine is accompanied by the claim to inspiration: 'Nectar vt Ingenium'. The Latin makes its own social claim, and the upper part of the picture establishes all the usual connections with the august sources of inspiration from the classical world. By contrast, the Thames-side alehouse in the lower picture is allowed only a bagpipe, a notoriously unrefined instrument, and a bit of a jig on the right hand side, while the streams of water above the company on the ale bench look far from clean. In this good-humoured disposition of symbolic spaces, the Herrick/Jonson imaging is that of the upper scene, whilst the connection with poetry is denied to the alehouse. That which inclusively spans different social groups serves as a definition of exclusivity, and what is defined by drink and by literature appears to be the same.[20]

---

[20] For further discussion of this image, see Michelle O'Callaghan, 'Tavern Societies, the Inns of Court, and the Culture of Conviviality in early seventeenth-century London', below.

2

The *Anacreontea* and a Tradition of
Refined Male Sociability

STELLA ACHILLEOS

A COMMUNICATION that appears in the *Gentleman's Magazine* in 1780
provides a range of valuable information about the formation and
proceedings of the *Anacreontic Society*, a gentleman's social club that flourished in London during the final decades of the eighteenth century.[1]
Addressing 'Mr. Urban' – as the editor of the magazine was called throughout
the entire period of its publication – this *History of the Anacreontic Society*
begins with the following comment:

> I will not pay you so ill a compliment to suppose you have never heard of the
> Anacreontic Society. I therefore flatter myself the following account of its insti-
> tution and progress will not be unacceptable to you or your polite readers.[2]

In the first instance, this comment pays tribute to the popularity of the *Anacreontic Society*. At the same time, it attests to an eighteenth-century growing
preoccupation with the pursuit of gentility and refinement. In particular, the
use of the word 'polite' to qualify the readership of the magazine projects a
certain kind of social self-image.

A similar kind of language is used throughout the communication to
describe the *Anacreontic Society*. With regard to the establishments where the

---

[1] The *Anacreontic Society* has occasionally been listed as a music or singing society. See, for
instance, Peter Clark, *British Clubs and Societies 1580–1800. The Origins of an Associational
World* (Oxford: Clarendon Press, 2000), p. 122. Stanley Sadie refers to the *Anacreontic Society*
as one of the catch clubs that flourished in eighteenth-century England, which also include the
Noblemen and Gentlemens' Catch Club and two societies called Glee Club. Stanley Sadie,
'Music in the Home II', in *Music in Britain. The Eighteenth Century*, ed. H. Diack Johnstone
and Roger Fiske, The Blackwell History of Music in Britain, IV (Oxford & Cambridge:
Blackwell, 1990), pp. 313–54 (p. 320). This classification no doubt reflects the considerable
output of the society in various kinds of music, vocal and instrumental.
[2] *Gentleman's Magazine*, 50 (1780), 224.

society was initially housed, we are told that the *Anacreontic Society* 'was begot and christened . . . at a *genteel* public-house near the Mansion house'. Then describing the entertainments provided during the meetings, the correspondent refers to the '*elegant* supper provided'. Readers are also informed that the membership of the club consists of 'Peers, Commoners, Aldermen, Gentlemen, Proctors, Actors, and *Polite* Tradesmen'.[3] This vocabulary is clearly applied to distinguish the club in terms of stylishness and refined manners.

Of course the *Anacreontic Society* was not a unique phenomenon. A large number of clubs and societies were established in Britain in the eighteenth century and gradually became a distinctive feature of the social life of urban centres.[4] Many clubs held their meetings in public drinking houses while the great majority attracted a male membership. Some clubs had a small membership and maintained some degree of intimacy and exclusivity. A considerable number of clubs, though – including the *Anacreontic Society* – grew into bigger, socially inclusive institutions that often had to move to dedicated premises to accommodate their increasing memberships. As social historians have noted, the financial prosperity of increasing parts of the population in eighteenth-century Britain brought about an explosion in the demand for such kind of high-status forms of public sociability.[5]

While the *Anacreontic Society* may be placed within a wider group of practices that marked the development of a 'polite' culture, it also has a distinctive identity that is established by the association of the club with the anacreontic model. The *Anacreontea* are made up of a relatively small collection of short and elegant Greek lyrics that mainly celebrate the pleasures of love and wine. Modern scholarship has proved that the anacreontic corpus was actually composed by a number of poets from the Hellenistic ages to the Byzantine era. In the early modern period, though, it was largely believed that the poems belonged to the Greek lyric poet Anacreon who is also the governing figure in the corpus. The members of the *Anacreontic Society* would call up the poet as

---

3   The italics in these quotations are mine.
4   Clark, *British Clubs and Societies*. Clark provides a wide-ranging study that looks at the development of clubs from their early stages in the late sixteenth century to the late eighteenth century when they became formalised institutions. He covers a broad range of associations, from literary and political to music, singing, philanthropic, hunting societies, and so on. In the last few years, the formation of clubs and societies in the early modern period has also been noted by other social historians, though not dealt with thoroughly. See, for instance, R.J. Morris, 'Voluntary societies and British urban elites 1780–1850: an analysis', in *The Eighteenth-Century Town. A Reader in English Urban History 1688–1820*, ed. Peter Borsay (London & New York: Longman, 1990), pp. 338–66.
5   Peter Borsay uses the term 'Urban Renaissance' to describe the transformation of the public life of urban centres during this period. Peter Borsay, *The English Urban Renaissance. Culture and Society in the Provincial Town 1660–1770* (Oxford: Clarendon Press, 1989). See also *The Birth of a Consumer Society. The Commercialization of Eighteenth Century England*, ed. N. McKendrick, J. Brewer and J.H. Plumb (London: Europa, 1982).

their presiding figure pledging themselves as 'Sons of Anacreon' and they would regularly open up their meetings, as the correspondent to the *Gentleman's Magazine* informs us, with a group recitation of the '*Anacreontic Song*'. This was a very popular song, which at some point became known in America, where with new words it provided what we nowadays know as the 'Star-Spangled Banner'. The song begins with the members requesting the patronage of the 'jolly old Grecian':

> To Anacreon, in Heaven, where he sat in full glee,
> A few sons of Harmony sent a petition,
> That he their inspirer and patron would be;
> When this answer arriv'd from the jolly old Grecian:
> 'Voice, fiddle, and flute, no longer be mute,
> I'll lend you my name, and inspire you to boot;
> And besides, I'll instruct you, like me, to entwine
> The myrtle of Venus with Bacchus's vine.'
>
> ('*Anacreontic Song*', stanza 1, lines 1–8)

This figurative act of ritual induction clearly provides an element of humour suiting the convivial spirit of the meetings. But besides that, it suggests a conscious act of public fashioning that involves the appropriation of the anacreontic symposium as a topos of polite sociability.

In the original corpus, Anacreon is presented as an old man who utters perpetual exhortations to an ever-available world of wine and women. Yet these pleasures are treated in a rather gentle way. They are kept within the bounds of propriety and are not allowed to transgress the fine line beyond which they would prove unsettling or harmful. So despite the endless array of potential lovers that feature in the corpus, Anacreon's sexual yearning is never consummated. Rather the object of his desire is always snatched out of his hands. Along similar lines, drinking in the *Anacreontea* is presented as a refined discourse that encodes a sense of temperance and is carefully regulated by attendance to the proper ritual. Before starting to drink, for instance, wine and water have to be mixed in the due proportions.[6] Attention to ritual activities preserves an equilibrium of the right amounts of drink and constructs a symposiastic occasion where immoderate indulgence is not allowed to interfere with the spirit of conviviality and companionship. 'στυγέω μάχας παροίνους' (*Anacreontea* 42, line 13), 'I hate arguments while drinking,' Anacreon says.

> πολυκώμους κατὰ δαῖτας
> νεοθηλέσιν ἅμα κούραις
> ὑπὸ βαρβίτῳ χορεύων
> βίν ἥσυχον φέροιμι.　　　　(*Anacreontea* 42, lines 14–17)[7]

6　*Anacreontea* 38, lines 11–12; *Anacreontea* 47, lines 10–12; *Anacreontea* 60B, line 1.
7　The *Anacreontea* are quoted from *Anacreon, Anacreontea, Choral Lyric from Olympus to*

> At merry parties with youthful girls,
> dancing to the lyre, may I take life easy.

In effect, the concept of the anacreontic symposium provides an idiom of civility that could be seen to define a particular kind of social identity.

While there has been recent scholarly interest in drink literature and the use of drink as a social marker, the social and political implications of the reappropriation of the anacreontic in early modern England have only been scantily considered by scholars.[8] My purpose is to open up this largely over-looked area of study, dealing with the dissemination of the *Anacreontea* though not strictly in terms of literary history. Rather I look at the anacreontic in a much broader fashion as the marker of a conceptual area. Because of its connection to the classical world, the anacreontic provides a very distinct form of symposiastic poetry that may be set against other, perhaps more robust, forms of drinking verses or ballads. My suggestion is that the reproduction of the genre in early modern England is symptomatic of a wider set of social and cultural discourses, providing the identifier for a polite form of male sociability that may, at least in the first instance, be marked out by education and class.

In fact, knowledge of the anacreontic corpus became available as early as 1554, when it was first published by Henricus Stephanus. It does not appear to have had an immediate impact on English poets and initially it might have been looked on as a rather archaic form, available only to a social or educational elite who could read either the Greek original or a Latin translation. The genre follows a somewhat slow process of assimilation into the corpus of Renaissance literature and increasingly becomes more widely reproduced in the vernacular, with several translations in the first half of the seventeenth century.

By the eighteenth century it had become a very recognisable mode that was not so strictly or exclusively adherent to the original corpus. Rather it came to represent more broadly a kind of 'light' and carefree, yet elegant, symposiastic space that defined various aspects of male bonding. As I suggested earlier on, the anacreontic may primarily be looked at within the context of such polite and refined gentlemen's clubs as the *Anacreontic Society*. Besides that, the genre was often considered as a *jeu d'esprit*, a light-hearted kind of literary composition that gentlemen would often indulge in at leisure. A number of broadly anacreontic verses were sent for publication to the *Gentleman's*

Alcman, ed. D.A. Campbell, Loeb Classical Library: Greek Lyric, II (Cambridge, MA: Harvard University Press; London: Heinemann, 1988). The translations that accompany the Greek texts are also taken from this edition.

8   For an exception, see Joshua Scodel, *Excess and the Mean in Early Modern English Literature* (Princeton & Oxford: Princeton University Press, 2002), chapter 7: 'Drinking and Politics of Poetic Identity from Jonson to Herrick', pp. 199–224.

Magazine where Anacreon, together with Horace, is one of the most widely represented classical authors.

Yet the formative moments for this tradition may actually be found in the early years of the seventeenth century. In particular, this wider set of social and cultural discourses identified by the reproduction and circulation of the anacreontic may be traced back to Ben Jonson and the groups that flourished around him. By the eighteenth century, Jonson and his 'sons' would often be nostalgically invoked as archetypal exemplars providing the model for a civilised and refined form of male sociability, anacreontic in spirit. A poem from an early eighteenth-century miscellany entitled '*On Ben Johnson's Club-Room, call'd the Apollo; at the Devil-Tavern in Fleet-street*' calls up from the past the figure of Jonson presiding over a convivial drinking-session in the Apollo room at the St Dunstan and the Devil tavern near Temple Bar.[9] There Jonson and his 'sons' frequently held their meetings in the late 1620s and the 1630s:

> Once on a Time, as plac'd supream in State,
> Amidst his Sons old merry *Ben* was sate [.]   (lines 1–2)

The image of 'old merry *Ben*' stately seated as an authoritative figure among his young followers bears a striking resemblance to the image of the 'jolly old Grecian' in the opening lines of the '*Anacreontic Song*'.

In fact the poem here playfully rewrites the anacreontic 'recusatio', in which the bard professes his intent to sing in heroic measures. His lyre though refuses to obey, constantly changing the tune to the 'light' lyric measures of symposiastic verse.[10] '*On Ben Johnson's Club-Room*' is a variation of the same topos. Jonson attempts to compose 'At some rare Strain' (line 3) but without success: Apollo, the patron god of poetry, and the Muses will not come to his aid. Humorously puzzled by this, the 'jovial Bard', as Jonson is called in line three, soon makes a graceful gesture of resigning to the overwhelming power of symposiastic poetry:

> At some rare Strain the jovial Bard essay'd,
> And call'd the Muse and *Phoebus* to his Aid:
> In vain; nor *Phoebus* nor the Muse obey'd.
> Nonplust at this, and in a strange Quandary,
> He fill'd a lusty Bumper of Canary.
> Soon as this Nectar glided o'er his Tongue,
> He rous'd, and tun'd his Lyre, and sweetly sung.
> Then to the Room which the rich Juice supply'd,
> Henceforth be thou *Apollo* call'd, he cry'd;
> *Apollo* let thy Name for ever be,
> That lab'ring Bards, in Time to come, may see,

---

9   *Miscellaneous Poems, by Several Hands*, 2 vols (London: D. Lewis, 1726–30), I, p. 71.
10 See *Anacreontea* 23. The anacreontic corpus contains various other verses defined by dialogical opposition.

> If they their Father *Ben*'s Advice will take,
> The best Inspirer is delicious Sack.   (lines 3–15)

The story about the naming of the tavern room after Apollo represents it as a venue for a choice and refined kind of merry-making that includes literary activity. The select nature of this symposium is also suggested by the consumption of canary and sack, wines usually imported in England from Spain and the Canary Islands, rather than the cheaper, locally produced ale. In the text, canary and sack are notably called in line eight 'Nectar', the drink of gods in mythology, and in line ten 'rich Juice'. As other chapters in this volume suggest, a similar distinction might exist between the tavern that would serve wine and the alehouse that could only serve beer.

Like the 'jolly old Grecian' of the '*Anacreontic Song*', 'old merry *Ben*' is thus idealised as a mythical figure that represents an urbane and select kind of male tavern-clubbing. Along similar lines, Richard Steele describes Jonson and the Apollo as invested with a sacred aura of civility. Referring to the entertainments he thought suitable to provide to celebrate his sister's wedding, Isaac Bickerstaff – the narrative voice of *The Tatler* – comments:

> The Wedding was wholly under my Care. After the ceremony at Church, I was resolv'd to entertain the Company with a Dinner suitable to the Occasion, and pitch'd upon the *Apollo*, at the *Old Devil* at *Temple-Bar*, as a Place sacred to Mirth, temper'd with Discretion, where *Ben Johnson* and his Sons us'd to make their liberal Meetings.   (*The Tatler*, no. 79, October 1709)[11]

The associations with Jonson and his circle clearly mark the room as a space for polite merry-making, branding it as 'a Place sacred to Mirth, temper'd with Discretion'. The traces of this early seventeenth-century group would still be present in the room, as Bickerstaff is commended for his choice of venue:

> Here the Chief of the *Staffian* Race appear'd; and as soon as the Company were come into that ample Room, *Lepidus Wagstaff* began to make me compliments for chusing that Place, and fell into a discourse upon the Subject of Pleasure and Entertainment, drawn from the Rules of *Ben*'s Club, which are in Gold Letters over the Chimney.

The rules referred to here are apparently Jonson's '*Leges Convivales*', his 'Sociable Rules for the Apollo'. This code, engraved in gold letters on a tablet made of marble and placed over the fireplace in the Apollo room, suggests a confined and rather elitist view of tavern-clubbing. It describes an intimate and enclosed group of choice, male companions who indulge in a civil kind of entertainment and in learned merry-making. One imagines that Jonson would choose his boon companions to be educated and clever enough to appreciate

---

[11] *The Tatler*, ed. Donald F. Bond, 3 vols (Oxford: Clarendon Press, 1987), II, p. 5.

his display of learning and witticisms and perhaps expected them to challenge his intellect by contributing their own part.

The fact that the rules were initially written in Latin and contain numerous echoes of classical authors suggests the elitist nature of the Apollo.[12] They were a few years later translated in the vernacular by Alexander Brome, who was probably too young in the 1620s and early 1630s to have shared the company of Jonson at the Apollo, but nevertheless counted himself among his 'sons'.[13] The code invites those who are learned, urbane and in cheerful spirit to join in. Fools and ignorant men with vulgar and gloomy disposition are asked to keep away:

1. Nemo asymbolus, nisi umbra, huc venito.
2. Idiota insulus, tristis, turpis, abesto.
3. Eruditi, Urbani, hilares, honesti, adsciscuntor.
4. Nec lectæ fœminæ repudiantor.   (*'Leges Convivales'*, lines 1–4)[14]

Brome's translation turns the list of rules into verse form – rhyming couplets – that does not preserve the numerical division:

Let none but *Guests* or *Clubbers* hither come;
Let *Dunces, Fools, sad, sordid* men keep home;
Let learned, civil, merry men b' invited,
And modest too; nor the choice *Ladies* slighted:
(Alexander Brome's translation of the *'Leges Convivales*,
Ben Johnson's sociable rules for the Apollo', lines 1–4)

The fourth rule that refers to women is often found to be rather ambiguous. No evidence exists to support the participation of women in the Apollo. Though in the first instance the rule may seem to allow female involvement, it is possible that the Latin 'repudiantor' – 'slighted' in line four of the translation – means that women should not be referred to in an offensive manner

---

[12] In particular Jonson's code often alludes to a number of passages from Horace and Martial that provide invitations to a dinner.

[13] Brome was born in 1620, so his translation of the *'Leges Convivales'* cannot be dated earlier than the late 1630s. The translation was first published in Brome's *Songs and other Poems* (1661). The original code had probably already been composed and used at the Apollo by the mid-1620s. Percy Simpson suggests that it was composed in 1624, when the Apollo room was supposedly built. See Percy Simpson, 'Ben Jonson and the Devil Tavern', *MLR*, 24 (1939), 367–73 (p. 368). John Buxton however argues that the evidence used by Simpson is misleading and that the *'Leges Convivales'* might have been composed a few years earlier. John Buxton, 'The Poets' Hall Called Apollo', *MLR*, 48 (1953), 52–4. On the whole, it appears that surviving evidence about the date of composition of the code or when the Apollo started to be used by Jonson and his 'sons' is scanty.

[14] Jonson's works are cited from *Ben Jonson*, ed. C.H. Herford, Percy Simpson and Evelyn Simpson, 11 vols (Oxford: Clarendon Press, 1925–52). Alexander Brome's translation of the *'Leges Convivales'* is also quoted from this edition.

by male members of the club.[15] In any case, Jonson's rule still marks an element of elitism, as he only refers to 'lectæ' or 'choice' ladies.

The exclusiveness of the symposium is preserved by not allowing any external intrusion, like fiddlers who may wish to play without being asked (rule 15). Members of the group themselves are sworn to an oath of secrecy, that they will not publicly disclose any information about what is said or done during the meetings of the group (which is probably the reason why so little is known about it):

> 23. Qui foràs vel dicta, vel facta, eliminat, eliminator.
> ('*Leges Convivales*', line 26)

> Who ere shall publish what's here done or said,
> From our Society must be banished.
> (Brome's translation, lines 31–2)

Other individuals who may happen for various reasons to be around, mostly as servants, are asked to keep their proper places and not attempt to interrupt the symposium. Waiters are notably expected to be quick-sighted, so as to refill provisions of wine that have run out, and 'muti' (dumb):

> 9. Ministri à dapibus oculati & muti; à poculis auriti,
> & celeres, sunto.   ('*Leges Convivales*', lines 9–10)

> Our waiters must quick-sighted be, and dumb;
> And let the *drawers* quickly hear and come.
> (Brome's translation, lines 9–10)

Despite the assurance that there is never a shortage of wine, Jonson recommends moderation in merry-making, guarding his companions against excessive drinking and riotous behaviour. In practice, of course, things could always go wrong. Jonson himself is portrayed in various contemporary sources as a hearty drinker.[16] As he often does in his works though, Jonson describes an ideal set of values. Here he provides an idealised space for refined drinking that offers a fine occasion for polite conversation and literary activity. So he urges

---

15 The Latin verb 'repudio', generally taken to mean 'to reject / refuse to accept / repudiate', may be said to allow the possibility of some female engagement even though it carries some ambiguity. Brome's translation is also ambiguous as the verb 'to sleight' may be given a range of interpretations here.

16 Jonson's habit of indulging in drink, often to the point of excess, is suggested in the *Conversations with William Drummond*, but also by various other comments made by Jonson's contemporaries. The notes of John Aubrey and Archdeacon Plume, reproduced by Herford and Simpson in their edition of Jonson, support the reputation of the poet as a heavy drinker. See *Ben Jonson*, ed. Herford and Simpson, I, pp. 178–88. Also Frances Teague in 'Jonson's Drunken Escapade', *Medieval and Renaissance Drama in England*, 6 (1993), 129–37, discusses a particular incident during which Jonson got drunk in France, where he served as a tutor to the young Walter Raleigh. Young Raleigh reportedly took advantage of his tutor's disposition to get him drunk and parade him around the streets.

those who partake in the symposium to compete in 'outwitting' rather than in 'outdrinking' each other and to be guided by a sense of measure:

> 11. Moderatis poculis provocare sodales, fas esto.
> 12. At fabulis magis, quàm vino, velitatio fiat.
> 13. Convivæ nec muti, nec loquaces sunto.
>
> ('*Leges Convivales*', lines 12–14)

> And let our only emulation be,
> Not drinking much, but *talking* wittily.
> Let it be voted lawful to stir up
> Each other with a moderate *chirping* cup;
> Let none of us be mute, or talk too much.
>
> (Brome's translation, lines 13–17)

In subsequent rules Jonson banishes any kind of behaviour that may disrupt the spirit of conviviality and companionship:

> 20. Argumentationis totus strepitus abesto.
> 21. Amatoriis querelis, ac suspiriis, liber angulus esto.
> 22. Lapitharum more scyphis pugnare, vitrea collidere,
> fenestras excutere, supellectilem dilacerare, nefas esto.
>
> ('*Leges Convivales*', lines 22–5)

> All noise of vain *disputes* must be forborne,
> And let no lover in a *corner* mourn.
> To fight and brawl (like *Hectors*) let none dare,
> Glasses or windows break, or hangings tare.
>
> (Brome's translation, lines 27–30)

In the verses that were painted on a panel and placed over the entrance of the Apollo welcoming its guests, the room is euphemistically invested with the connotations of a sacred space where all practices resemble a religious ritual:

> Welcome, all who lead or follow
> To the Oracle of Apollo:
> Here he speaks out of his Pottle,
> Or the Tripos, his Tower Bottle;
> All his Answers are Divine:
> Truth itself doth flow in Wine.
>
> ('*Over the Door at the Entrance into the Apollo*', lines 1–6)

Here drinking is a mild and controlled practice that is kept within the refined limits of this sacred place. Similarly wine is not a purpose in itself. It is not consumed just for its own sake to cause drunkenness but to induce literary activity:

> Wine it is the Milk of Venus,
> And the Poets' Horse accounted.

> Ply it, and you all are mounted;
>> ('*Over the Door at the Entrance into the Apollo*', lines 12–14)

Notably the use of wine, as opposed to any other form of drink, defines the circle of the Apollo and signifies its exclusivity through both classical associations, and wine's relative exclusivity in early modern England as a largely imported drink. As in antiquity, wine is considered the drink of poets, related to literary composition and classical moderation.

This ideal practice of moderate drinking associated by Jonson with companionship, friendly emulation and literary composition may be contrasted to what the poet calls elsewhere 'the wild anarchy of drink'. In '*An Epistle Answering to one that asked to be Sealed of the Tribe of Ben*' Jonson defines himself against those who have no sense of measure and are hypocritical. This category apparently does not have the right attributes to be admitted in Jonson's circle:

> Let those that meerely talke, and never thinke,
>> That live in the wild Anarchie of Drinke,
> Subject to quarrell only; or else such
>> As make it their proficiencie, how much
> They' <h>ave glutted in, and letcher'd out that weeke,
>> That never yet did friend, or friendship seeke
> But for a Sealing: let these men protest.　　　　　　　　(lines 9–15)

A similar concept is used in *Epigrams 115* ('*On the Town's Honest Man*') to provide the description of an ideal man who may indulge in drinking and merry-making, but knows how to keep the limits that will cause trouble if transgressed. This man can 'Do all that 'longs to the Anarchie of Drinke, / Except the duel. Can sing songs and catches, / Give everyone his dose of mirth' (lines 12–14).

Jonson's commendation of temperate drinking is reminiscent of Horatian exhortations. Moderation was celebrated by Horace as an essential element for the preservation of a spirit of mirthfulness and fellowship in the symposium. Proper attention to the rites of drinking becomes a recurrent feature in the *Odes*, as that safeguards against excessive consumption of alcohol and unruly behaviour. In *Ode 18* (Book I) Horace warns his audience to avoid the example of the Centaurs and the Lapiths whose fight was caused because of their failure to observe the rules of the ritual:

> Lest anyone take too much of moderate Liber's gift,
> be warned by the Centaurs' and Lapiths' brawl
> that was fuelled and fought on unmixed wine;
>> (Book I, *Ode 18, Nullam, Vare, sacra*, lines 8–10)[17]

---

[17]　*Horace. The Complete Odes and Epodes with the Centennial Hymn*, trans. W.G. Shepherd (Harmondsworth: Penguin Books, 1983).

In *Ode 10* (Book II) to Licinius, Horace extends this concept beyond the immediate context of the symposium to the wider public arena, making use of the metaphor of weather to demonstrate the importance of finding a middle ground that ensures the existence of equilibrium in life:

> The proper course in life, Licinius,
> is neither always to dare the deep, nor,
> timidly chary of storms, to hug
> the dangerous shore.
>
> Who values most the middle way
> avoids discreetly both the squalor
> of the slum and a palace liable
> to excite envy.   (Book II, *Ode 10, Rectius vives*, lines 1–8)

This concept of moderation was taken up by various English poets in the Renaissance. One recalls the sense of refined elegance and Horatian temperance echoed in Milton's *Sonnet XVII* ('To Edward Laurence'), or, coming back to Jonson, '*Inviting a Friend to Supper*'.

Rather than applying to Bacchus for more drink, Robert Herrick's 'A Hymne to Bacchus' in *Hesperides* subverts traditional conventions by making an explicit call for moderate drinking. Only thus will the speaker be able to fulfil his duties to the god and give up flowers in supplication. The metaphor of foul weather and stormy sea probably alludes to Horace:

> *Bacchus*, let me drink no more;
> Wild are Seas, that want shore.
> When our drinking has no stint,
> There is no one pleasure in't.
> I have drank up for to please
> Thee, that great cup *Hercules*:
> Urge no more; and there shall be
> Daffadills g'en up to Thee.[18]

In various descriptions of genial symposiastic scenes by Jonson and his 'sons', the model of Anacreon is often blended with the Horatian model, providing an elegant space of moderation and urbane conviviality. Turning to Robert Herrick again, 'An Ode to Sir Clipsebie Crew' calls upon both poets to grace his jovial gathering:

> . . . then call upon
> *Anacreon*
> To grace the frantick Thyrse:
> And having drunk, we raise a shout

---

[18] Texts from Herrick's *Hesperides* are cited from *The Poetical Works of Robert Herrick*, ed. L.C. Martin (Oxford: Clarendon Press, 1956).

> Throughout
> To praise his Verse.
>
> Then cause we *Horace* to be read,
> Which sung, or seyd,
> A Goblet, to the brim,
> Of Lyrick Wine, both swell'd and crown'd,
> A Round,
> We quaffe to him.   (lines 7–18)

Another example can be found in Herrick's anacreontic '*A Lyrick to Mirth*', where Anacreon and Horace are called up from the dead to join the merry-making:

> Rouze *Anacreon* from the dead;
> And return him drunk to bed:
> Sing o're *Horace*; for ere long
> Death will come and mar the song: (lines 9–12)

A number of such convivial verses by the 'sons of Ben', verses that evoke anacreontic in mood images of tavern-clubbing, were probably composed within the context of the Apollo in the 1620s and 1630s. It is tempting to suggest, for instance, that a number of Herrick's anacreontics actually date back to the time when the poet joined the company of Jonson and other poets in jovial drinking sessions of the Apollo. Together with verses produced later on though, they were presented in a definitive act of publication in *Hesperides* in 1648.

During this period the concept of social bonding in the anacreontic assumes greater political urgency. Produced within networks of poets like Abraham Cowley, Thomas Stanley, Richard Lovelace, Charles Cotton and Alexander Brome, the genre is invested with royalist connotations. Singing in the 'light' yet refined measures of the anacreontic, these poets attempt to produce a sense of continuity with the past and to provide moral affirmation of a prewar court culture. In more ways than one, the assumption of the anacreontic stance of the dejected old man who longs for the joys of bygone days becomes a Cavalier 'marker'.

This is a stance Herrick often assumes in *Hesperides*. Many of his verses nostalgically look back to Jonson and the Apollo as part of an ideal, carefree past. Turning on the figure of the older man who presides over a group of younger companions, Herrick's '*An Ode for Him*' (that is, Ben Jonson) provides a wonderful version of an anacreontic scene at the Apollo. The lines suggest the spirit of geniality and elegance that defines this choice symposiastic group:

> Ah *Ben*!
> Say how, or when
> Shall we thy Guests

Meet at those *Lyrick* Feasts,
Made at the *Sun,*
The *Dog,* the triple *Tunne?*
Where we such clusters had,
As made us nobly wild, not mad;
And yet each Verse of thine
Out-did the meate, out-did the frolick wine.   (lines 1–10)

The image of Jonson and his 'sons' being made 'nobly wild' rather than 'mad' highlights the element of refinement and civility that defined this exclusive culture of tavern-clubbing. The lines here are reminiscent of the anacreontic bard in *Anacreontea* 53 who wants to drink and dance among youths and to 'go mad gracefully' ('χαριέντως τε μαγῆαι', line 14). This is a notion strongly associated in Herrick's mind with Jonson. In '*Upon M. Ben. Johnson*', Herrick expresses his grief for the loss of his master, but also for the fact that 'No Holy-Rage, or frantick-fires did stirre', as he says in line nine, after Jonson's death.

The oxymoron of drinking as a refined form of madness is again picked up by Herrick in '*His fare-well to Sack*' in *Hesperides*.[19] This poem suggests a public gesture of resignation from the pleasures of drinking and possibly from poetic composition that is so closely associated with it. Here wine is exalted as 'the drink of Gods, and Angels!' (line 11) that has the power to suspend life's care and grief, arousing what is here called 'the sacred madnesse' of the soul (line 25):

'Tis thou, alone, who with thy Mistick Fan,
Work'st more then Wisdome, Art, or Nature can,
To rouze the sacred madnesse; and awake
The frost-bound-blood, and spirits; and to make
Them frantick with thy raptures, flashing through
The soule, like lightning, and as active too.
                    ('*His fare-well to Sack*', lines 22–8)

This he suggests later on was the inspiring force for poets like Horace and Anacreon who 'both had lost their fame, / Hadst thou [wine] not fill'd them with thy fire and fame' (lines 31–2). The same force no doubt inspired a number of verses in Herrick's collection.

In this light the poet's renunciation of drinking appears almost like an all the more painful attempt to hold on to a set of pleasures that is in fact taken away because of external factors. Herrick's poem was probably written at a time when drinking and merry-making came under attack by the Puritan

---

19 A similar concept is used by Herrick in various other places in *Hesperides*. In '*Delight in Disorder*', for instance, he refers to the 'wilde civility' (line 11) of a 'carelesse shooe-string' (line 12). Also in '*Art Above Nature, to Julia*', he describes 'those Lawnie Filmes' (line 13) that 'play with a wild civility' (line 14).

constitution. The practices of drinking and merry-making, as experienced by Herrick in the company of Jonson and other poets at the Apollo, come to signify an ideal past that Herrick now gives up, though apparently not by his own accord:

> But why? why longer doe I gaze upon
> Thee with the eye of admiration?
> Since I must leave thee; and enforc'd, must say
> To all thy witching beauties, Goe, Away.
> But if thy whimpring looks doe ask me why?
> Then know, that Nature bids thee goe, not I.
>
> ('*His fare-well to Sack*', lines 37–42)

Of course like various other poems in *Hesperides*, a few poems down the line '*His fare-well to Sack*' is paired off with another poem, '*The Welcome to Sack*', that soon denounces the poet's former declaration. Here Herrick addresses sack as though a mistress. He courts it so as to win its affections back. 'Welcome, O welcome my illustrious Spouse', he hails it in line thirteen. This poem pledges a renewed and lasting affection for wine that once again in Herrick's verses provides a social marker. Wine, as opposed to other drinks, prescribes an elite space that involves polite conversation and literary composition.[20] In this context, being called the 'sonne of Beere' (line 87) sounds like an insult or a curse that should come upon the poet if he proves unfaithful to wine, depriving him of his ability to compose.

The concept of exclusivity is also suggested in '*Upon Love*'. The poem rewrites those little Cupid narratives in the *Anacreontea* in which the poet professes to be tricked by Cupid and to succumb to his overwhelming power.[21] '*Upon Love*' provides another version of the anacreontic 'recusatio' in which poetic intent is stated by means of contradistinction. The poet professes to

---

[20] Susan J. Owen suggests that this distinction between wine and beer can also be found in texts written in the latter part of the seventeenth century, when it appears to have been used as a social and political marker. Owen's discussion focuses in Restoration Drama, arguing that the image of beer drinking was used by Tory dramatists to satirise the Whigs. As she comments with regard to Aphra Behn and the Earl of Rochester, 'the drinking of wine is a marker of good taste; an upper-class good taste that can encompass bawdy badinage and bisexual antics, but not vulgarity or beer drinking'. Whig dramatists, on the other hand, satirised Cavaliers as over-indulgent in French wine. See Susan J. Owen, 'The Politics of Drink in Restoration Drama', in *A Babel of Bottles*, pp. 41–51 (p. 42), and also her chapter in this present volume. Note also Angela McShane Jones's chapter, 'Roaring Royalists and Ranting Brewers', below.

[21] The anacreontic 'recusatio' in *Anacreontea* 23 provides one of these narratives. *Anacreontea* 33, in which Cupid unexpectedly knocks on the poet's door to return his hospitality with a blow in the heart, is another well-known example. *Anacreontea* 6, 11, 30 and 31 also provide different versions of the topos. The story in *Anacreontea* 6 in particular has some similarity to Herrick's '*Upon Love*'. There the poet finds Cupid among the roses while he weaves a garland. Holding him by the wings, he then plunges Cupid in his wine and drinks him up to be thereafter constantly tickled by him inside his body.

want to avoid the power of love. Instead of that he is handed Cupid's crystal glass. This of course is a figurative act that signifies the poet's initiation into erotic verse:

> A Christall Violl *Cupid* brought,
>   Which had a juice in it:
> Of which who drank, he said no thought
>   Of Love he sho'd admit.
>
> I greedy of the prize, did drinke,
>   And emptied soon the glasse;
> Which burnt me so, that I do thinke
>   The fire of hell it was.   ('*Upon Love*', lines 1–8)

The crystal glass of poetic composition is then contrasted to the 'earthen Cups' of common mortals. Even though the poet professes that he wishes to abdicate his crystal glass for an earthen one, his jestful gesturing in fact encodes an attitude of superiority:

> Give me my earthen Cups again,
>   The Christall I contemne;
> Which, though enchas'd with Pearls, contain
>   A deadly draught in them.   ('*Upon Love*', lines 9–12)

As I have already noted, the reappropriation of the anacreontic in the mid-seventeenth century acquired some very distinct political resonances. Yet the reproduction of the genre continued to mark a rather intimate and exclusive kind of male sociability as that found in the Apollo. For the greatest part of the seventeenth century the anacreontic may be identified with choice groups of learned or sophisticated figures. In later periods the anacreontic followed a course of broader dissemination, during which the boundaries between the elite and the popular were perhaps renegotiated. The late-eighteenth-century example of the Anacreontic Society attests to a more formal kind of institution, significantly bigger than the seventeenth-century societies and more socially inclusive. Certainly the discourse remained urbane, but perhaps not quite so select.

3

Tavern Societies, the Inns of Court, and the Culture of Conviviality in Early Seventeenth-Century London

MICHELLE O'CALLAGHAN

THE public drinking house was a vital social space in early modern society. Inns, taverns, and alehouses were, in the words of Peter Clark, 'indispensable social agencies', focal meeting places for the community where business and trade could be conducted, information exchanged, political issues debated, and social rituals performed.[1] Yet, out of the various forms of drinking house in the early seventeenth century, it was the tavern that played a particularly prominent role in fostering new forms of sociability among an urban elite. This was partly owing to the unique legal and institutional situation of the tavern within the drink trade, and to the entrepreneurial role of certain London tavern keepers whose taverns had gained a reputation as places renowned for attracting gallant company and men of wit. The growth of London into a populous metropolis had placed new pressures on an urban elite to distinguish itself from the commonality, particularly since dress was no longer a reliable marker of social status. Attention turned to the cultivation of city manners, typified in satiric fashion by the gallant, and the formation of elite communal identities through sociable activity that brought together civil gentlemen.[2] The early seventeenth-century tavern societies were at the centre of this new elite urbane social world, and have their social basis in the Inns of Court that, during the course of the sixteenth century, had undergone a process of gentrification to become an urban centre of civility. At the same time, the Inns were home to a new class of lawyers eager to fashion a professional identity in which notions of fellowship, civility, and gentility were vital

---

[1] Peter Clark, *The English Alehouse: A Social History, 1200–1830* (London & New York: Longman, 1983), p. 2. The most recent account of drinking spaces is Beat Kümin and B. Ann Tlusty (eds), *The World of the Tavern* (Aldershot: Ashgate, 2002). See also the notes in the Introduction to this present volume.

[2] Anna Bryson, *From Courtesy to Civility: Changing Codes of Conduct in Early Modern England* (Oxford: Clarendon Press, 1998), p. 133.

constituents. The tavern societies that met at the Mitre and Mermaid taverns on Bread Street in the early seventeenth century were largely, if not exclusively, gatherings of urban professional men, and provided an arena in which to act out rituals of social identification, based as much on the pleasures of conviviality as forms of civility and gentility.

I

Much has been written on the hierarchy of drinking establishments in the early modern period. Within this hierarchy, there was a clear social and legal distinction between the lower class and heavily regulated alehouse and the socially elite and self-regulating tavern.[3] The early Stuart period saw the tightening of licensing laws relating to alehouses that limited new buildings, drinking hours, and closely regulated alehouse keepers and their customers. Alehouses were perceived to be a threat to public order and a source of social ills, and therefore in constant need of policing. The same licensing regulations did not apply to taverns, partly because the Vintners' Company held the monopoly over the buying and selling of wine and so policed their own trade in close co-operation with the city authorities. Hence, in the 1580s the Vintners' Company petitioned the City of London over the increasing number of unregulated back-street taverns that had not only resulted in unwelcome competition and the lowering of standards, but also meant that the exclusive space of the tavern was being opened to those of lower social status.[4] It was similarly in the interests of individual tavern keepers to co-operate with the City by keeping a respectable establishment, and they, in turn, rose in wealth and status during the sixteenth and seventeenth centuries.[5] In July 1600, a case was brought before the Star Chamber by the City of London against Sir Edmond Baynham, Captain Dutton, and others, and William Williamson, a vintner, for riotous and unlawful assembly at Williamson's tavern, the Mermaid on Bread Street. The gentlemen were fined £200 and imprisoned. After much debate, Williamson was acquitted on the testimonies of his neighbours: Robert Sheppard told the court that 'Williamson hath, ever since he was a householder there, behaved himself very honestly and orderly in the well ordering of his house and family as any man of his trade in London, and doth not maintain any carding or dicing in his house'; a view corroborated by one of Sir Edmond's company, who was said to have exclaimed, 'God's wounds! What shall we do in this house? For here we shall have neither music nor

---

3 See the Introduction to this present volume. Also note, for example, Clark, *English Alehouse*, pp. 5–15; Judith Hunter, 'Legislation, Royal Proclamations and other National Directives affecting Inns, Taverns, Alehouses, Brandy Shops and Punch Houses, 1552–1757', Ph. D., University of Reading, 1994, pp. 10–19.

4 Hunter, 'Legislation', p. 117.

5 Clark, *English Alehouse*, p. 12.

dicing, for the good man of this house is the precisest man in England. We had better have gone to any tavern in London than to have come hither.'[6]

Respectable taverns could provide a relatively privileged space for the performance of a range of elite social identities. The tavern was divided into distinct public and private areas, and private rooms were made available for dinners and entertainment, such as music and gaming. Drawers in George Wilkins's *Miseries of Enforced Marriage* (1607), in a scene set at the Mitre tavern on Bread Street, run between the Dolphin room and the Pomegranate room bringing wine to clients such as William Scarborrow who calls for 'a full gallon of Sacke' so that Sir Francis Ilford can 'pledge it to the health of a friend of thine'.[7] These rooms, set off from the more public communal drinking areas, offered drinking companions and the more formal drinking societies a space of relative privacy and exclusivity, closed to those outside its circle, to act out rituals of social intimacy and identification. The 'convivium philosophicum' held at the Mitre tavern around 1611 was a self-conscious revival of the Roman convivium. By combining *convivia* and *amicitia*, the convivium cultivated an idealised space of social equality in which social boundaries could be relaxed, permitting liberties of speech and the enjoyment of pleasure, although not to the extent that conviviality degenerated into the incivilities of drunkenness.[8]

The 'success of a city tavern', as David Shields points out, 'depended on it possessing some distinguishing quality: good wine, good food, good lodging, good talk, good tobacco, a notable clientele'.[9] The dramatisation of the Mitre tavern on stage in Wilkins's *Miseries of Enforced Marriage* was not an isolated incidence, nor was it the only tavern to make such an appearance. Between 1599 and 1616 the Mitre and Mermaid taverns were advertised as the fashion-able place to be seen in plays such as Ben Jonson's *Every Man Out of His Humour* (1599), *Bartholomew Fair* (1614), and *The Devil is an Ass* (1616), Thomas Dekker's and John Webster's *Westward Hoe* (1607), and Thomas Middleton's *Your Five Gallants* (1608). The Mitre and Mermaid taverns are dramatised in a remarkably similar form across all these plays, and are typecast as the favoured resort of the gallant and men of wit. Brief allusions to these taverns in plays are particularly telling, since they rely on the audience instantly recognising the name Mermaid or Mitre and what they signify – in these cases, the conspicuous consumption, the fashionable manners, and modes of licence and revelry associated with the stage figure of the gallant. The

---

[6] Leslie Hotson, *Shakespeare's Sonnets Dated and other essays* (London: Rupert Hart-Davis, 1949), pp. 80, 91–3; John Hawarde, *Reportes del Cases in Camera Stellata*, ed. W.P. Baildon. (London: Spottiswoode, 1894), pp. 114–15.

[7] George Wilkins, *Miseries of Enforced Marriage* (1607), sigs E2r, E3r.

[8] John D'Arms, 'The Roman *Convivium* and the Idea of Equality', in *Sympotica: A Symposium on the Symposion* (Oxford: Clarendon Press, 1994), pp. 312–14.

[9] David Shields, *Civil Tongues and Polite Letters in British America* (Chapel Hill & London: University of North Carolina Press, 1997), p. 18.

gallant had emerged in the 1590s as an urbane figure, albeit in satiric dress, a caricature of fashionable London Society.[10] The local detail and privileged knowledge that structure these dramatisations of the Mitre and Mermaid give very precise shape to a new dramatic space appearing on the London stage, and allow a wider audience to participate vicariously in an elite culture of fashion, conviviality, and leisure put on display. George, a character said to be a drawer at the Mitre, seems to have attained celebrity status, and made appearances in Jonson's *Every Man Out of His Humour* and Dekker's and Webster's *Westward Hoe.*

Jonson's play, Middleton's *Your Five Gallants*, and Thomas Coryate's letters from Ajmere all identify Friday night as the night when gallants and wits, such as the Sireniacal Fraternity, gathered at either the Mitre or Mermaid tavern. Friday night may have been Mitre and Mermaid night because these taverns were distinguishing themselves from competitors by skilfully marketing their fish suppers. Friday night was fish night, even in post-Reformation London.[11] The Mitre and Mermaid taverns on Bread Street appear to have exploited their proximity to the Fish Market on Old Fish Street, and the Mermaid, in particular, was a popular venue among guilds for their formal dinners in the sixteenth century.[12] William Johnson, the tavern keeper of the Mermaid in the early seventeenth century, seems to have made considerable effort to establish a reputation not just for the food his tavern could offer, but more particularly for being willing to take risks to cater to his patron's individual tastes and appetites; Johnson was charged with selling meat on Fridays over a seven-month period in 1613.[13] In Act 5, scene 5 of Jonson's *Every Man Out of His Humour*, Carlo Buffone is served a 'loyne of porke' by George, his favourite drawer at the Mitre, on Friday night and this meat, forbidden to 'the *Iewes*', signifies a particularly greasy combination of gluttony and conspicuous consumption.[14] Despite this transgression, Johnson, like his predecessor and former master at the Mermaid, William Williamson, appears to have kept a respectable house. Even though Williamson banned gaming and itinerant musicians, the Mermaid was able to attract the society Inns of Court gentlemen in the late sixteenth century and early seventeenth century.[15] It may have been that both Williamson and Johnson marketed their tavern as a

---

10 Bryson, *Courtesy to Civility*, pp. 129–30.

11 The Statute of 27 Elizabeth outlawed the sale of meat 'upon any Friday, Saturday, or other days appointed to be Fish Days, or any day in time of Lent' (Hotson, *Shakespeare's Sonnets Dated*, p. 84).

12 Kenneth Rogers, *The Mermaid and Mitre Taverns in Old London* (London: Homeland Association, 1928), pp. 8, 14–15, 119.

13 Hotson, *Shakespeare's Sonnets Dated*, p. 84.

14 Jonson, *Every Man Out of His Humour*, in *Ben Jonson*, ed. C.H. Herford, Percy Simpson and Evelyn Simpson, 11 vols (Oxford: Clarendon Press, 1925–52), III, p. 580.

15 *Le Prince d'Amour, or the Prince of Love* (1660), p. 42; Thomas Coryate, *Travailer For the English Wits, and the good of this Kingdom* (1616), pp. 40–5.

respectable elite establishment noted for the quality of its wine, food, and clientele, rather than for riotous activity, such as gaming, and in this way clearly distinguished their tavern in terms of social class from other, 'common' drinking houses that would tolerate disorderly conduct.

Both the Mitre and the Mermaid are portrayed in contemporary texts as the favoured meeting place for men of wit. It is likely that these taverns cultivated the society of the nearby Inns of Court men, who in turn cultivated a reputation for wit. One of the key preconditions for the emergence of new modes of public sociability, as Peter Clark points out, was 'significant clusters of resident gentry', since voluntary societies, in particular, depended on the leisured elite's commitment of time and money to ensure their long-term viability.[16] The Inns of Court in the sixteenth and early seventeenth century housed the most significant cluster of resident gentry in London, even outnumbering the court.[17] The Inns were ideally positioned geographically, socially, and economically to take advantage of the new forms of leisure activity increasingly available in London. In fact, they appear to be the main consumers of new forms of leisure activity. Sir Hugh Cholmley, a Gray's Inn student in the mid-1610s, recalled that the year after he left the Inn he took a house in Fleet Street and 'lived at large all the winter about the towne'. By the early seventeenth century, there was a distinct London season that followed the law year and began in autumn, ended in June, and reached its height at Christmas. During this time, he played bowls in indoor bowling alleys and on outdoor bowling grounds, presumably in parks such as Spring Garden where spectators and players could also drink wine, and frequented gaming houses. While still at Gray's Inn, he met his future wife when promenading with friends in Hyde Park. From the vantage point of middle age, he regretted the way he had 'totally misspent my tyme' at Gray's Inn by playing and gaming.[18] These notions of prodigality form the basis of the standard satiric portrait of the Inns of Court man. Fungoso, the Inns of Court student in Jonson's *Every Man Out of His Humour*, extorts money out of his father to ape the fashionable apparel of the court clothes-horse Fastidius Briske. Like the stage gallant, Fungoso stands in for a newly emergent and troubling urban culture of fashionable consumption.

[16] Peter Clark, *British Clubs and Societies 1580–1800: The Origins of an Associational World* (Oxford: Clarendon Press, 2000), p. 46.

[17] Philip Finkelpearl, *John Marston of the Middle Temple: An Elizabethan Dramatist in his Social Setting* (Cambridge, MA: Harvard University Press, 1969), p. 5.

[18] *The Memoirs and Memorials of Sir Hugh Cholmley of Whitby, 1600–1657*, ed. J. Binns (York: The Boydell Press for Yorkshire Archaeological Record Society, 2000), p. 83; F.J. Fisher, 'The Development of London as a Centre of Consumption in the Sixteenth and Seventeenth Centuries', *Transactions of the Royal Historical Society*, 30 (1948), 41–2, p. 47.

II

When the tavern became a place of fashion, it simultaneously underwent a process of aestheticisation. The societies that frequented the Mitre and the Mermaid were characterised by their wit and versifying. Poetry in these spaces, in part, appears to function as an aesthetic commodity, a pleasure available to a cultivated elite possessing the requisite education, leisure, and, above all, civility for its appreciation. Pascal Brioist makes a similar point when he argues that wit became a marker of social distinction among the seventeenth-century tavern societies, identifying an aristocracy of intellect based on style or linguistic fashion.[19] This is not to argue for the emergence of a separate aesthetic sphere in this period. I.A. Shapiro concluded from his study of the composition the Mitre and Mermaid tavern societies that it did not gather for the purposes of appreciation of *belles lettres*, since it did not include a professional writer, such as Ben Jonson, but was dominated by lawyers, merchants, and former members of Prince Henry's household.[20] There are important distinctions to be made between the complexion and functioning of early seventeenth-century tavern societies and the private societies and salon culture of the eighteenth century. Yet, Shapiro assumes a separation of politics and literature that was not yet in place. An interest in literature was widespread among the social elite, and the composition of poetry was one of the social accomplishments that distinguished the gentleman.[21] The tavern societies that frequented the Mitre and the Mermaid may have been talking politics, but all the available evidence indicates that they were also making poetry.[22] Writers in this period speak of taverns as places where the drinking of wine went hand in hand with the making of poetry. George Wither, a young Lincoln's Inn poet, recalled that he first met his friend, William Browne, a student at the Inner Temple, at a gathering held at the St Dunstan and the Devil tavern in Fleet Street in the early 1610s, when verses were read and exchanged 'Sitting by the Crimson Streame'.[23] A 1617 engraving by William Marshall, 'Lawes of Drinking' (Fig. 1.1, above), which compares the world of the tavern and the alehouse, uses poetry as a marker of social distinction that signifies the social and cultural differences between 'the leisured quality and the working

---

[19] Pascal Brioist, 'Que de choses avons nous vues et vécues à la Sirène', *Histoire et Civilisation*, 4 (1991), 113.

[20] I.A. Shapiro, 'The "Mermaid Club"', *Modern Language Review*, 15 (1950), 8.

[21] R.W. Wienpahl, *Music at the Inns of Court during the reigns of Elizabeth, James and Charles* (Ann Arbor: University Microfilms International, 1979), p. 8.

[22] Annabel Patterson coins the phrase 'talking politics' to characterise the activities of these tavern societies in 'All Donne', in *Soliciting Interpretation: Literary Theory and Seventeenth-Century English Poetry*, ed. E.D. Harvey and K.E. Maus (Chicago & London: University of Chicago Press, 1990), pp. 37–67.

[23] William Browne, *The Shepheards Pipe* (1614).

commonality'.[24] The tavern is the socially elite home to the muses, and gathered around the table are stylishly dressed gentlemen, some smoking pipes, served by a Roman wine bearer carrying a lyre, the musical instrument of the gods. Wine flows from the Helicon and is 'Nectar vt Ingenium', alluding to the notion that wine stimulates the creative imagination. The tavern sign is a dolphin, perhaps a reference to the Dolphin room at the Mitre, and is inscribed with the words 'Poets Impalled wth Lawrell Coranets'. The lower-class alehouse, at the sign of the rose, is frequented by rustics who drink ale trickling from the rather earthier Puddlewharf and entertain themselves with jigs and music from the bagpipe, associated with the ballad. The different modes of entertainment are carefully socially inflected, and function to establish a clear distinction between elite and popular cultures.[25]

Marshall's engraving accompanies *A Solemne Ioviall Disputation, Theoreticke and Practicke; briefly shadowing the Law of Drinking* (1617), Richard Brathwaite's highly self-conscious contribution to the very German genre of drink literature (*Trinkliteratur*). Brathwaite and his publisher correctly envisioned a market for this type of literature, and there were at least three editions of this work, in Latin and English, between 1616 and 1617, and a further edition appeared in 1627. For the 1617 English version, Brathwaite composed a new companion text to the *Law of Drinking, The Smoking Age, or, the Man in the Mist: with the life and death of Tobacco*. By englishing *Trinkliteratur*, Brathwaite was disseminating the cultural fictions and rituals of elite sociable drinking that were the basis of this genre. The type of reader and uses that this text was put to is suggested by the inscription on fly leaf of a copy of the *Laws of Drinking* in the Bodleian Library:

> To my woothelye esteem[ed *page damaged*] frind Tho: Stradling esq [*page damaged*] and other my ancient frin [d *page damaged*] and familier accquaintance in Glamorgan sheere
> I pray see this Straunger well entertayned and th[at *page damaged*] hee receaue safe conduct from place to place.[26]

In this case, the act of gift-giving and the book's circulation among an intimate readership is translated into the language of friendship and conviviality whereby the text is a 'stranger' requiring the hospitality of friends to be admitted into their circle. Elite drinking rituals relied on the cultivation of social manners and modes of sociability, and thereby enabled members of an

---

[24] Shields uses this phrase in a different context (*Civil Tongues*, p. xx). See Cedric C. Brown's chapter, above, for further notes on Marshall's engraving.

[25] Brioist has argued that the tavern sign portrayed in the engraving is that of the Mermaid tavern ('Choses', p. 103).

[26] *Laws of Drinking* and *The Smoaking Age* (1617), Bodleian Douce D. 34. Page reference to this text will be given in parentheses.

elite to identify themselves with gentlemen of equal status.[27] Brathwaite's *Law of Drinking* primarily addresses a student audience, and the tract sets out the codes of behaviour and modes of sociability appropriate to a student-based tavern society. Its governing principle is that social drinking is intrinsic to civility. There is evidence that by the late sixteenth century, Inns of Court drinking societies were explicitly employing such notions of 'civil conversation', a term that referred to civility in manners as well as speech, to distinguish their convivial gatherings. The Gray's Inn revels of 1594–5, in a tone of light mockery, set out a programme of reading, '*Guizo*, the *French* Academy, *Galiatto* the Courtier, *Plutarch*, the *Arcadia* and Neoterical writers', that should be accompanied by 'Conference' at the 'better sort of Ord'naries . . ., whereby they may . . . become accomplished with Civil Conversations, and able to govern a Table with Discourse'.[28] Brathwaite's *Law of Drinking* is closely related to a classic of *Trinkliteratur*, Vincentius Obsopoeus' *Ars Bibendi* (1536), and may have drawn its inspiration and title from the German text. Obsopoeus' *Ars Bibendi* is a book of manners, a type of humanist conduct book, as its title suggests, designed to teach the arts of drinking and accommodate the custom of health pledges to ideals of civility that characterise polite society. Obsopoeus advocates moderation in drinking, the careful choice of cultivated drinking companions drawn from one's class, since the 'public's opinion of you arises from your friends', temperate speech while drinking, good-mannered social behaviour, such as avoiding grimacing, belching, and spitting, and setting limits when health pledging in such a way that honour is not compromised.[29] If this fails, then Obsopoeus gives advice on how to deceive others and maintain face during bouts of competitive drinking. Competitive social drinking in Germany appears to have provided an outlet for elite masculine aggression and the display and defence of masculine honour following the decline of the martial forms of medieval chivalry at court and aristocratic households.[30]

The aggressive display of aristocratic honour, enshrined in the custom of health pledging, which *Ars Bibendi* sought to reform and civilize, is subsumed to the milder and more temperate imperatives of friendship and '*Morall Civilitie*' in Brathwaite's *Law of Drinking*: social drinking arises out of a '*liberalitie* [that] is occasioned either out of *pure affection*, as mutuall courtesies are shewne among friends for no other cause than merely for friendship' (3).

---

27 B.A. Tlusty, *Bacchus and Civic Order: the Culture of Drink in Early Modern Germany* (Charlottesville & London: University Press of Virginia, 2001), p. 212; Bryson, *Courtesy to Civility*, pp. 133–9.

28 *Gesta Grayorum 1688*, edited by W.W. Greg (Oxford: Malone Society Reprints, 1914), pp. 29–30.

29 *The Art of Drinking. Three Books by the Author Vincentius Obsopoeus the German*, trans. Helen F. Simpson, in E.M. Jellinek, 'A Specimen of the Sixteenth-Century German Drink Literature – Obsopoeus's *Art of Drinking*', *Quarterly Journal of Studies on Alcohol*, 5 (1944–5), 666–72.

30 Tlusty, *Bacchus*, p. 91.

The *Law of Drinking* sets out the various types of pledges that provide a ritualised medium of social cohesion and are said to have superseded other ceremonies and signs of alliance and fraternity, such as 'the reciprocal salutation, joining of hands, sociable and familiar conversation' (12). The list of pledges begins with the health cup, which provides a very public display of the close social bonds and group solidarity forged by kinship ties among the elite: 'Yea, oft times it is held incivility, for anyone to suffer the health of his neere kinsman to be begun without a ceremoniall protestation of indeered amity and affection' (11). The sincerity of this pledge does appear to be open to question, leaving the impression that the health cup has become an empty aristocratic ceremonial form. By contrast, sincerity is key to the Cup of Brotherhood. The author advises that this pledge should not be invoked in the company of someone to whom 'you conceive any distaste . . . unless you freely desire reconciliation' (13). *Law of Drinking* is less interested in the social values of blood and honour that underpin aristocratic pledges, and instead concerns itself with the sincerity and '*pure affection*' (3) that motivate the pledge of brotherhood. This dissemination of a civil notion of fraternity, arising out of the intimate bonds of friendship rather than blood, is appropriate to a student tavern society that has a different social composition from an aristocratic drinking society, which places greater value on kinship ties, and hence is structured by different forms of sociability.

In principle, fraternity describes social relationships that are equal rather than hierarchical. Yet, there is a social limit to this equality that admits a concept of hierarchy. The discourse of fraternity reconceptualises social bonds. When the *Law of Drinking* considers the question of appropriate drinking companions, the social distinctions the text elaborates have complex inflections that are not necessarily dependent on social status, but are also related to education, perhaps not surprisingly given the university context. For example, the author considers whether a senior student should drink with a freshman and concludes that he should not lest the elder brother fall down to his younger brother's level. The use of a fraternal metaphor in this context suggests the ways in which an intellectual hierarchy structures the concept of brotherhood. Education has at least equal value to claims of blood in this process of reformulating social status and distinctions; a nobleman can profitably drink with a student without damaging his status or reputation, in fact, he 'addes ornament to his dignity', and the author gives the example of 'how great Monarches have sought the friendship of learned men; that being instructed by their counsell and learning, they might more happily sit at the sterne of state, and governe their kingdomes' (17). Here, the text is drawing on a civic humanist concept of counsel to structure the relationship between the aristocracy and men of learning within an expanded governing class. A meritocratic notion of nobility accompanies this account of counsel, and, interestingly, is offered as a particular feature of students who 'apply themselves to the study of the Law' in a manner that is strongly reminiscent of Inns of Court writings on the subject: 'Which Nobility being obtained by his owne proper worth, is held much more excellent than that which commeth by descent, according to that: *He is truely noble, whom his owne worth doth ennoble*' (17).

III

Evidence for the existence of the tavern societies that met at the Mitre and Mermaid largely derives from texts associated with the well-known traveller Thomas Coryate: a Latin poem circulating in manuscript records a 'Convivium Philosophicum' held at the Mitre tavern probably in late 1611; and in his letters from Ajmere to the 'English wits', Coryate, a guest at the Mitre convivium, gave details of meetings of the 'Fraternitie of Sireniacal Gentlemen' at the Mermaid tavern. The textual nature of these traces of a tavern society or societies suggests that it was as much a textual space as a lived space. Coryate's published letters from Ajmere tend to situate these tavern gatherings in a distinctly urban environment. Tavern societies in the early to mid seventeenth century were almost exclusively an urban phenomenon. In new urban centres, older forms of community were rapidly breaking down, giving rise to new communities and new modes of social organisation.[31] Thomas Coryate's letters from Ajmere characterise London in terms of a series of social exchanges among a cohesive group of educated professional male friends. The third letter addressed to Lawrence Whitaker directs the letter-bearer to convey his greetings to a list of individuals including:

> ... M. George Speake my generous & ingenuous contriman, the Sonne and heyre apparent of Sir George Speake in Sommersetshire: him you are like to finde in any Terme, eyther at the middle Temple, or in some Barbers house neere to the Temple.
> ... M. Iohn Donne, the author of two most elegant Latine Bookes, *Pseudo martyr*, and *Ignatii Conclaue*: of his abode either in the Stra[n]d, or elsewhere in London: I thinke you shall bee easily informed by the meanes of my friend, M. *L. W.*
> ... M. Richard Martin, Counsellor, at his chamber in the middle Temple, but in the Terme time, scarse else.
> ... M. Christopher Brooke of the city of Yorke, Councellor, at his chamber in Lincolnes Inne, or neere it.
> ... M. *Iohn Hoskins*, alias *Aequinoctial Pasticrust*, of the citie of Hereford, Councellor at this chamber in the middle Temple.
> ... M. George Garrat; of whose beeing you shal vnderstand by Master Donne aforesaide.
> ... M. William Hackwell, at his chamber in Lincolnes Inne.
> ... Master Beniamin Iohnson the Poet, at his chamber at the Blacke Friars.
> ... Maist. Iohn Bond my countreyman, chiefe Secretarie vnto my Lord Chancellour.

---

31 Shields, *Civil Tongues*, p. xiv.

...M. Doctor Mocket, resident perhappes in my Lord of *Canterburies* house at Lambeth, where I left him.

...M. *Inigo Jones*, there where Maister *Martin* shall direct you.

...M. *Iohn Williams* the Kings Gold-[...] at this house in Cheapside.

...M. *Hugh Holland*, at his lodging, where M. *Martin* shall direct you.

...M. *Robert Bing* at *Yongs* ordinarie, neere the Exchange.

...M. *William Stansby*, the Printer of my *Crudities* and *Crambe*, at his house in Thames street: also to his childlesse wife.

...all the Stationers in *Paules Churchyard*; but especially those by name, Mast. *Norton*, Mast. *Waterson*, M. *Mathew Lownes*, M. *Edward Blount*, and M. *Barrat*, &c.[32]

Coryate identifies his countrymen George Speake and John Bond through kinship and patronage ties that tend to be the basis of 'country' modes of sociability, but it is clear in the case of Speake that this 'contriman' has been transformed in this urban environment, and is now at home in the barber's shop.[33] Coryate's letters map patterns of sociability on to the geography of London. It is, in fact, a very specific area of London around the Inns of Court to the west and east, an area that includes taverns, such as the Mitre and Mermaid on Bread Street, the newly fashionable area in the west around the Strand and Blackfriars, and St Paul's Cathedral, with its aisles, a place for exchanging gossip and news, and the stationers' shops in the churchyard. The letters give a very concrete sense of the way that physical space is constituted by social practices and social relationships through the way that it carefully maps occupations, and patterns of social activity and interaction.

I.A. Shapiro, Baird Whitelock and Pascal Brioist have closely studied the composition of the societies said to have held meetings at the Mitre and Mermaid taverns in the early seventeenth century. Their research has produced a picture of a fluid gathering of individuals that coalesced into more formalised societies meeting regularly on Fridays at the Mitre and Mermaid. The majority of those who dined together at the Mitre *convivium* are also named by Thomas Coryate as Mermaid Sireniacs; as Whitelock points out, just as it 'is not always possible to keep the groups separate, nor is it ever possible to establish them as essentially the same society'.[34] These fluid textual and social gatherings are most productively viewed not in terms of the fixity of the self-enclosed circle but through the conceptual framework of the network. One particular gathering of individuals, for example, the Sireniacal Fraternity, threads out into a dynamic web of associations that includes Prince Henry's court, the Inns of Court, the House of Commons, and the Society of

---

[32] Coryate, *Travailer For the English Wits, and the good of this Kingdom* (1616), pp. 44–5.

[33] Bryson distinguishes between 'country' and urban modes of sociability (*Courtesy to Civility*, pp. 139–40).

[34] Baird Whitelock, *John Hoskyns, Serjeant-at-Law* (Washington, DC: University Press of America, 1982), p. 381; Shapiro, "Mermaid Club", pp. 6–17; Brioist, 'Choses', pp. 89–132.

Antiquaries. The nexus is to be found at the Middle Temple and Lincoln's Inn. Those named among the Mitre convivium and the Mermaid Sireniacal Fraternity, and those who placed verses before *Coryate's Crudities* (1610), were overwhelmingly Middle Temple and Lincoln's Inn men. Friendship between the two Inns had a long history; Sir George Buc spoke of the Middle Temple as the 'ancient friend and ally' of Lincoln's Inn, and the two Inns regularly held 'convivial meetings – "a drinking"', in the words of the Black Books of Lincoln's Inn.[35] One such 'drinking' had led to the creation of the Prince of Love who presided over the 1597–8 Middle Temple Christmas Revels. It is possible that these Revels began to formalise and give structure to friendships among a group of 'Linconians' and their 'noble confederates' the Middle Templarians that subsequently developed into the later tavern societies.[36] Key members of the Sireniacal Fraternity took major roles in these revels: Richard Martin, the Prince of Love, was attended by a court that included John Hoskins, Lord President of the Council, and other, unidentified officers, such as the Lord Chancellor and Lord Marshall, and it may have been the case that Linconians, like Christopher Brooke and his close friend John Donne, played a strong supporting role in the revels. It is possible that the structure of this court was translated into the Sireniacal Fraternity, which also had officers: for example, we know from Coryate's letters that Lawrence Whitaker held the office of High Seneschal, a steward in a prince's household.

A court, however, has a very different social and symbolic formation from a fraternity. The mock-courtly form taken by the grand Christmas Revels was, in part, a consequence of the way the Inns of Court in the course of the sixteenth century had been turned into an academy for the training of courtiers, a place where the nobility were, in the words of John Fortescue, 'taught. . . to practice dancing and all games proper for nobles, as those brought up in the king's household are accustomed to practice'.[37] These noble social manners and courtly graces underwent a transformation in the socially mixed environment of the Inns of Court. Although it appears that 88 per cent of those entering the Inns between 1590 and 1640 styled themselves gentlemen, the use of this title had become widespread among the middling sort to the extent that, as Christopher Brooks concludes, 'it is likely that a significant number of those who entered the inns should be regarded as of bourgeois or plebeian stock rather than as sons of country gentlemen'.[38] There is an assumption that there was a clear social distinction at the Inns between the 'plebeian' professional lawyer and the gentleman amateur, who 'aggressively' distinguished himself from the

---

35 E. Williams, *Early Holborn and the Legal Quarter of London* (London: Street and Maxwell, 1927), I, p. 37.

36 *The Memoirs of Sir Benjamin Rudyerd, Knt.* ed. J.A. Manning (London, 1841), p. 9.

37 Quoted in Wienpahl, *Music at the Inns of Court*, p. 8.

38 C.W. Brooks, 'The Common Lawyers in England, c. 1558–1642', in Wilfred Prest (ed.), *Lawyers in Early Modern Europe and America* (London: Croom Helm, 1981), pp. 42–64, p. 54.

former through wit and versifying, the cultural markers of gentility.[39] Yet, the majority of Coryate's English wits were professional lawyers well known for their versifying, men such as Richard Martin, John Hoskins, and Christopher Brooke. As well as adopting the cultural markers of gentility, professional lawyers turned their craft into a form of *civilitas*, identifying with the educated and well-born '*iuris prudente* or *iuris consulti* of the Roman Republic', whose legal knowledge fitted them for an active life in government.[40] Sir Hugh Cholmley's meditation on the consequences of his failure to pursue his legal studies indicates the extent to which this professional ideal had become commonplace in the early seventeenth century:

> every man that hath but a smackering of the law though of no fortune or quallety shall bee a leader or director to the greatest and best gentlemen on the bench, which hath often put in to my mynde a sayeing of my father in law Sir W. Twisden a very great scholler that there were two. . . things worth spending a mans tyme and studdy in, the one the law of god to teach him the way to heaven, the other the law of the Nation to direct how to deport him self in this life and to manage his cyvell affayres.[41]

The Inns of Court in the late sixteenth and early seventeenth century arguably provided an environment in which mock courts could become professional fraternities and fellowships.

In 1598, many of those Middle Templarians and Linconians later identified by Coryate as Sireniacal gentleman, such as Richard Martin, John Hoskins, Christopher Brooke, John Donne, and William Hakewill, were in their mid to late twenties and seeking to establish a career, many in the legal profession.[42] The Sireniacal Fraternity brought together lawyers, members of the House of Commons, individuals attached to Prince Henry's court or important official households, like that of Sir Thomas Egerton, the Lord Chancellor, and merchants and financiers, and it is possible that it functioned as a type of mutual society, a support network designed to further the personal, business, and professional interests of its members. The period from around 1606 to 1614, when the tavern societies associated with the Middle Temple and Lincoln's Inn were most active, coincides with the period when the core Sireniacs (Hoskins, Brooke, Sir Robert Phelips, Hakewill, and Martin) were working together in parliament. All were members of the 1604 to 1610 parliaments and, apart from Martin, the 1614 'addled' Parliament. Martin did speak in this parliament on behalf of the Virginia Company, and he was supported by Hoskins and Brooke, who had forwarded the motion that the business of

---

[39] W. Prest, *The Inns of Court under Elizabeth I and the Early Stuarts, 1590–1640* (London: Longman, 1972), pp. 41–2; Finkelpearl, *John Marston*, p. 46.
[40] Brooks, 'Common Lawyers', pp. 54–5.
[41] *Memoirs and Memorials*, p. 83.
[42] Hoskins was in his early thirties.

the Company be heard.[43] These individuals frequently appeared on the same committees, supported each other's speeches, and took similar stances on issues such as the Union of the Kingdoms, impositions, parliamentary privileges, and extent of the royal prerogative. Impositions, taxes on imported goods used to raise revenue for the Crown, brought together a range of issues from constitutional questions regarding the legislative role of parliament and the extent of the absolute prerogative to the business interests of merchants. It was a hot issue from around 1604 until 1614, and Brooke, Martin, Hakewill, and Hoskins formed a particularly effective lobby group in the Commons against impositions in the 1610 parliament. The Sireniacal Fraternity therefore appears to have facilitated a working relationship between its members in the House of Commons and may have provided a sounding board for discussion of contentious issues currently debated in parliament and, in this way, have proved instrumental in the formation of political opinion among this group of lawyers in the Commons.[44]

This chapter has tended to produce an image of rather sober tavern societies that bear a close resemblance to the mutual societies that flourish within a Habermasian public sphere. Such rational sobriety belies their conviviality, and does not take adequate account of how formative pleasure was to the nature of these societies. These societies were as much about play and pleasure as they were about professional interests and civility. As noted earlier in this chapter, one of the models for these early seventeenth-century tavern societies was the Roman *convivium*, which sought to maintain a state between sobriety and drunkenness that could stimulate liberty of speech and an epicurean suspension of reason, in order to explore states of pleasure.[45] Liberty of speech within these societies found its expression through wit. Part of the pleasure of wit is that it can confirm an individual's membership of a community when that individual is able to recognise its in-jokes, formulae, codes, and rituals, and thereby clearly distinguish themselves from those who are its unwitting victims.[46] The pleasure of wit, however, can also derive from its scurrility. The liberty and ease of speech enjoyed within the tavern society could be dangerous in other environments. Richard Martin and John Hoskins, in particular, were well known in the Commons for their wit, but both also took the parliamentary privilege of freedom of speech into dangerous territory: Martin was censured by the House in 1614 for presuming to lecture on the Virginia Company, and Hoskins was imprisoned by the King at the dissolution

---

[43] *Proceedings in Parliament 1614*, ed. M. Jansson (Philadelphia: American Philosophical Society, 1988), pp. 257, 276.

[44] M. O'Callaghan, ' "Talking Politics": Tyranny, parliament, and Christopher Brooke's *The ghost of Richard the third*', *The Historical Journal*, 41 (1998), 105–7; Brioist, 'Choses', p. 125.

[45] Ezio Pellizer, 'Outlines of a Morphology of Sympotic Entertainment', in *Sympotica*, pp. 178–9.

[46] Noel Malcolm, *The Origins of English Nonsense* (London, 1997), p. 119.

of this parliament for drawing a potentially treasonous analogy between the situation of James I and his Scottish favourites and that of Charles of Anjou who was driven out of Sicily and his French followers massacred. The popular scatalogical satire, the 'Censure of a Parliament Fart', also called 'A Parliament Libel', which circulated widely in manuscript, is a vivid example of the way that political languages and spaces could be shaped by the wit, humour, theatricality, and satire that characterise the culture of the tavern societies. One manuscript version closely identifies the satire with members of the Sireniacal fraternity – Inigo Jones, Martin, Hoskins, and Brooke – and ends with the lines:

> Ned Jones, Dick Martyn, Hopkins, [sic] & Brooke
> The fower compilers of this booke
> Fower of like witte, fower of like arte.
> And all fower not worth a fart.[47]

The satire was occasioned by a fart let by member of the Commons, Henry Ludlow, which interrupted the Chief Messenger of the House of Lords, Sir John Crook, who was delivering his message during debates on the Union in March 1607. The poem consists of a series of couplets, variously ordered and numbering anywhere from fifty to one hundred in different versions, that give the characteristic response of members of the Commons to Ludlow's fart. In this sense, it takes a similar form to that other contemporary tavern society poem, 'Convivium Philosophicum', in that the couplets gather together those present to create a space of sociability in which individuals are united by wit and common political interests. The 'Parliament Fart' turns the House of Commons into a raucous tavern meeting, and gives the impression of an institutional self-consciousness and confidence among members of parliament, by paradoxically taking great liberties with the House and its members. Texts like 'The Censure of a Parliament Fart', and the actions of Martin and Hoskins, strongly suggest that we need to consider the way that wit, humour, and a playful theatricality shaped political life in the early seventeenth century, and how the civil spaces emerging in the period were as much places for convivial pleasures as rational deliberation.

---

[47] British Library, Add. MSS 23,339, f. 17b.

Politicised Drink

4

Wine for Comfort:
Drinking and the Royalist Exile Experience, 1642–1660

MARIKA KEBLUSEK

IN March 1658, the exiled royalist Sir Robert Moray, writing from his lodgings in Maastricht, assured his friend Sir Alexander Bruce, living in Bremen: 'You pay me with a clairet complement for drinking your health. I will take it as if it were true Canary'.[1] Going out to dinner with the physician Dr Massenet, an acquaintance of his, Moray promised Bruce two months later that 'we mean to remember you and Will as often as we drink as we use to do'.[2] The custom of drinking someone's health is referred to time and again in this correspondence, not merely as a sign of respect, or a cursory ending to a letter, but as a confirmation of friendship, of shared intimacy, sometimes even of consolation. 'Here I dined & we drank your health,' Moray jokingly complained: 'a debt you are pretty deep ingaged in'.[3] On another occasion, a story too complicated to tell on paper was described as a 'tale of 2 drinkes', to be saved until the time when the two friends could sit down together.[4] For Moray, toasting his friends *in absentia* was a powerful way to keep a company emotionally together, while physically apart.

Deeply resonant in the Moray letters is the notion of drinking as an integral part of friendship, conviviality and mirth. Its literary counterpart, of course, had long been established in poetic traditions celebrating the pleasures of alcohol and intoxication, laughter and wit. In the 1640s and 1650s, anacreontic traditions intensified, and drink and drunkenness became crucial features of the fictional Cavalier character – with heavy political overtones, as recent criticism has shown.[5] This royalist 'cult of drinking' operated on various levels.

---

1 London, Royal Society, MS 246 (Transcript Kincardine Papers), p. 219: Moray to Bruce, 19–3–1658 (NS).
2 Ibid., p. 318: Moray to Bruce, 3–5–1658 (NS).
3 Ibid., p. 245: Moray to Bruce, 29–3–1658 (NS).
4 Ibid., p. 223: Moray to Bruce, 21–3–1658 (NS).
5 Lois Potter, *Secret Rites and Secret Writing. Royalist Literature, 1641–1660* (Cambridge:

Drinking wine as opposed to the common pint of beer emphasised the aristocratic, courtly status of the Cavalier. Richard Flecknoe, a Catholic royalist refugee, urged in one of his poems:

> Let then Divines, if they would mend it, preach
> Gainst small beer only, and no Doctrine teach,
> But drinking *wine*, no other vice dispraise,
> But *Beer*, and we may hope for better days.[6]

One of the most prolific poets on the subject of wine and intoxication, Alexander Brome declared claret to be

> . . . the means and the end of our study,
> It does make our invention oreflow,
> While the channel of ale makes it muddy.[7]

In a society that was roughly divided into the camps of royalists and parliamentarians, one's choice of drink could, therefore, mark one's political affiliation.[8] According to Brome,

> Beer and Ale makes you prate
> Of the Kirk and the State
> Wanting other discourse worth the hearing (. . .)
> And your talk's all diurnals and Gunpowder matter,

whereas wine drinkers were loyal to the king's cause, and ready to fight for it:

> But we while old sack does divinely inspire us
> Are active to do what our Ruler require us.[9]

Cambridge University Press, 1989); Alexander Brome, *Poems*, ed. Roman R. Dubinski (Toronto, Buffalo & London: University of Toronto Press, 1982), I, pp. 18–22; Adam Smyth, *Profit and Delight: Printed Miscellanies in England, 1640–1682* (Detroit: Wayne State University Press, 2004); Jason McElligott, 'John Crouch, *The Man in the Moon*, and Royalism in Interregnum England' (forthcoming). I thank both Dr Smyth and Dr McElligott for generously allowing me to read their unpublished work.

6   'In Small Beer', in Richard Flecknoe, *Miscellania. Or, Poems of all sorts, with divers other Pieces* (1653), p. 29. Compare Alexander's Brome's song 'To his Friend that had vow'd Small-Bear', in Brome, *Poems*, I, pp. 83–4.

7   'On the fall of the prices of wine', in Brome, *Poems*, I, p. 97. See Dubinski, 'Wine and the Happy Life' in his introduction to Brome's *Poems*, pp. 18–22. On Brome, see further, Raymond A. Anselment, 'Alexander Brome and the search for the "Safe Estate" ', *Renaissance and Reformation*, 20 (1984), 39–51.

8   See Smyth, *'Profit and Delight'*.

9   'The Answer', in Brome, *Poems*, I, p. 126. Some poets made an exception for good-quality beer, however, possibly because of 'nationalistic' associations: 'our wholsome and Heroic *English* juice', in 'The Answer to the Curse against Ale', in Brome, *Poems*, I, pp. 160–2. Here, the poet pointed out that corrupted ale had been one of the causes of the rebellion: ''Twas not this loyal liquor shut / Our Gates against our Soveraign, but / Strange drinks into one tub together put'. Equally, corrupted sack was perceived as upsetting the social order: 'Against

In royalist writing, drinking beer was often associated with the Roundheads' base behaviour.[10] In his account of the destruction of Norwich Cathedral during the Civil Wars, Bishop Joseph Hall lamented the sacrilegious behaviour of the soldiers who had turned the church into an 'Ale-house', 'drinking and tobacconing (. . .) freely'.[11] Getting them drunk was the only way to make parliamentary soldiers fight and 'to pour out their blood in the act of rebellion', the royalist newspaper *Mercurius Aulicus* scorned.[12] Pamphleteers exploited to the fullest Oliver Cromwell's former career as a brewer.[13] Wine, then, was the drink of the king's supporters, and it was sack, 'princely' canary and claret, 'born of the royal vine', which was celebrated and immortalised by royalist poets.[14]

At first glance, many of these poems seem simply to extol the pleasures of alcohol and the company of wits, or to suggest drink as an excellent remedy against a melancholy mind. In 'The Club', for example, Alexander Brome admonished:

> Prithee ben't so sad and serious,
> Nothing's got by grief or care,
> Melancholy's too imperious,
> Where it comes 'twil domineer,
> If thou hast a cloudy breast,
> In which thy cares would build a nest,
> Then drink good sack, 'twill make thee rest,
> Where sorrows come not near.[15]

However, the political stance of these poems is unmistakable. The sorrows Brome alluded to, albeit in a veiled manner, were those of loyal royalists, facing the bankruptcy of the Stuart cause. In other poems, he spoke in less general

Corrupted Sack', in Brome, *Poems*, I, pp. 168–70: 'Treasons committed and contriv'd by thee, / Kingdoms and Kings subverted'.

10 For examples from printed miscellanies, see Smyth, *'Profit and Delight'*.

11 Joseph Hall, *The Shaking of the Olive Tree: The remaining Works of . . . J. H. . . . With some Specialities of Divine Providence in his Life, noted by his own hand. Together with his Hard Measure, written also by himself* (1660), p. 64. Compare a similar report about events in Cambridge, where parliamentary troops were said to abuse the colleges as 'meer Spittles and Bawdy-houses': [John Barwick], *Querula Cantabrigiensis*, part 3 of Bruno Ryves, *Angliae ruina: Or, English ruine, represented in the barbarous, and sacrilegious outrages of the sectaries of this kingdome* ([1648]), p. 15.

12 Quoted in Charles Carlton, *Going to the Wars. The Experience of the British Civil Wars, 1638–1651* (London & New York: Routledge, 1995), p. 82. See also pp. 163 and 193 for examples of excessive drinking by both parliamentarian and royalist troops.

13 See Laura Lunger Knoppers, *Constructing Cromwell. Ceremony, Portrait, and Print 1645–1661* (Cambridge: Cambridge University Press, 2000), pp. 26 and 49.

14 'On Canary', in Brome, *Poems*, I, p. 140; 'On Claret', in Brome, *Poems*, I, p. 84.

15 'The Club', in Brome, *Poems*, I, p. 153. Compare, for instance, his 'The Trouper', at pp. 121–2: 'Come, come let us drink, / 'Tis in vain to think, / Like fools on grief or sadness / (. . .) All wordly care is madness'.

terms about the causes for suffering, for example in 'The Cheerful Heart'.[16] Referring to the sequestration of estates, and the subsequent poverty of royalists, he urged them to seek comfort and joy in the bottle:

> What though we are made, both beggars and slaves,
> Let us stoutly endure it and drink on't.[17]

Despite 'these ill times', Brome reminded his audience, 'our hearts are our own' – referring both to the loss of all other possessions, and to the figurative state of imprisonment many a royalist felt himself to be in under puritanical rule. The connection between the literary motives of drinking and imprisonment has been noted by recent critics.[18] In Brome's poem 'The Prisoners', a band of Cavaliers, locked up over debts caused by sequestration, spends the time behind bars singing and drinking 'each health to our King'. These men defy Parliament, which has put a ban on the ritual of toasting:

> They Vote that we shall
> Drink no healths at all
> Nor to King nor to Common-wealth,
> So that now we must venture to drink 'um in stealth.[19]

Toasting the king and his cause represented an act of loyalty, and defined one as a full member of an underground community. Thus, drinking became a genuine act of resistance. This is evident in 'The Royalist', one of Brome's most outspoken poems on the subject:

> Come, pass about the bowl to me,
> A health to our distressed King;
> Though we're in hold, let cups go free,
> Birds in a cage may freely sing.

---

[16] 'The Cheerful Heart', in Brome, *Poems*, I, pp. 158–9.

[17] Echoes of these lines are found in William Cavendish's 'A Songe': 'Sweet harte we are beggers, our Comfort tis seene / That we are undunne, for the King, and the Queene (. . .) Wee can not borrow, nor take up a Crust / So water weele drinke, and bite a hard Cruste', in Peter Davidson (ed.), *Poetry and Revolution. An Anthology of British and Irish verse, 1625–1660* (Oxford: Clarendon Press, 1998), no. 239. Cavendish, Duke of Newcastle, was one of the most notorious royalist exiles.

[18] Potter, *Secret Rites*, pp. 134–8, esp. p. 137: 'For other writers, like those in overcrowded London prisons, it was possible to create collective rituals (. . .) This is part of the point of their constant references to drinking.' Following Leah Marcus' suggestion that royalists retreated into a safe world of private rituals and 'protective enclosures' (Leah Marcus, *The Politics of Mirth. Jonson, Herrick, Milton, Marvell, and the Defense of Old Holiday Pastimes* (Chicago & London: University of Chicago Press, 1986), p. 214), Potter concludes that both prison and tavern were such spaces, where 'with the help of alcohol, the cavalier can carry on rituals of loyalty'.

[19] 'The Prisoners. Written when O[liver] C[romwell] attempted to be King', in Brome, *Poems*, I, pp. 150–1. Compare, for example, 'The contented Prisoner his praise of Sack', in *Choyce Drollery* (1656), pp. 93–6.

[...]
A sorrow dares not shew its face,
When we are ships and sack's the sea.[20]

Careless of the consequences, the royalist challenges the new authorities:

Pox on this grief, hang wealth, let's sing,
Shall's kill our selves for fear of death?

and ridicules them:

When we are larded well with drink,
Our heads shall turn as round as theirs.

Drinking could even be a means to mislead and undermine government, for example in 'The Prisoners', where the Cavaliers have

... found out a way that's beyond all their [= Parliament] thinking,
To keep up Good-fellowship still
We'l drink their destruction that would destroy drinking,
Let 'um Vote that a health if they will.

Parliament was also mockingly toasted in the anonymous drinking song 'On the Goldsmith Committee':

And next, let a Glasse
To our undoers passe,
Attended with two or three Curses:
May plagues sent from Hell
Stuff their bodies as well
As the Cavaliers coyn doth their purses.

A company of 'joviall Compounders' has returned from an unsuccessful trip to Goldsmith Hall, where they had hoped to redeem their estates by swearing allegiance to Parliament. Back in the pub, they 'make the house ring / With healths to our KING', declaring that alchohol-induced pledges invalidated any oath sworn before Parliament:

Since Goldsmiths Committee
Affords us no pitty,
Our sorrows in Wine we will steep 'um,
They force us to take
Two Oaths, but wee'll make
A third, that we ne'er meant to keep 'um.[21]

---

20 'The Royalist. Written in 1646', in Brome, *Poems*, I, pp. 117–18.
21 'On the Goldsmiths Committee', in *Rump: Or an Exact Collection of the Choycest Poems and Songs relating to the Late Times. By the most Eminents Wits, from Anno 1639. to Anno 1661* (1662), pp. 235–7.

Thus, in royalist texts, the image of the drinking Cavalier contained a host of meanings: a blissful retreat from daily sorrows and depressing thoughts; a way to overcome the sense of general defeat of the Stuart cause; a means to defy and ridicule the puritan government; and an attempt to reaffirm the royalist identity. In short, to be a Cavalier meant 'to be loyal and drink in defence of our King'.[22]

Conversely, in parliamentary writings the motifs of alcohol, and to some extent tobacco, were used to demonstrate the royalists' debauchery and lewdness. Parliamentary newsbook writers, for example, accused their royalist colleagues of being drunks who made up their news in the tavern.[23] In *The Cavaliers Jubilee* (1651), a satire on defecting royalists seeking a general pardon after Parliament's 'gracious Act of Oblivion', two former exiles, Sir Timothy Turn-coat and Sir Rowland Resolute, meet on English soil after deciding to 'leave the service of the ioung Charles Stuart'.[24] In his very first lines, Resolute confirms the image of the hard-drinking Stuart sympathiser:

> Well Noble Heart, and fellow Cavalier, as I am glad to see thee, so my heart leaps for joy that I have this liberty to live at home again; but since we are met, let's not part with dry lips, 'twas our custome (thou knowest) to take off the taplash, though we have been lash'd for't, and I have half a Crown left still in my pocket.[25]

Putting word into deed, he drags his friend off to the 'Sign of the Black Boy' – probably a reference to Charles II – where they discuss their adventures. Embittered by the king's ungrateful behaviour during the Civil Wars ('*Slighted, not knighted*'), Turn-Coat enlightens his friend about

> my sufferings, and travells and marchings, and journeys from Countrey to Countrey, and what miseries of hunger and cold, with wounds and imprisonment I have undergone, 'twould be past belief, I was so hasty, that I mortgaged my estate to be furnished with moneys: Oh how I bestirred my self, to undo my self, my wife, and children, to procure horses, and Armes, and Ammunition, for those which never gave me thanks.

---

22 'The New-Courtier. Written in 1648', in Brome, *Poems*, I, p. 129.
23 Potter, *Secret Rites*, p. 29. Thomas N. Corns, *Uncloistered Virtue. English Political Literature, 1640–1660* (Oxford: Clarendon Press, 1992), p. 70, mentions parliamentary attacks on Lord Goring that 'highlighted his alcoholism'. Lord Goring's drinking problem is also referred to in Carlton, *Going to the Wars*, p. 195, citing a report that 'he was up and sober for but an hour or two a day'.
24 *The Cavaliers Jubilee: Or, Long look'd for come at last: viz. The Generall Pardon. In a pleasant dialogue between Sir Timothy Turn-coat, and Sir Rowland Resolute, two Cavaliers that met accidentally, and were lately come over from beyond Sea, upon the noise of a Generall Pardon, and their Resolution to leave the service of the ioung Charles Stuart, and imbrace the Parliaments protection in their gracious Act of Oblivion* (1652 [= 1651]).
25 *The Cavaliers Jubilee*, p. 1.

Rather, the ungrateful courtiers 'help'd to devoure that which was left, in drunkennesse, whoredome, and rioting (the common use and custom of our Cavaliers)'.[26]

The image of the hard-drinking Cavalier is presented, then, in both royalist and parliamentarian texts, with entirely opposite connotations. However, examining the papers and correspondence of royalists, especially of those living in exile, it is clear that their attitude towards drinking is not always as unequivocally positive as could be deduced from Cavalier literature.[27]

In real life, drunk Cavaliers could pose a serious threat to the stability of Charles II's exiled court. Inertia and boredom drove courtiers to drink, and under the influence they became aggressive, challenging each other, or their hosts, to fights and duels. Sir Edward Nicholas, Secretary of State to Charles II, was greatly alarmed by the indiscreet behaviour of Lord Rochester in Ratisbon, which could potentially have harmed diplomatic relations:

> There they say he is frequently drunk in public, and in his drink talks at random against the House of Austria and the evil office the late K[ing] received from it.[28]

Parliamentary spies on the Continent were keen to report on anything upsetting the precarious balance of social order and hierarchy established in the banished court community. One spy – possibly Henry Manning – concluded that 'there are such factions among them, as if the three kingdoms were all their own, and to be divided by them'.[29] Glimpses of the life of Charles II's retinue can be found in Manning's letter of intelligence to John Thurloe, Secretary of State under Cromwell, recording a drinking party at which Charles II toasted the Queen of Sweden, and the 'health went round with many laughs and ceremonies; the most part of that night spent in mirth, singing, dancing, and drinking'. However, alcohol could severely undermine the unanimity among the exiled royalists, as the rest of his intelligence report revealed:

> Our lords and cavaliers here fall out one with another. The lord Wilmot and lord Newbourg fell out last day eagerly; they were to fight, but RC [= Charles II] having notice of it, hinder'd their duel. The lord Wentworth and one major Boswel quarrell'd and knock'd one another last night, in the next room to RC's bed-chamber: the one cannot endure the other; the wine makes them mad.

---

[26] Ibid., p. 2.

[27] On the intellectual and literary life of royalists in exile, see my *The Exile Experience. The Book Culture of Royalists in Exile in the Low Countries, 1642–1660* (forthcoming).

[28] *The Nicholas Papers: Correspondence of Sir Edward Nicholas, Secretary of State*, ed. George F. Warner (London: Camden Society, 1886–1920), II, p. 7: Edward Hyde to Edward Nicholas, 5–3–1653.

[29] *A Collection of the State Papers of John Thurloe* (1742), II, p. 586: Letter of intelligence from Aachen, [August] 1654.

Similarly, an exiled royalist in The Hague had to intervene to prevent a duel. A 'misunderstanding' had arisen between Lord Culpeper and Hannibal Sestade, Viceroy of Norway, in July 1655,

> after a meeting they had where they dined together, with my Lord Taffe and others, after plenty of Cups on all hands, wch proceeded so farre that a challenge was sent by Culpeper but not delivered to the other, being prevented by the charitable care of Doctor Morley.[30]

That excessive drinking often led to violent and outrageous behaviour was demonstrated by a horrible and sensational story, which a royalist in France, having heard it from 'a very honest and worthy English knight' in St Malo, sent on to a friend in London. Three Catholic men in Brittany had been drinking heavily, when one of them 'grew mad in his drink', and

> espying a picture of our blessed lady in the chamber, fell a-drinking healths to it, and at last, in disdaine, threw a glass of wine in her face, using some scurrilous words.

Having slept for about an hour, he was suddenly pulled out of bed by an invisible force, and 'dragged up and downe the roome upon his face, having it distorted and drawn severall wayes, and both it, and all the rest of his body singed'. Three days later, the man died 'most penitently'. This, certainly, was a story from which a lesson could be learned.[31]

Because the temptations of alcohol, as well as tobacco, affected young men especially, royalist tutors closely monitored their pupils. The Anglican divine Robert Creighton frequently reported on the habits of Edmund (Mun) Verney. Mun was 'no ill conditioned youth', Creighton reassured Sir Ralph Verney in February 1653, and appeared 'not inclined to any vice in the world'.[32] A year later, Creighton confirmed with a sense of relief that Mun 'never took a pipe of Tobacco (. . .) I know he hates wyne, and seldom*me* drinks at meales but beere'.[33] When an alarming story of a drunken quarrel in which his son might have been involved had reached Sir Ralph Verney, Creighton hastened to explain the occasion. Mun had been 'late out wth some gentlemen English and a mixt company', and on their way home from the tavern, two of his friends had heatedly argued with a Dutchman. There had been some punching and window smashing, but Mun had not had any part in

---

[30] London, British Library (BL), Egerton MS 2535, f. 322: Hume to Nicholas, 12–7–1655 (NS). George Morley, an Anglican divine who spent over a decade in exile, became Dean of Winchester Cathedral after the Restoration.

[31] *Thurloe State Papers*, II, p. 341: Intercepted letter, W.H. to John Walton, 11–6–1654.

[32] BL, Verney Papers, Microfilm MS 636/12 (Jan. 1653 – Dec. 1654): Creighton to Verney, 14–2–1653 (NS).

[33] Ibid., Creighton to Verney, 13–3–1654 (NS). Compare 15–5–1654 (NS), where Creighton states that although Mun is incredibly lazy, he does not swear, smoke or drink.

the brawl. Still, Creighton was extremely concerned about the incident, and promised to keep a better eye on his pupil in the future.[34] Members of the royalist exile community, then, fully realised the often damaging consequences of excessive drinking, and certainly did not endorse the positive symbolism of the Cavalier falling over with drink, with cheeks 'as starred as the skies'.[35]

Yet taken in moderation, alcohol did serve important social functions within the community of exiles, functions that mirror those referred to in royalist literature. Drinking and 'being merry' could drive sombre thoughts away and provide consolation. This was certainly how Charles II's wandering courtiers kept up their spirits: 'our court begins to be more calm; yet we drink more Rhenish wine to comfort ourselves'.[36] In a freezing Calais, John Evelyn encountered Lord Wentworth 'who drives away sorrow, or drownes it, with Sack and hott water'.[37] Drinking could reaffirm and strengthen relationships, which the letters of Sir Robert Moray demonstrate as poignantly as do the poems of Alexander Brome. Even when a friend, or a family member, was not physically present – as was the case for so many of the exiles – toasting each other's health on paper was felt to have the same effect. The poet Abraham Cowley, living in Paris in the 1650s, informed Henry Bennet, secretary to James, Duke of York, that 'as for the *Piedmont* wine we are now such moderate Men, as to content our selves with that of the *Rhine*, in which I suddenly hope to drink your Health'.[38] In Utrecht, a group of exiles regularly met in the library of Michael Honywood to talk politics, discuss books, exchange gossip and drink each other's health:

> We ar heere in the old manner, all your true servants, and at night Robinibus shall not be forgotten in a cup of London Canary; which was brought by Sr Roger Burgoyne, whom your Pupil Dr Paman, Senior of St. Johns, accompanyed hether.[39]

Here, the intimacy of the drinking ritual is intensified by inside references to mutual friends and acquaintances, and to the company's traditions and history ('the old manner').

---

34 Ibid., Creighton to Verney, 15–12–1654 (NS).
35 'The Companion', in Brome, *Poems*, I, p. 131.
36 *Thurloe State Papers* II, p. 515: Letter of intelligence from Spa, 12–8–1654.
37 BL, Add. MS 78298 (Letterbook John Evelyn, 1644–1686), f. 52v: John Evelyn to Sir Richard Browne, 4–2–1652.
38 T. Brown (ed.), *Miscellanea Aulica: Or, a Collection of State-Treatises, never before publish'd* (1702), p. 157: Cowley to Bennet, 5–12–1650. Cowley himself wrote a poem on the pleasures of drinking, simply entitled 'Drinking'. Compare a letter by Endymion Porter to Sir Richard Browne: 'I hope (. . .) that you will give William a rouse at the "Spread Eagle" and not forget me, but dash me in one glass as you do an orange peel, and I believe William will not like the wine the worse.' Quoted in Gervas Huxley, *Endymion Porter. The Life of a Courtier, 1587–1649* (London: Chatto & Windus, 1959), p. 235.
39 BL, Harl. MS 3783, f. 244: Honywood to William Sancroft, 14–10–1659 (NS).

The political implications of drinking that can be traced in royalist verse, however, do not seem to have existed so much within the mental world of Stuart refugees. Although most of the references are indeed to drinking wine, the social and political status of beer, as displayed so contemptuously in royalist literature, is absent in exiles' accounts. On the contrary, beer is sometimes heralded as the 'English' drink *par excellence*, thus gaining a patriotic significance.[40] In August 1659, after a hazardous and uncomfortable journey through Germany and Switzerland, 'often forct to lie in yᵉ straw, & found noe drink but wine, or water', William Sancroft finally reached Geneva. There, to his utmost relief and joy, he found lodgings with

> one, who indeed was borne heere, but lived 14, or 15 yeares in England, speakes English as well as wee, & who's wife is a Welsh woman, & brewes beere after yᵉ English fashion.[41]

Edward Martin, the ejected dean of Ely Cathedral, spent his many years abroad in 'nothing but Prisons, Ships, wandrings, and solitude', surviving on

> one Meal a day, and at night a Crust of Bread, and a Cup of any Drink. That I most desire every where is Cider, or indefect of that, Water (if it bee any thing neer so good as here at Paris) for I drunk no Wine for thirteen years together, before I came out of England.[42]

References to toasting the king as an explicit act of resistance barely occur in correspondence or memoirs, which of course does not necessarily mean that the ritual was not performed in royalist circles on the Continent. The curious broadsheet *An extemporary answer to a cluster of drunkards, met together at Schiedam*, published in April 1648, certainly seems to point to its existence.[43] Probably a product of the parliamentary propaganda machine, it relates the story of (the fictional?) Timothy Gunton, who, upon his refusal to drink Charles I's health with a band of royalist exiles in Holland, was forced to explain his anti-Stuart behaviour. Gunton's main argument is that alcohol benefits neither the body nor the soul; thus, drinking another person's health, even the king's, is to impair one's own. Concluding with an explanation in verse, the author turns the royalist ritual into an act of sacrilege:

40 See Charlotte McBride, 'A Natural Drink for an English Man: National Stereotyping in Early Modern Culture', below.

41 Oxford, Bodleian Library, Tanner MS 51, f. 55: Sancroft to his brother Thomas Sancroft, 9–8–1659. Alas, Sancroft found 'this March beere & too stale & strong'.

42 Edward Martin, *Doctor Martin, Dean Ely, his Opinion* (1662), ff. E2r–v. Compare Edward Hyde's remark that although he could not complain about the French air, 'otherwise I am not at all taken with the delights of it, and on my worde, for all that I have seene, give me old Englande, for meate, drinke, and lodging, and even for wyne too': *Calendar of the Manuscripts of the Marquis of Bath* (London: Historical Manuscript Commission, 1904), II, p. 82: Hyde to his wife, 12–8–1649 (NS).

43 Timothy Gunton, *An extemporary answer to a cluster of drunkards* ([London] 1648). Date on Thomason copy: 13–4–1648 (BL: 669, f. 12(4)).

By these let all men know 'tis worse then sordid stealth,
To fawn upon a friend, and swallow down his health.
Yet some audacious Rogues dare in their drunken notes
Pour King, and Kingdomes health down their ungodly throats
And stove it in their stinking paunch an hour, or twain,
And then they'l spew, and cag, and pisse it out again.
Oh then how sick art thou poore King, and common-wealth,
While drunken sots daily drink, pisse, and spew thy health.

In the safety of exile, the ceremonial toast to Stuart monarchy could be performed without any danger, thus losing its heroic association. Still, in a poetic account of a pub crawl in The Hague, an 'unknown Ladye' (perhaps Henrietta Maria) is toasted in secret, and the drinking Cavaliers subsequently deny that this could be perceived as 'a plote upon the common wealth'.[44]

It is quite possible that this particular poem was composed by Thomas Killigrew, the courtier and dramatist whose colourful years of exile were marked by scandals, court intrigue, illegal business deals, drinking and debts.[45] In Killigrew's plays, written during his years abroad, drinking is a favourite theme, almost always associated with soldiers or, more specifically, exiled Cavaliers. While *The Princesse: Or, Love at first Sight* is set in Naples and Sicily, the soldier who exclaims 'no covenants, no conditions for drinking while you live, drink freely', obviously voices royalist sentiments.[46] Killigrew used his exile experiences, and those of his friends, in his semi-autobiographical play *Thomaso, Or, The Wanderer*.[47] The story focuses on the amorous adventures of three English soldiers, Thomaso, Edwardo and Ferdinando, in Madrid. Having recently arrived in town, they look up the 'sober English Gentleman' Harrigo, to whom Thomaso reveals the Cavalier identity of his friends:

They are true blades, Hall. — Remnants of the broken Regiments; Royal and Loyal Fugitives, highly guilty of the Royal Crime [= being a royalist], Poor and

---

[44] Nancy Cutbirth, 'Thomas Killigrew's Commonplace Book?', *The Library Chronicle of the University of Texas at Austin*, new series, 13 (1980), 31–8, esp. p. 38. I have not seen the commonplace book, and the interpretation given here is Cutbirth's.

[45] On his life, and especially the exile period, see Alfred Harbage, *Thomas Killigrew: Cavalier dramatist, 1612–83* (Philadelphia: University of Pennsylvania Press, 1930); J.-P. vander Motten, 'Thomas Killigrew: A Biographical Note', *Revue Belge de Philologie et d'Histoire*, 53 (1975), 769–75, and 'Thomas Killigrew's "Lost Years", 1655–1660', *Neophilologus*, 82 (1998), 311–34.

[46] Thomas Killigrew, *The Princesse: Or, Love at first Sight: The Scene Naples and Sicily. Written in Naples by Thomas Killigrew. Dedicated to his dear Niece the Lady Anne Wentworth, wife to the Lord Lovelace*, in Killigrew, *Comedies, and Tragedies. Written by Thomas Killigrew, Page of Honour to King Charles the First. And Groom of the Bed-Chamber to King Charles the Second* (1664), p. 56. Drinking songs by soldiers on pp. 34–7 and 54–5.

[47] Thomas Killigrew, *Thomaso, Or, The Wanderer: A Comedy. The Scene Madrid. Written in Madrid. In two Parts. Dedicated to the Fair and Kind Friends to Prince Palatine Polixander*, in Killigrew, *Comedies, and Tragedies*. According to Vander Motten, ' "Lost Years" ', p. 316, part II was composed in the Spring of 1654, a few months before Killigrew settled in The Hague.

Honest, *Hall*; you see his Majesties marks upon us, English, and that gave us a safe Conduct.[48]

The most obvious autobiographical element in *Thomaso* – apart from the pun on the playwright's own name, and some rather obscure references to characteristics of real-life persons – is a Dutch tavern scene. Recalling their wanderings in France and Holland, Thomaso and his friends commemorate how they stole a pig in Rotterdam,

> out of the Cradle where the kind Nurse had hid it (. . .) 'twas cruel *Ned* that kill'd it: the Neighbours ran together at the cry; and as if we had kill'd her first born, it put all the house in mourning, till Sack and Sugar allay'd the grief.

The pig is eaten in the St John's Head tavern, where Thomaso and his companions run into the company of 'Embassadour *Will*, and Resident *Tom*, with M. Sheriffs Secretary, *John* the Poet with the Nose; all *Gondiberts* dire Foes'. A marginal gloss reveals their identity: William Murray, William, Lord Crofts, Thomas Killigrew and John Denham.[49] These men, all royalist exiles, had performed various diplomatic missions for the Stuart cause: in 1650, Denham and Crofts had travelled to Poland in order to raise money for Charles II; Killigrew had served as English ambassador in Italy between 1649 and 1652; and Murray was acting as a secret agent, going back and forth between Scotland and the Low Countries. Their friendship, immortalised by Killigrew in this particular scene, dated back to pre-Civil War times, when they had formed a 'cavalier drinking circle', dubbed 'the maddest of the Land' by its leader William Murray.[50] Killigrew's predilection for wine was well known within the exile community. In November 1653, the English resident in Paris, Sir Richard Browne, had sent him a 'butt of canary divided into three barrells', to be distributed at court. It never arrived there; as Edward Hyde gossiped to the diarist John Evelyn, 'the Canary Wyne is come to Paris, but no mencion of the delivery of it, being conceaved to be Mr. Killigrew's owne wyne, so that I expect a very small share of it'.[51]

The company's festive reunion in a Dutch pub may also have been the

---

[48] Killigrew, *Thomaso*, p. 320. In the list of characters, Thomaso is identified as an 'English cavaleer'; Ferdinando and Edwardo as 'English Gentlemen, his Friends, late Commanders in that Army' and Harrigo as a 'sober English Gentleman, attending the English Ambassadour'. Harrigo has been identified by Harbage, *Thomas Killigrew*, p. 227, as Henry Proger, steward to Edward Hyde and Francis Cottington during their Madrid embassy in 1649–50.

[49] Killigrew, *Thomaso*, p. 456. This implies, of course, that Killigrew ran into his fictional alter-ego Thomaso. William Crofts is not mentioned as a separate character, only in the marginal note – he belonged to the group of poets, headed by John Denham, who had made fun of William Davenant's *Gondibert*. See Timothy Raylor, *Cavaliers, Clubs, and Literary Culture. Sir John Mennes, James Smith, and the Order of the Fancy* (Newark, London & Toronto: Associated University Presses, 1994), pp. 198–9.

[50] Raylor, *Cavaliers, Clubs*, pp. 66 and 96.

[51] Quoted in Harbage, *Thomas Killigrew*, p. 104.

subject of the anonymous poem in Killigrew's commonplace book, mentioned above; it certainly was alluded to by John Denham. As in the case of Killigrew, Denham's years in exile provided ample material for topical poems, for example his rhymed account of his and Croft's fund-raising mission to Poland.[52] In another poem he jokingly recalled a rather wet and trying journey from Calais to Boulogne, where his friend Sir John Mennes was to attend a dinner party – the menu promising a pig.[53] In 1652, 'Resident Tom' and William Murray's return to The Hague from their royalist missions in Venice and Scotland gave Denham opportunity for another commemorative poem. Warmly mocking his friends, he pictured their little group as a typical band of merry Cavaliers, drinking their way through exile:

> These three when they drink,
> How little do they think
> Of Banishment, Debts, or dying?
> Not old with their years,
> Nor cold with their fears;
> But their angry Stars still defying.
>
> Mirth makes them not mad,
> Nor Sobriety sad;
> But of that they are seldom in danger:
> At *Paris*, at *Rome*,
> At the *Hague* they are at home;
> The good Fellow is no where a stranger.[54]

Although 'mad drinking' certainly implied negative associations, royalist poets and dramatists in exile seem to have proudly adopted the literary image of the merry, intoxicated Cavalier as a patriotic symbol.[55] The poetic representation of royalist drinking as a social ritual, as a means to keep old solidarities intact, resonated in the exiles' daily life. Toasting absent friends in letters assured them that they were as much part of the royalist community as when they had been physically there. Thus, in the exile experience, drinking did not so much serve to confirm a political affiliation, or to demonstrate an act of loyalty, as to provide an opportunity, especially in the company of friends with whom one had shared the happy pre-war years, to remember an England which seemed

---

52 'On my Lord *Croft's* and my Journey into *Poland*, from whence we brought *10000 L*. For his Majesty by the Decimation of His Scottish Subjects there': John Denham, *The Poetical Works of Sir John Denham*, ed. Theodore Howard Banks (2nd edn, Hamden, CT: Archon Books, 1969), pp. 107–10.

53 'To Sir *John Mennis* being Invited from *Calice* to *Bologne* to Eat a Pig', in Denham, *Works*, pp. 100–2.

54 'On Mr. *Tho. Killigrew's* Return from his Embassie from *Venice*, and Mr. *William Murray's* from Scotland', in Denham, *Works*, pp. 111–12.

55 Even Killigrew touched upon the dangers of drinking excessively in a violent scene where a heavily intoxicated Edwardo sexually assaults a girl: Killigrew, *Thomaso*, pp. 355–9.

lost forever.[56] Drinking, for those wandering 'good fellows', was an effective way to forget about the poverty, homesickness and illness with which they were confronted while abroad. Perhaps too effective, as Angellica realized when she contemplated her future with Thomaso:

> We shall never eat again (. . .) for he'l have all in drink; nay, 'tis an English Souldier too, and one of the King's party, three titles to perpetual poverty; a race of men who have left praying, or hoping for daily bread; and only relye upon nightly drink.[57]

[56] See, for example, Richard Flecknoe's poem 'To Colonell Jos. Rutter, inviting him to a Feast in *Lisbon*', in Flecknoe, *Miscellania*, pp. 55–7, which promised 'of Lads a Joviall Crew, / Who never care nor sorrow knew'. Wine would flow freely and 'make those who drink it younger, / And in spight of death live longer'.

[57] Killigrew, *Thomaso*, p. 342.

5

Roaring Royalists and Ranting Brewers:
The Politicisation of Drink and Drunkenness in
Political Broadside Ballads from 1640 to 1689*

ANGELA McSHANE JONES

FROM the lone staggering reveller merrily weaving his way home to the massed harmonious (though perhaps not salubrious) efforts of the victorious rugby club, drink and song have a natural affinity. In the early modern period drinking and singing were often essential to entertainment when the public met to enjoy themselves. This continued to be the case even when in the seventeenth century reforming governors tried to eradicate such ungodly and unseemly behaviour.[1]

Thousands of early modern songs and ballads were far from being 'traditional' in the romantic sense that later nineteenth-century collectors and folklorists such as Francis Child would have understood, that is, passed on orally over decades or longer – though some of the tunes may have been.[2] Many ballads were topical and printed in broadsheet form. Child referred to collections of such ballads as 'veritable dunghills', and certainly many may have

---

* Ballad citations are made by date (where possible) and collection. Collections consulted for this chapter were the Pepys, Roxburghe, Bagford, Lutterell, Thomason, Manchester, Crawford, Wood, and others in the Bodleian and British Library. Ballads in American Libraries available on Early English Books Online were also used. Roxburghe, Pepys and Euing ballads are cited as they appear in the widely available printed or facsimile collections. It should be noted that woodcuts in the Roxburghe volumes edited by J.W.E. Ebsworth are rarely connected to the ballads they illustrate on the originals; the dating and referencing is also frequently inaccurate. Euing ballads are in black letter. Most of the ballads in the Bodleian collections can be accessed on their website, www.bodley.ox.ac.uk/ballads.

1 See for example J. Eales and C. Durston (eds), *The Culture of English Puritanism* (Basingstoke: Macmillan, 1996), and D. Underdown, *Fire From Heaven: Life in an English Town in the Seventeenth Century* (London: HarperCollins, 1992).

2 F.J. Child, *The English and Scottish Popular Ballads* (Boston & New York: Houghton Mifflin, 1882), 5 vols.

ended up there.[3] Nevertheless, however un-romantic they may have been, as a genre, broadside ballads bridged the gap between orality and literacy, and between centre and periphery. They could be heard or read, bought or memorised and were available at a small cost, or free as they were performed publicly at markets and fairs, on the street or in local hostelries. They were also pasted or pinned to the walls in homes, in alehouses and taverns or to posts in public spaces.[4] From the mid-seventeenth century onwards, in a substantial number of these ballads the perennial duo of drink and song became a threesome – with politics or 'state affairs' making the third member of the 'jovial crew'.

Throughout the seventeenth century there was a thriving trade in broadside ballads that dealt with all aspects of life from the heart to the soul. Taking ballads from all the main collections (amounting to between 9,000 and 10,000 ballad sheets), about one-third are concerned either entirely or partly with politics. One of the best-known collections, made by Samuel Pepys, reflects a similar pattern. Of the 1,775 ballads in his collection (mainly ballads from the 1670s to the 1690s), Pepys himself listed 315 as being on 'State and Times' and 215 on drinking. Only 'Love (pleasant)' is a bigger category, with over 600. Pepys's criteria and mine are clearly different, however, as I have come up with rather more 'state' ballads than he suggests from his collection. Partly, this is because many of the drinking ballads were in fact political – or were anti-political, as I shall discuss below.[5]

By political broadside ballads, I mean ballads that concerned themselves with 'affairs of State' – to use a term these texts themselves employ – and which were published as single-page items for the price of half to one penny. Ballads or songs might also be collected into books, while some could be several pages long and were sold as chap books or pamphlets. As books, these items were too inaccessible and too expensive for the lowest in society. However, many of the songs had been printed singly, or were widely sung.[6] Even single-sheet broadside ballads could be expensive – Luttrell paid 6d for a version of *The Cabal* printed in 1680.[7] Other broadside ballads required an intimate knowledge of parliamentary procedure, personalities and gossip, and were therefore in some

---

3   Letter to Grundtvig, 25 August 1872, quoted in A. Bold, *The Ballad* (London: Methuen, 1979), p. 96.

4   On distribution, see A. Fox, *Oral and Literate Culture in England 1500–1700* (Oxford: Clarendon Press, 2000); T. Watt, *Cheap Print and Popular Piety 1550–1640* (Cambridge: Cambridge University Press, 1991); N. Wurzbach, *The Rise of The English Street Ballad, 1550–1650* (Cambridge: Cambridge University Press, 1990).

5   W.G. Day (ed.), *Catalogue of the Pepys Library. The Pepys Ballads*, vols I–V (Cambridge: Brewer, 1987), (henceforward *Pepys*).

6   Martin Parker's ballad *When the King enjoys his own again* is a case in point. There is no printed sheet extant of this ballad before it appears in the 1662 edition of *Rump Songs* entitled 'Upon Defacing of Whitehall'. However, references to it or its tune before that date make it clear that it was already in wide circulation as a song by 1643, and was then widely adapted in printed ballads after the Restoration.

7   BL. C20.f4 (23). Luttrell added 6d in manuscript to his copy of the ballad.

ways elite texts. My analysis here concentrates on ballads that would have been accessible to a majority, at least in London.[8]

Tessa Watt's study of cheap print suggests that those most likely to be able to buy ballads would have ranged from the husbandman and artisan upwards.[9] The internal evidence certainly supports this. Some ballads printed to 'prevent scandal' have husbandmen listed as part of the group who have decided to have the ballad printed.[10] However, the young as well as the lowly were also key buyers. It is well known that apprentices and maids were ballad enthusiasts – both frequently appear in ballads – and in plays ballads are bought as presents for sweethearts as in *A Winters Tale*. Many ballads were aimed at tradesmen and middling sorts of all kinds. The cost of new ballads may be irrelevant in tracing readership as this ignores the lending of items, the second-hand trade and the accessing of the song simply by being in the right place at the right time.

It is difficult to place ballads of any kind in the hands of the middling or lower sort of reader, or to trace readings of them as Sharpe, Ginzberg or Seaver have done in other contexts.[11] Balladeers and ballads are mentioned in sources such as plays, pamphlets, diaries and court records and are depicted in wood-cuts, but on the whole I have had to rely upon the ubiquity of the ballad discourses discussed here. Over 200 ballads were used in constructing this chapter. This is the only security for a historian dealing in what is, theoretically, a literary minefield.

Drinking played an important role in ballad culture. Alehouses, inns and taverns were important as stopping-off points for ballad traders. As Michael Frearson's analysis of chapmen's and pedlars' trade routes has shown, it was through using inns and taverns as trading posts that printed matter was distributed, effectively and speedily throughout the country.[12] Many sources suggest that the events hostelries depended on for business, such as markets

---

8   There is no easy way to categorise 'popular' and 'elite' ballads, seepage from one to the other in either direction being constant. Print types – black letter or Roman letter – are unhelpful as categories as the production of ballads of all kinds was moving towards the more modern roman type throughout the period, and in any case the same ballad was frequently published in a variety of formats (cf. n. 39 below). The use of common language, imagery, level of detail and rhythm in ballads is the only way of distinguishing between what was really poetical satire and what was popular song.

9   Watt, *Cheap Print*, pp. 261–2.

10 For example, *Strange and True News from Westmoreland* (n.d.), is 'signed' by 1 esquire, 2 gents, 5 yeomen and 5 husbandmen.

11 K. Sharpe, *Reading Revolutions* (New Haven & London: Yale University Press, 2000); C. Ginzburg, *Cheese and the Worms* (London: Penguin, 1992); P. Seaver, *Wallington's World* (London: Methuen, 1985).

12 M. Frearson, 'The Distribution and Readership of London Corantos in the 1620's', in R. Myers and M. Harris (eds), *Serials and their Readers 1620–1914* (Winchester: St Paul's Bibliographies, 1993). M. Knights, *Politics and Opinion in Crisis, 1678–81* (Cambridge: Cambridge University Press, 1994) is also useful on this for the later period.

and fairs, were invariably also popular arenas for performance. Ballads themselves demonstrate this connection through their content, by both attacking and encouraging drinking, and by reflecting and providing subject matter for discussion or song wherever conviviality took place.

Drink and balladeers enjoyed a symbiotic relationship. Ballads were notoriously composed by drinkers or 'pot poets', for the purposes of earning their drink money. In one ballad Lady Pecunia points out: 'Some think the Poet for applause doth sing, / When for my sake he undertakes this thing, / A cup of Sack doth make his spirits glad; / But without me there's no Sack to be had.'[13] This can be illustrated in the epitaphs of three well-known balladeers. First, William Elderton, the great sixteenth-century balladeer: 'Dead drunk here Elderton doth lye, / of him it may well be said, / here he but not his thirst is laid.' Second, Martin Parker, king of seventeenth-century balladeers: 'the distillations of his quill, /. . . did kindly greet, / the peoples ears as they did pass the street/ . . . was not every song/ of thine applauded by the thirsty throng/ . . . He always bathed his beak in ale, / Toping whole tubs off, like some thirsty whale.' Third, playwright and songwriter of the late seventeenth and early eighteenth century, Tom D'Urfey: 'His Tale was pleasant, and his Song was sweet, / His heart was cheerful – but his thirst was great.'[14]

From 1649 onwards a new relationship between drink and song emerged. Broadside balladeers took a political stance on drink and drinking. They politicised drink and then drunkenness, personified radical political leaders in terms of drink and drunkenness and, in so doing, depicted the social and cultural landscape in which 'political drinking' took place.[15]

Many ballads point out that to drive away melancholy and lift the spirits was one of the most important reasons for drinking. For example, in *The Twelve Brave Bells of Bow* the royalist balladeer declares,

> Come Noble Hearts
> To show your loyall parts,
> Lets drink a lovely cup and banish care
> Why should not we
> Which are of spirits free
> Dround grief with sack and cast off all dispare[.][16]

13 *The Lady Pecunia's Journey into Hell* (1654), Thomason, 669.f17 (75).
14 Elderton in W. Camden, *Remaines of a greater worke, concerning Britaine* (1605), p. 56. Parker in S.F., *Death in a New Dress: or Sportive Funeral Elegies* (1656), sig. A4 and B. D'Urfey, quoted in J.W.E. Ebsworth (ed.), *Roxburghe Ballads* (New York: AMS Press, 1966 edn), vol. 8, p. cxlii* (henceforward *Rox.*).
15 Drinking and politics had always been connected in elections, and Cavaliers had been drinking in defeat since 1646, but I have not found the political separation of drinks in ballads before 1649. It may be significant that rumours about Cromwell's brewing activities did not begin to circulate until February 1649 (cf. n. 58 below).
16 (n.d.), Manchester Ballads (henceforward MB.), II (14). H.E. Rollins, *Cavalier and Puritan* (New York: New York University Press, 1923), p. 251, suggests 1649 as the publication date.

The interregnum years were a time when the morale of the royalists was inevitably low. Defeated in battle; the King dead; deprived of their estates through sequestration (a theme consistently brought up in ballads during the period); their 'natural' position in society was gone and they had been replaced by socially inferior commonwealth men. Cavaliers feared that the king of their hearts, Charles II, would never be able to return.

In *A Royall Health to the Rising Sun* both text and image suggested that there was only one way to pass the time before the hoped for change in fortune might come:

> Let us cheare up each other then,
> And show ourselves true Englishmen
> . . .
>
> The Father of our Kingdoms dead,
> His Royall Sun from England's fled,
> . . .
>
> A Royall Health I then begun,
> Unto the Rising of the sun.[17]

In this miserable condition, the Cavaliers caroused and soused, drinking sorrows away in gallons of wine – canary, malago, sack, claret and sherry. Drinking in company (and the singing that inevitably entailed) became an important part of the political culture of the royalist. Consequently, it made its way into political discourse and into songs and ballads, a medium almost impossible for the state to control.[18] As drinking became politicised, a musical attack was launched on the ale and beer that upstart 'mechanics' drank as opposed to the more refined and royalist wine. *Canary's Coronation*, for example, decried 'anarchic Ale' and promoted Canary – or other wine – as the proper drink for monarchists:

> From Hopps and Grains let us purge our brains;
> They do smell of Anarchie.
> Let us choose a king from whose blood may spring
> Such a royal progenie
> That it befits no true wine-bred witts
> Whose brains are bright and clear,
> To tye their hands in Dray-men's bands,
> When as they may goe freer:
> Why should we droope or basely stoope
> To popular ale or beere?

---

[17] (1649), MB.I (44).

[18] C.H. Firth, 'The Royalists Under the Protectorate', *English Historical Review*, 52 (1937), 634–48 mentions a case in the Thurloe papers of anti-Cromwell ballads heard in London and copied down by Major General Overton, 'that Cromwell himself had seen and laughed at', p. 647.

The imagery of 'popular' ale and beer and wine as the natural drink of an elite, was an ideal vehicle with which to express dissatisfaction with government by the lower classes and the exile of the rightful king whose rights were bound up with the Cavaliers' own. The final call of the song was to approve young blades who 'waste away their cash/ In wine and recreation, who hate dull beere' and 'will allow Canary's Coronation'.[19]

Other songs by Thomas Jordan described the sorry state of sousing Cavaliers:

> There with a sack-incensed face
> In speckled state and flaming grace,
> With dabbled doublet doth appear
> The curral front of Cavalier,
> With a bowle
> Full of sack, such as can
> In the most dying man
> Raise a soul.

He also explained the reason for their drunkenness:

> There will we sit and fret a while,
> Cursing the puddle of their brains
> That pull'd down grapes and put up grains,
> Who bagpipes for Shalmes
> Deal in small Beer and Psalmes
> Through the Nose [.][20]

This imagery was further augmented in ballads by the linking of Cromwell and his government with the brewing trade. Whatever the real relation of Cromwell to a 'brewer of Huntingdon', brewing played an important role in propping up godly government in towns like Dorchester and Salisbury. Clarendon was to describe Dorchester as the 'most malignant' town in England, 'entirely disaffected to the King'. Renowned as a centre of parliamentarian control, it funded its godly reform, a hospital, education schemes, and many other charitable and godly causes with the help of the Brewhouse, a town-run brewery. Deliberately destroyed by 'Goring's crew' when they entered the town in 1645, it was swiftly rebuilt as the New Brewhouse in the same year, enabling Dorchester's beery reform to continue. It is clear that the notion of ale or beer as a radical, disloyal, political entity had a real as well as a figurative meaning.[21]

---

19 Originally a song from *Fancy's Festivals a Masque* (1657) by Thomas Jordan, and later reprinted in *The Loyal Garland* (1673) and elsewhere, which suggests it was sold separately as a song.

20 'The Leaguer' in Thomas Jordan, *Musick and Poetry mixed in a variety of songs and poems* (1663), p. 13. See also *Bacchus Festival or a New Medley* (1660), Thomason, 669.f24 (63).

21 Underdown, *Fire from Heaven*, pp. 199 and 209.

Some songs emphasised the different effects that wine and beer or ale had on the individual. Ale and beer 'makes our spirits muddy', sang one ballad, while another declared 'When Ale's in his head then wit is out'.[22] A song printed in 1654 declared 'your hops, yest and malt, / When they're mingled together, / make our fancies to halt, / Or reele any wither/ It fluffs up our brains with froth and with yest'.[23] Wine, however, was reported to sharpen up the brain, it was 'the Muses nectar' and, as *The Delights of the Bottle* said, "Tis a way that's gentile, and is found to be good, / Both to quicken the Wit, and enliven the blood'.[24] During the interregnum period this gave carousing Cavaliers a distinct advantage over the ale-drinking, godly mechanic. Dull and dreary – a sot – he was no match for a sparkling young blade in his cups and could never rise to the wit of a royalist even if, temporarily, he had the upper hand politically. Later in the period any alcohol was said to be able to sharpen the wit, although wine usually had the edge. For a Cavalier or loyalist however, the worst thing for the wit, was not to drink at all.

The drinking was not over once the 'King enjoyed his own again', as the Martin Parker chorus went. Far from it, though there was a call for moderation as in *A Country Song, intituled the Restoration*:

> Let's render our praise for these happy dayes,
> To God and our Soveraign;
> Your Drinking give o're, Swear not as before:
> For the King bears not the Sword in vain.[25]

Nevertheless, after the return of the king, numerous toasts were drunk and ballads sung in praise of the newly restored monarchy and a properly ordered society. *The Noble Prodigal* declared 'Let's call, and drink the cellar dry/ There's nothing sober underneath the sky'.[26] And no wonder, in *The Royal Entertainment* the balladeer tells us 'Conduits did shine/with liquor divine, / the people did bear away hat fulls of wine'.[27] Wine had won pride of place as the loyal tipple and anarchic ale had returned to its proper place. In *The Country-Mans Vive le Roy* Jack and Dick go 'To mother Mabs old Tipling house/ where we will take a smart carrouse, / of the brown nappy stuff, till we/ Are full of Ale and Loyalty'. By 1666 *England's Royal Conquest* reported that 'The bells did ring and bone-fires shine, / and healths carous'd in beer and wine'.[28]

---

22 *Sack for my Money* (n.d.), *Rox.* VI, 319. *Two Penny-worth of Wit for a Penny* (n.d.), Crawford Ballads (henceforward CB.), 25/1.
23 'On Canary' in T.W., *Songs and Poems of Love and Drollery* (1654), pp. 66–7.
24 *The Loyal Subject* (n.d.). Anthony Wood wrote on his 1660s copy of *The Delights of the Bottle* that it was originally published in 1650.
25 *Rox.* VIII, p. xxvi*. The official line is recorded in *A Proclamation against Vicious Debauch'd and Profane Persons* (13 May 1660), promulgated to prevent unofficial retribution by drunken royalists.
26 (1660), *Rox.* VI, 490.
27 (1660), MB.I (7).
28 (1660), BL. C20.f2 (41). (1666), Wood, E25 (56).

Fig. 5.1: The beastly and disruptive effects of drunkenness. *A Looking-Glass for Drunkards: Or, The Good-Fellows Folly* (1660). Copyright Bodleian Library, University of Oxford, Wood, E 25 f. 52.

The politicisation of drink that had developed in the mid-century soon reappeared, providing the imagery for further polemical attacks as upheavals returned with the Popish Plot, the Exclusion Crisis and the Glorious Revolution. During the interregnum, only royalist ballads had used drink as a political image. By the late 1670s and 1680s, the political divide between ale and wine gave way to a politicisation of drunkenness. Whigs and Tories now attacked each other in terms of their consumption of drink, using established ballad-drinking discourses.

The old drunken behaviour of the Cavaliers – with all its moral undertones – was now hurled at the Tories, while, in their turn, the Tories imposed a 'double-whammy' on the Whigs. Continuing the image of drinking and loyalty, Tories made a virtue of their revelling. They claimed a major difference between their merry, loyal carousing and the miserable, seditious sobriety or hypocritical sousing of the Whigs. Thus, the Whigs were doubly damned either as miserable misers who would not buy or enjoy a drink, or as the worst kind of drinkers, who did not drink to be merry or in good company but to be drunk and cause trouble.

Ballads had always dealt with drinking in two opposing strands of discourse. First, there was the godly strand, which warned against the waste and dissipation, the roaring, swearing, whoring and beastliness drinking could lead to. In *Looking Glass for Drunkards* (see Fig. 5.1), for example, a strong message in the ballad – 'Drunkards how dare ye boast of your hard drinking? / Think you there is neither heaven nor helle?' – is combined with woodcuts of drunken roistering men and beasts dressed in men's clothing, drinking, vomiting and fighting.[29] Many ballads referred to drunks who had neglected their wives and children, had drunk away their estates and could not now afford anything, including drink itself, as alewives and tapsters would not give credit to a poverty-stricken drunkard, however good a customer he had been. In some ballads the 'macho' image of men (and sometimes women) holding their drink, smoking, whoring and generally having a riotous night was held up for disapproval.

This strong moral tone fitted in with the many problems drunkenness inflicted on early modern society. In all English towns a large proportion of cases brought before magistrates related to riotous drunkenness, tippling, unlawful entertainment, or the selling of ale without a licence. In Restoration London, drunken 'jest and frolic' was becoming a real problem as 'wild hectorian gentlemen' smashed up property (including the King's own sundial – by the Earl of Rochester), duelled, murdered each other in drunken brawls and attacked women.[30]

---

[29] (n.d.), Wood, E25 (52) has the best woodcuts. Beastliness as an outcome of drinking was a very common image in ballads, broadsides and sermons throughout the seventeenth century, for example, *The Drunkards Character* (1646), Thomason, 669.f10 (51).

[30] J. Spurr, *England in the 1670s* (Oxford: Blackwell, 2000), p. 70.

The other line of discourse was that of good company and generous spirit. *The Young Gallant's Tutor* commended 'The life of Canary', the company of ladies and the 'joyes of good fellowship'.[31] Another song explained 'For Vine keeps joie and unity, / and loves its own society, / So well, that seldom it is known, / That e're a Bottle's drunk alone'.[32] From earliest times, traditional ballads of all kinds had ended with a prayer for the royal family. Thus, in traditional ballad discourse the linking of singing and drinking with the loyal health was well established. Sobriety, on the other hand, was a different matter. 'The Grave and the Dul [were] by sobriety curs'd'.[33] Non-drinkers were depicted as miserable, miserly and bad company. By implication, sobriety was also disloyal. After all, godly sectarians had tried to curb merriment during the Civil War and interregnum years. One balladeer exclaimed, 'these hypocritick knaves/denounced our harmlesse joys / and silenc'd all the loyall staves/ chorus'd by roaring boys'.[34] That there was a connection between sobriety and sedition was clear.

Though, from the later 1670s, this attitude was sometimes expressed in ballads against the 'coffee house crew', it was more often simply related to non-drinkers – and non-participators in loyal health drinking.[35] The refusal to drink a loyal health marked out the seditious and could lead to threats of violence in ballads and in real life. Tim Harris has described many potentially violent scenes in London during the Popish Plot and Exclusion crises. Gangs of Whig and Tory apprentices stopped coaches and passers-by to demand money for healths and the participation of the victim in their loyal tippling. They also attacked pub signs and taverns that were seen as either Whig or Tory strongholds.[36]

Whig balladeers drew upon this strong moral strand of discourse in their attacks on Tories, and made links to papist tippling on communion wine. Tories were roarers and swearers, the town 'bullies', who stupidly preferred to waste their powers and riches in mindless roistering. 'We care not for such sots, as are the crew of papists',[37] sang one ballad; 'Their time is spent Quaffing and cursing',[38] sang another; and yet another 'Now damme is good manners

---

31 *Pepys*, IV, 246.

32 This was copied into the Duke of Monmouth's notebook, quoted by Ebsworth, *Rox.* V, 395.

33 *Delights of the Bottle* (1675), Wood, E25 (58).

34 *The Merry Boys of Christmas* (n.d.), *Rox.* V, 82.

35 In coffee ballads both ale and wine are accused of criminality and rebellion. 'Rapes, murders, thefts and thousand crimes/ Are gender'd by foul Ale and Vines; / These are but trifles to the Woe, / That Wine and Ale and Beer can do, / From whence, unless from these, do daily spring, / Rebellion, Treason, and sham-plotting Sin?' *Rebellions Antidote: or a Dialogue between Coffee and Tea* (1685), CB.29/1.

36 T. Harris, *London Crowds in the Reign of Charles II* (Cambridge: Cambridge University Press, 1987), esp. chapter 7.

37 *Jemmy and Anthony* (1682), *Rox.* V, 169.

38 *An Answer to the Tories pamphlet called the Loyal Feast* (1682), BL. 1876.f1 (20).

grown'. Tories were also depicted drinking the health of the Pope – 'When all the Zealous Whigs are down/ we'll drink and fall a roaring/ And then set up the triple crown/ will saint us all for whoring'.[39]

This was a potent attack. The Whigs had the advantage of a reputation already widely imputed against the Cavaliers. One loyal ballad of 1660 referred to the 'fear of Cavaliers/ that sleep all night and drink all day'.[40] A much reprinted and neutral ballad (blaming both sides for disturbing the peace) described Tories as swearers, who had been 'turn'd to sack and to claret' by the Rump. They had wasted their wealth, 'would fain be at strife,/ In drinking healths do take a great pride' and though they swear they would be loyal – 'this with their actions can not agree right'.[41]

However, Tories could use the convivial strand of drinking discourse in self-defence and as a counter-attack on the Whigs. They took pride in their revelry, which, they claimed, was not drunken but showed 'loyalty without excess'.[42] Only loyalists would merrily drink healths to the king and Duke of York – and in the process augment the royal income through contributing to the excise. The king's income, and thus his independence from parliament, was a major political issue between Whig and Tory. Loyalists were 'trying to drink us out of debt', as *The Loyal London Prentice* put it.[43] 'Our drinking shall him tribute bring', sang *England's Triumph*.[44]

What a Whig needed, Tory ballads argued, was several drinks and the immediate improvement in his spirits would soon convince him to be loyal too. *The Courtier's Health* suggested, 'He that denies the brimmer/ we'll drown him in canary/ and make him all our own,/And when his heart is merry/ he'l drink to Charles in's throne'.[45]

In an 'anti-political' argument (which brings to mind the soma of Huxley's *Brave New World*), a large number of Tory ballads pointed out that a major benefit of drinking was that those who drank made themselves incapable of political designs and plotting. *In Praise of the Bottle* summarised the frequently made argument thus: 'What a Pox d'ye tell me of the Papists' Design, / Would to God you'd leave talking and drink off your wine, / . . . /When the head's full of wine, there's no room left for thinking, / 'Tis naught but an empty and

39 *The Popish Torys Confession; or An Answer to the Whigg's Exaltation* (1682), Douce Ballads, 2 (182a). This ballad and the one it answered were printed both in 'popular' black letter format and 'elite' white letter.

40 *England's Joy, for the coming in of our Gratious Sovereign King Charles II* (1660), Rox.VIII, p. xxiv*.

41 *Religion made a Cloak for Villany* (n.d.), Wood, E25 (78).

42 *A Health to the Royal Family* (1683), *Pepys*, II, 217. Not always though, as in *A New Song* (1685), *Rox.* V, 549, 'We'd rather expire with overmuch drinking, / Than Plotting and Sotting should have a new birth'.

43 (1681), BL. C20.f6 (10).

44 (n.d.), *The Euing Collection of Broadside Ballads* (Glasgow: University of Glasgow Publications, 1971), (henceforward *Euing.*), 102.

45 (n.d.), Firth, b.19 (4).

whimsical pate, / that makes fools run giddy with notions of state.'[46] It was sedition and not drink that created the giddy effects of drunkenness; therefore, the best place for any disaffected mechanic, or fanatick whose 'crazy brain' needed cooling, was in the alehouse or tavern drinking. Sedition and melancholy were connected. To drink was to drive away melancholy and thus drive away sedition. As *The Loyal Subject (as it is reason) Drinks good sack and is free from Treason* put it:

> We that drink good sack in plate
> To make us blithe and jolly
> Never plot against the state
> To be punished for such folly
> But the merry glass and pipe
> Makes our senses quick and ripe
> And expels melancholy [.][47]

Through a fortuitous series of events, Tory songsters could also accuse Whigs of hypocritical drunkenness. It was not an entirely new idea. In the 1660s the charge had appeared in a number of 'discontented cavalier' ballads such as *The Cavaliers Genius*. This sang of disloyal, turncoat, Presbyterians who had gained places or patents at court and who secretly feasted and drank healths in wine to the 'brethren' and against the king. Meanwhile 'stout and loyal' Cavaliers were only able to toast the king with herrings, bread and ale, an interesting reversal of the interregnum imagery.[48]

In 1675, Sir Thomas Armstrong, a notorious womaniser and possibly a rapist, committed a murder – his third – during a drunken brawl. He had been with Monmouth, Albermarle and Dunbar at the time – all courtiers with Whig connections by 1680. Armstrong was finally executed in 1684 as a Whig conspirator, and the epitome of the 'Whig Bully'. Armstrong's activities demonstrated that Whigs (like the Presbyterians) were the most dangerous kind of drinkers: 'In a corner they'l be drunk/ With drinking healths unto the Rump,'[49] 'common hirelings, cheats and knaves, heroes in stews, stabbers and alley braves'[50] who sported 'a bi-fronted conscience' like an alehouse sign.[51] Tories wrote of the 'sullen Whig and trimmer/ that boggles at a loyal health/ Yet will not bawk a brimmer'[52] – not the good fellows or jovial blades of loyal Tory drinking songs but low-class ranters and hotheaded bullies who were such a danger to community and political order. Thus, though the Whigs claimed sobriety, they in fact indulged in the worst kind of miserable 'sotting

---

46 *Rox.* V, 503.
47 (n.d.), *Pepys*, IV, 243.
48 (1660), Wood, 416 (78).
49 *The Loyal Tories Delight* (n.d.), *Rox.* IV, 636.
50 *A Loyal Satyr against Whiggism* (1682), BL. 1872.a.1 (86).
51 *The Loyal Subjects Litany* (1680), BL. 1876.f1 (7).
52 *Tangiers Lamentation* (n.d.), *Rox.* V, 474.

and plotting', 'smoaking and soaking . . . sadly looking' and not singing but 'croaking'.[53]

Tory balladeers also had an answer to Whig accusations of whoring. Several ballads, as the nineteenth-century editor of the Roxburghe ballads Ebsworth put it, 'gave precedence to Bacchus over Cupid'. Here the essential argument was: who needs a woman when you can have drink? As *The Courtier's Health* pointed out, 'we mind not the beautiful lasses' it is 'sack we are wooing' and the King that they adored.[54] Whether an acceptance of the inevitable results of too much drink or a real preference, it meant Tory attacks on Whig sobriety could also be expressed in accusations of womanising or 'Whigs with their lasses'.[55] Whigs, like Presbyterians, were accused of seducing just about anyone. In *The Whig Rampant*, Whigs are made to declare 'We'l make their plump young daughters fall'.[56] If Tories did have sex it was good-fellow, drunken intercourse with the fair-game 'misses' of the taverns. Sober Whigs, however, threatened respectable wives and daughters with their 'presbyterian itch', and were a danger to good society and to innocent women. Again, the evidence was against them, for any man not in the alehouse or tavern drinking himself incapable, as any loyal subject would be, must be available for whoring – and must, therefore, be a Whig.[57]

Happy circumstances also enabled Tory balladeers to exploit drink imagery in their attacks on the radical protestant leaders. These happy circumstances were that while on the one hand there was a widespread rumour of a family link between Oliver Cromwell and brewing in Huntingdon, on the other hand, there was a reference to the making of wine barrels in the family name of the demagogic Earl of Shaftesbury, leader of the Whigs – Anthony Ashley Cooper.[58]

The Protecting Brewer[59] personified the drink revolution that had taken

---

53 *Well-wishers to the Royal Family* (1682), Firth, c.15 (19).
54 (n.d.), Firth, b.19 (4).
55 *The Oxford Health or the Jovial Loyalist* (n.d.), Wood, E25 (27).
56 *Rox.* IV, 265.
57 See *The Whig Rampant* (1682), *Rox.* IV, 264 and *Few Words are Best* (n.d.), *Euing*, 123. The connection of illicit sex and puritanism was made constantly in ballads at least from the 1640s onwards. There are literally hundreds of examples. *The Courtiers Health* put it thus: 'Quakers and Anabaptists, we'll sink them in a glass,/ He deals most plain and flattest that says he loves a lass/ Then Tumble down canary, and let your brains go round,/ For he that won't be merry / He can't at heart be sound.'
58 The only biographers who deal with this question are: A. Fraser, *Cromwell Our Chief of Men* (London: Weidenfeld & Nicolson, 1973), p. 14, who suggests the first mention of this connection was in *Mercurius Elenticus* in February 1649; P. Gregg, *Oliver Cromwell* (London: Dent, 1988), p. 15, who states that Cromwell's mother supervised brewing on the Huntingdon estate; and C. Hill, *God's Englishman* (London: Weidenfeld & Nicolson, 1970), p. 43, n. 5, who references the royalist propagandist Marmaduke Rawsdon as the originator of the rumour.
59 There were many versions of this ballad printed in collections, mostly entitled *The Brewer*. This version (1656?) is printed in *Rox.* VIII, p. c*, another can be found in *Rump: or an Exact Collection of the choycest Poems and Songs relating to the late Times* (1662), pp. 336–9.

place when mechanic ale took over from aristocratic wine. Numerous ballads claimed that Oliver Cromwell was a brewer's son.[60] His red warty nose or 'Naples face' was a continual victim of attacks by royalist writers who read it as the sure sign of a tippler. Many drinking ballads referred to the 'dirty nose' and the 'carbuncles that do shine' of the drunkard. *The Traytors Downfal* described how power had 'caused fire to rise in Oliver's nose: / this ruling nose did bear such sway/ it cast such a heat and shining ray / That England scarce knew night from day'.[61] Major figures were also attacked in these terms, such as Pride 'the drayman', while Whitehall was referred to as 'the Brewhouse'.[62] *Canary's Coronation* deplored that 'A Tavern . . . shall be the court' and, prophetically as it turned out, that 'A Cooper . . . with a red nose . . . shall be . . . keeper of the crown'.[63] In a dialogue between Queen Fairfax and Mrs Cromwell published at the end of a pamphlet called *The Cuckoos Nest*, Mrs Cromwell points out that Cromwell 'will grace a crown being naturally adorned with Diamonds and Rubies' while Queen Fairfax retorts 'a Brewers wife a Queen; that Kingdom must need be full of drunkards when the King is a brewer?'[64] The family trait was inherited. Richard Cromwell, who failed to maintain his father's regime, was called 'Drunken Dick' who 'lov'd a cup of nectar'.[65]

By the time of the Popish plot, 'Old Noll' the brewer had been replaced by the Earl of Shaftesbury, leader of the exclusionists, or 'Toney' the 'Cooper' in ballad discourse. Shaftesbury was referred to as 'the vilest of bullies' and 'a Trayterous sot'.[66] The direct connection with beer was lost, but this was of less significance by the late 1670s and 1680s. Worth far more was the existence of Shaftesbury's 'tap'. Shaftesbury had bravely undergone surgery to install a colostemic tap in his side – a godsend to the political satirist – as in 'Did you not hear of a Peer that was try'd . . . / That looks like a cask with a Tap in his side?'[67]

Connections between the 'Good Old Cause', the brewer of the old cause and the Whigs were constantly reiterated. 'Sing you of the tap, I'll sing of the barrel' trilled one ballad: 'I'll not meddle with barrels of Ale and Beer/ For should they work again we may fear/ Too quick return of the Plutonic Tear.'[68] In *The Wine Cooper's Delight*, Shaftesbury declares, 'We'l kindle old plots by

60 One example of many is *The Royall Subjects warning-piece to all Traytors* (n.d.), *Euing*, 310.

61 (n.d.), *Euing*, 350.

62 See *Rox*. VIII, p.xcvii*–xcviii*.

63 *Op. cit.*

64 (1648), p. 8. Laura Knoppers offers an extensive study of the literary treatment of Cromwell's body and image, including his nose, in *Constructing Cromwell* (Cambridge: Cambridge University Press, 2000).

65 *A New Ballade: To an Old Tune* (1660), Wood, 416 (31). *The Traytors Downfal* (n.d.), *Euing*, 350.

66 *Jack Ketch's New Song* (n.d.), *Rox*. V, 319. *A Song of the New Plot* (n.d.), Ashm. G.16 (101).

67 *Ignoramus Justice* (1682) BL. c.38. i. 25 (4). There are frequent mentions of the 'Tap of sedition' in ballads from 1680 to 1684.

68 *The Meal Tubb Plot* (1679), *Rox*. IV, 179.

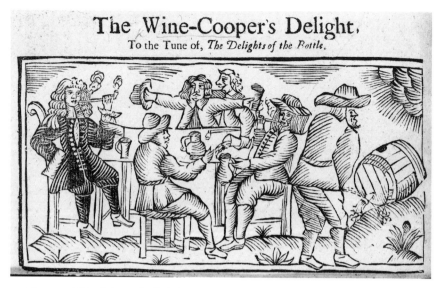

Fig. 5.2: A black-letter ballad sheet making graphic the tainting of wine with the outpourings of Shaftesbury's 'Tap'. Most editions of *The Wine-Cooper* were in roman letter and were not illustrated. Traditional black-letter ballads supported Shaftesbury, which may account for the trouble taken to produce an illustrated edition. *The Wine-Cooper's Delight* (1681). By permission of The British Library, C20. F9, Roxburghe.

inventing of new' and is referred to as a 'second Red Nose'. His demagogic appeal to the 'Rabble', a reminder of Cromwell's 'mechanic rule', was consistently highlighted, here and elsewhere: 'Tinkers and Coblers, the Broom-men and Sweep, / Before this Wine-Cooper in flocks they did meet.'[69]

The imagery surrounding Shaftesbury was complicated, reflecting the multi-faceted use of both drunkenness and sobriety by the Tories in their attacks. *The Wine Cooper's Delight* (Fig. 5.2) used both imagery and image of drunkenness in attack. It aimed to show that Shaftesbury and his followers did not participate in good drinking nor did they drink good wine or beer. They are depicted and described as contaminating drink. Many ballads exploited the image of Shaftesbury's tap, which, instead of good drink, poured out the poison of seditious sobriety. *A New Song on the old Plot* addressed 'Ye Tapland Crew! That Treason Brew'.[70] 'He broached the tap, and it ran apace/ To make a solemn treat for all the town' sings *The Loyal Feast*.[71] *A Litany from Geneva* offered the prayer 'From the Tap in the guts of the honourable stump/ From which runs rebellion, that stinks like the Rump, / On purpose to leaven the

---

69 *The Wine Coopers Delight* (1681) BL. C20. f6 (7).
70 (1682), *Rox*. V, 455.
71 (1682) Ashm. G.16 (144).

Factious Lump; / Libera nos, Domine'.[72] Shaftesbury's 'treats' had led to a 'croud drunk with sedition'.[73]

Finally, we might investigate what ballads can tell us of the cultural landscape of political drinking. Who was singing or hearing these highly political ballads, and where? Once wine had reappropriated politics, were those singing these songs elite wine tipplers while the lower and middling sorts returned to unpoliticised ale, as advised by Tory rhetoric? It seems unlikely. Woodcuts and texts of political and other drinking ballads make it quite clear that wine was widely drunk by all sorts and that in the late seventeenth century a socially widespread, political dialogue concerning 'state affairs' was going on in the hostelries of England and especially in London.

Recent work by Judith Hunter on the habits of drinkers and the sale and licensing of wine and ale in England shows that in towns, at least, establishments would often sell a wide variety of drinks.[74] Ballads too make this point very clear. Drinking ballads rarely make distinctions between ale and beer, and frequently list ale, beer and wine when describing drinking. In *The Heavy Heart and a Light purse,* for example, a ballad warning against the snare of the alewife, the singer recalls 'in the Alehouse, / whilst I drank sack' and later 'Run tap, run tapster, I would cry, / hang sorrow lets be merry,/ . . . in both white wine and sherry.'[75] Even Robin Hood was 'a drinking beer, ale and wine' in his progress to Nottingham.[76] The people that drink wine in ballads range from the lower sorts to the aristocratic, the urban to the rural.

Women, too, are depicted as drinking, drinking wine and politically drinking in ballad discourses. In fact, in Cavalier and Tory discourse women who 'are not precise/ but will take a cup of the best' were more acceptable.[77] In *The Maidens Merry Meeting or the Maids Healths,* a Civil War ballad, the maids who were making merry 'with sack and good sherry'. . . 'did speak with a grace, / Let's drinke a good health to the King'. They are watched by two men 'who sat as demure as a sister', and who remonstrate 'its vainely, / to drink so prophanely'. The maids kick the men (who are as 'round as a ball') away and proceed to drink health after health in canary from a very ladylike 'pure silver boule'.[78]

The acceptable presence and behaviour of women in alehouses and taverns

---

72 (1682), Wood, 417 (89).

73 *A New Ballad of Jockey's Journey* (1681), BL. C20.f.4 (105).

74 J. Hunter, 'English Inns, Taverns, Alehouses and Brandy Shops: The Legislative Framework, 1495–1797' in B. Kümin and B.A. Tlusty (eds), *The World of the Tavern: Public Houses in Early Modern Europe* (Aldershot: Ashgate, 2002), pp. 65– 82.

75 (n.d.), *Euing,* 136.

76 *Robin Hoods Progress to Nottingham* (n.d.), *Pepys,* II, 105.

77 *Nick and Froth or The Good Fellows Complaint for want of full measure* (n.d.), CB. 45/1.

78 (n.d.), II. (55a). Several 1650s royalist ballads tell of loyal Cavalier women who run or are in alehouses and turn down the sexual propositions of puritans, remaining loyal to their royalist lovers and husbands.

is notoriously difficult to assess. This may be partly because the sources used are negative, usually court records of misbehaviour and criminality. A recent study by Martin Lynn, for example, focuses on lust and violence and the illicitness of female drinking.[79] Though Ann Tlusty's *Bacchus and Civic Order* does show women licitly present in taverns with their husbands, as working women and perhaps in groups and at festivals, her sources similarly lead her to emphasise the unacceptability and absence of a female drinking culture.[80] These negative themes are very much reflected in ballad tales and depictions, where female drinking is often part of an illicit sex negotiation of some kind, and many political drinking ballads are exclusively male.

However, there is a strong strand of licit female drinking in ballads – of both wine and ale. In *Councel of a Father to his sone newly married,* the advice is given: 'If she have occasion abroad to go, /with other women merry for to be, /Deny her not, this sometimes must be so, / when thou go forth she never hinders thee, /Answer me this, is she thy wife or slave?'[81] Licit female drinking in ballads often takes place at market or fair time, as *The Merry Market Women of Taunton,* or *Five merry wives of Lambeth* show. The Taunton women were sitting 'In an Alehouse, a drinking good Ale and strong Beer', while the Lambeth wives 'loved good wine, good ale and eke good cheer'.[82] In *Fowre wittie gossips disposed to be merry/ Refused muddy Ale, to drink a cup of sherrie,* the issue of cost is dealt with – 'If our opinions do not faile: / a quart twelve cups containeth, / Its cheaper then a dozen of ale, /where froth and snuffes remaineth'. They point out that the effects of sack are less injurious than ale. They will not be suffering from the effects of drinking as all their husbands currently are.[83] In ballads, women also drink licitly in public with men. In *Hey ho Hunt About* the ballad describes 'A pretty meeting of young men and maids/who went to the tavern by cupids strong aids/ they drank and were merry and sang a new song/ they talked and discoursed but did no body wrong'.[84] In this case they were merry with sugar and sherry, white wine, claret and sack.

Like men, after the Civil War and interregnum, women also continued to participate in 'political' drinking. This was deplored in *A New Satyricall Ballad of the Licentiousness of the Times* which sang: 'The women too prate of the pope

---

[79] M. Lynn, *Alcohol, Sex and Gender in Late Mediaeval and Early Modern Europe* (Basingstoke: Palgrave, 2001).

[80] B.A. Tlusty, *Bacchus and Civic Order. The Culture of Drink in Early Modern Germany* (Charlottesville: University Press of Virginia, 2001). B. Kümin, 'Public Houses and their Patronage in Early Modern Europe' in Kümin and Tlusty (eds), *World of the Tavern*, pp. 44–62, does place respectable women in public drinking houses.

[81] (n.d.), Johnson Ballads, 1251.

[82] (n.d.), Wood, E25 (95). (n.d.), Wood, E25 (120).

[83] (n.d.), *Pepys*, I, 436–7.

[84] (n.d.), 4° Rawl. 566 (122). In ballads drinks in a tavern are also used to seal a betrothal agreement, or as a venue for a proposal of marriage or there is much innocent drinking of wine and beer between lads and lasses – especially at weddings and outside in the summer. See the whole sequence of wedding ballads in *Pepys*, IV, 105–12.

THE

Happy Return:

OR,

The PARLIAMENTS *Wellcome to* London.

Which was Adjourned till the Ninth Day of *November*, 1685. But now Sitting again at *WESTMINSTER*.

To the Tune of, The fair One Let me in.

This may be Printed, R. L. S.

Te ye Noble Lords, and Gentlemen, who can but then but truly those well,
whose Faith and Loyalty, who sorrow did prevent,
Was always constant to your King, and pay allegiance to the King,
and bond of Treachery; and thank the Parliament.
Who humbly welcome you again, Bold Traytors then mutter all their tools
and wish you all content and vehement fail the main,
That Subjects still may reap the fruits This is the Boat now intends to France,
of this our Parliament. that Ship is bound to Spain:
Rebellion now is Rooted out, The tempests of the Sea are great,
Sedition's like to Dye, but nothing to a rent
With all the Trimmers of the Times Of State at Land that doth molest
intend to Vanish. both King and Parliament.

The cures that molest a state, Conjectures are no prophecies,
innumerable are, and chance informs to fate,
But there is none to be compar'd, For prudence concurreth all,
unto a Civil War: in Church as well as state:
When we are greatly bound to these Then should resolve to live content,
Who can't our Discontents: (time to God's Commandement,
We'll bask the King's good health in Ale and always pray God save the King,
in Ale the Parliament and bless the Parliament.

If peace and plenty be our fate, The chief estate which troubles us,
and truth be in our Land, results from ambitious eye,
A farthing for a forraign war, which doth most of the Kingdoms health
while James us both command: and small things magnifies:
Though all the Kings of Europe Bould Instead of mending up the boat,
frown us to't passions vent, we pick a contravent,
We have a remedy at hand, But let us pray, God save the King,
our King and Parliament. and bless the Parliament.

State Weather, wise men did conclude, May all the Members be insured,
when Charles the Court did sue, both honest, just, and true,
The tempests of the Church and State, Impartial bond of base pretence,
wou'd quite eclipse our Sky: all flees to subdue:
But James the second with his rays May all their acts be righteous,
quite the happiness seen, and good be their intent,
Then pray God save our Noble King, And then we'll pray God save the King,
and bless the Parliament. and O brave Parliament.

Printed for C. Dennisson, at the Stationers-Armes within Aldgate.

Fig. 5.3: On this political ballad one woodcut shows a woman drinking and reading along with a group of men in a tavern. *The Happy Return or The Parliaments Wellcome to London* (1685). By permission of The Pepys Library, Magdalene College, Cambridge, Pepys Ballads, vol. II, f. 234.

and the Turk/ who should play with their tails, or else be at work, / but two noble virtues they've attained to, I think, / To handle state matters, and take off their drink.'[85] More positively, in 1692 *An Excellent New Song call'd the Female Duel* described how a 'Williamite lady' of Yorkshire finding that another lady (a Jacobite) at a mixed dinner refused to partake in a loyal health challenged her to a duel.[86]

Ballads consistently place discussion of politics in taverns and alehouses in town and country. Songs such as *Tom and Will or News from the Country*[87] make that clear. Though the country bumpkin is often made to be the fool in ballad as in theatre discourse, often the 'bumpkin' is the one whose good sense asks the right questions. One ballad of 1688, *West Country Tom Tormented*, is especially telling. Tom, a loyal soldier, is 'vexed to the heart by the newsmongers of the town' and 'vow'd he'd neither talk nor prate/ or [any] news would give/ concerning affairs of State'.[88] As he walks through the streets of London he is constantly accosted by people, including a cobbler, a barber and gallants asking him for news of the Prince of Orange's army. He answers angrily 'I will neither meddle nor make' and goes to a tavern for a drink. There he finds it is worse than ever, with a regular debate going on. The only thing worth talking about in the tavern is politics. As with their texts, ballad wood-cuts can give us some idea of what was going on in public drinking spaces. They show men, and women, drinking, singing, reading and all, potentially, participating in the political singing this chapter has discussed.

One final point on the issue of the disloyalty of ale and beer. In 1685 *The Happy Return or The Parliaments Wellcome to London* (Fig. 5.3) suggested that the political separation of grape and grain was still apparent – 'We'l drink the King's good health in Wine/ In Ale the parliaments'[89] – but after the Revolution of 1688 the situation had greatly improved. There was an explosion of loyal political ballads during and after 1688 in which the portrayal of William III's relationship with drink is interesting. In one ballad, William buys his loyal soldiers a drink.[90] In another, often reprinted, ballad, *The Royal Frolic*, William, returning from Ireland with his court (obviously without his habitual flask of champagne), calls in at the house of a farmer and drinks 'nappy March Beer'. This recalls 'happy days, when great Caesars would be, / familiar with Subjects of e'ry degree/ Yet those that have govern'd these Kingdoms of late/ Has not been so pleasant since William the Great/. . . The high road he quitted for merriments sake.'[91] William thus restored ballad beer to loyalty and once more mixed the drinks of monarchy.

---

85 (1679), BL. C40.m11 (52).
86 *Pepys*, V, 128.
87 (1680), *Rox.* IV, 198.
88 *Pepys*, IV, 322.
89 *Pepys*, II, 234.
90 *King William's Welcome in Ireland* (1685), *Pepys*, V, 41.
91 *Pepys*, II, 312.

6

'Be sometimes to your country true': The Politics of Wine in England, 1660–1714

CHARLES C. LUDINGTON

THIS chapter attempts to show how wine, often early modern England's costliest import, became embroiled in the Tory–Whig divide of the late Stuart era, and how, as a consequence, claret became a symbol of Tories and port a symbol of Whigs. However, the original claret-versus-port debate was not merely about political affiliations, it was also about class; and it had nothing to do with personal preference or luxury wine. Instead, it was about competing Tory and Whig foreign policies and specifically, which wine was to be the tavern wine of England, or, as the economist Charles Davenant called it, the wine of the 'Middle Ranks of Men.'[1] Thus, while the claret-versus-port debate in early eighteenth-century England has often been referred to by historians and wine writers alike, the actual grounds of the debate have been consistently mis-stated.[2] Party affiliations informed one's foreign and commercial policy, but wealth and social class were the primary determinants of personal taste. This distinction must be investigated and explained if we are truly to understand the political, social and cultural meaning of wine in England from the Restoration through the reign of Queen Anne – and beyond.[3]

Before proceeding further it is important to elaborate upon the amplitude of change lest one imagine that it was subtle. The precise degree of claret's

---

[1] Charles Davenant, *A report to the Honourable Commissioners for Putting in Execution and Act, Intitled, An Act for Taking, Examining, and Stating the Publick Accounts of the Kingdom*, 2 vols (1712), II, p. 58.

[2] See, for example, Hugh Johnson, *Vintage: The Story of Wine* (New York: Simon & Schuster, 1989), pp. 220–9; A.D. Francis, *The Wine Trade* (London: Adam & Charles Black, 1972), pp. 99–142; Sarah Bradford, *The Englishman's Wine: The Story of Port* (London: Macmillan, 1969), pp. 34–45; André L. Simon, *Bottlescrew Days: Wine Drinking in England during the Eighteenth Century* (London: Duckworth, 1926), pp. 54–66 and 144–50.

[3] For a study of the politics of wine in England and Scotland that takes the story up to 1860, see Charles C. Ludington, 'Politics and the Taste for Wine in England and Scotland, 1660–1860' (Ph.D., Columbia University, 2003).

popularity among English wine drinkers at the outset of the Restoration cannot be proven through the use of import records, incomplete as they are, yet the general contours of English taste for wine during the early years of the Restoration – cosmopolitan but mostly claret – are attested to by the incoming ships' ports of origin. Bordeaux was the leading port of embarkation among ships bringing wine to England, although other boats came from the French ports of La Rochelle and Rouen, from Cadiz and Malaga in Spain, from the Canary Islands, and from various Mediterranean ports in Italy, Greece and the Levant.[4] When England was not at war with the Dutch, rhenish wines from Germany arrived via Rotterdam and other Low Country ports.[5]

Precisely this taste for wine, diversity with claret predominating, is seen in an entry to Samuel Pepys's *Diary* on 7 July 1665:

> Up, and having set my neighbour Mr. Hudson, wine cooper, at work drawing out a tierce of wine for the sending of some of it to my wife – I abroad, only taking notice to what a condition it hath pleased God to bring me, that at this time I have two tierces of claret – two quarter-cask of canary, and a smaller vessel of sack – a vessel of tent, another of Malaga, and another of white wine, all in my wine-cellar together – which I believe none of my friends of my name now alive ever had of his own at one time.[6]

The predominance of French wine was even more pronounced at the upper end of the English social scale, where aspirations to duplicate the court of the Louis XIV meant that all things French were fashionable. For example, in October 1666, the wine cellar of Robert Spencer, the second Earl of Sunderland, contained 12 bottles of white wine (type unspecified), 149 bottles of Lord Galloway's wine (unidentified),[7] 37 bottles of rhenish wine, two pints of Spanish wine (type unspecified), 38 bottles of mountain,[8] 41 bottles of Cyprus wine, 22 bottles of madeira, one bottle of Languedoc wine, 36 bottles of

---

4   The *Calendar of State Papers, Domestic Series*, of the reign of Charles II, 1660–1685, are full of records regarding the arrival of wine from various European ports. See, for example, vol. X (Jan.–Dec. 1670), pp. 3, 21, 62, 79, 82, 99, 146, 173, 182, 193, 199, 204, 212, 241, 292, 506, 551, 566, 579, 592.

5   Although rhenish wines were not the produce of the Netherlands but came from farther up the Rhine, the Navigation Acts allowed for their importation into England in Dutch vessels.

6   Samuel Pepys, *The Diary of Samuel Pepys, a new and complete transcription*, 10 vols, ed. Robert Latham and William Matthews (Berkeley: University of California Press, 1970–83), VI, p. 151. This quotation is also discussed in the Introduction to the present volume. For a more general description of Pepys's drinks and drinking habits, see Pepys, *Diary*, ed. Latham and Matthews, X, 'Drink,' pp. 104–8; Oscar Mendelsohn, *Drinking with Pepys* (London: Macmillan, 1963).

7   This wine is unidentified, but its name reveals that Lord Galloway imported the wine and gave or sold some to his friends, including Sunderland. Among seventeenth- and eighteenth-century aristocrats, it was common for one person, when abroad, to purchase a large amount of wine and have it sent to back to England or Scotland, thus saving his friends the difficulties involved in importing. This favor was then expected in return. For poorer noblemen, it was a respectable form of business to make a bit of a profit on each sale.

8   Mountain was the name for a popular, usually sweet white wine from near Malaga, Spain.

champagne, 40 bottles of côte-rôtie,[9] 84 bottles of burgundy, and finally, 191 bottles of claret (along with 24 pints of bitter water, 43 bottles of strong beer, and an unspecified amount of brandy).[10] In sum, over half of all his identifiable wine was French, and among these claret comprised a majority.

In 1675, the first year for which we have complete import figures for London (although not for English and Welsh provincial ports), French wines accounted for 62 per cent of all incoming wine, while Portuguese wines accounted for less than 1 per cent. And yet, twenty-five years later, French wines accounted for less than 10 per cent of the wine annually imported into England, while Portuguese wines – which did not even figure in Pepys's cellar in 1665,[11] and only made it into Sunderland's in the form of madeira – consistently accounted for roughly two-thirds of the total annual wine imports into England and Wales, and sometimes surpassed that amount. For example, during the War of the Spanish Succession, 1703–12, out of a per annum average of 15,677 tuns of legally imported wine, Portuguese wines, including madeira, accounted for 62 per cent of the total, Spanish wines for 16 per cent, Italian wines for 9 per cent and French wines for 8 per cent, while German wines, at 3 per cent, were almost negligible.[12] In short, by 1714 French wines remained the favorite of those who could afford them, but the Englishman's 'common draught' was no longer claret. Instead, it was a rough, red table wine from the Douro Valley in northern Portugal, a wine that was first known in England as 'priest's port' or 'porto-port,' but soon was known by the simple name of 'port.'

---

[9] I have regularized the spellings to reflect modern usage, because English spellings of wines in the seventeenth and eighteenth centuries was erratic at best. However, in instances where the original spelling is particularly colorful or inconsistent within the same cellar record, I have retained the original spelling by placing it in quotations, in parentheses or in a footnote. For example, in Sunderland's cellar record, madeira is spelled 'Madra,' Cyprus is spelled 'Ciprus,' and côte-rôtie is spelled 'Quoterots.' Finally, wines known commonly by their place of origin, such as bordeaux or burdundy, have not been capitalized.

[10] British Library (BL), Add. Ms. 61490, f. 203, 'An Account of Lord Sunderland's Wine Cellar, 14 October 1666.' Spencer's records do not indicate how much more wine he had in cask, but the amount was probably even greater, as prior to the late eighteenth century wine usually was purchased and stored in cask until a few months or weeks before being consumed.

[11] Pepys quit writing his diary in 1669; thus it is no surprise that it contains no references to port, a wine that was not yet known in England in the 1660s. When Pepys first drank port is unknown, but evidence from London Port records show that he did purchase some in March 1685, just after the death of King Charles, and ten gallons again in March 1686, just after the prohibition against French wines was ended. See Public Record Office (PRO), E 190/137/8, Port of London, Surveyor General of Tunnage and Poundage Overseas: imported wines, Christmas 1685–Christmas, 1686; and PRO, E 190/144/4, Port of London, Collector General of Tunnage and Poundage Overseas: imported wines, Christmas 1686–Christmas 1687.

[12] *Journal of the House of Commons* (*JHC*), XVII, 365, 'An Account shewing the Quantity of Wines imported in to London and the Outports of England, in Sixteen Years and one quarter, from Michaelmas 1696, to Christmas 1712' (report submitted 21 May 1713).

*

First and foremost, the dramatic change in popular English taste for wine from 1660 to 1714 was a result of legislation, embargoes, commercial treaties and wars upon the cost and availability of different wines. Specifically, French wines went from being the least taxed, least expensive and most often consumed wines during the reigns of Charles II and James II, to being the most taxed, most expensive and, while not the least consumed, the most often illicitly traded wines by the 1690s. Conversely, the same high political actions that effectively removed French wines (and especially claret) from English taverns and the tables of the middling sorts promoted Portuguese wines (and especially port) in their stead.

But just as the cost and availability of different wines influenced popular English taste, so too did wines' competing political affiliations. To be sure, wine in general had long been a symbol of the aristocracy in England, and in the mid-seventeenth century it was overtly linked to the Royalist cause.[13] However, it was the internecine political strife of the late Stuart era that gave first claret, and then port, their particular political affiliations. For example, when Parliament placed an embargo on all French goods in 1679, it was intended by the country interest within Parliament to punish Charles II for his clandestine alliance with Louis XIV of France, and also, to punish the French for steadily increasing the tariff on English cloth. As a result, claret, which was English consumers' favorite wine, was now overtly linked to the court and court party – who the embargo was intended to harm.

As the Exclusion Crisis of 1679–81 helped to crystallize the broad court and country political groupings into the Tory and Whig parties respectively, the claret–court link became a claret–Tory link. Nevertheless, in the early years of party politics, claret was as much a metaphor for Tory grievances as it was a symbol of Tory sentiments or consumption habits. This indirect link can be seen in a poem written by John Oldham in 1680 entitled 'The Claret Drinker's Song.' In this poem Oldham's Tory views are clear, as he reiterates the old royalist trope regarding wine drinking and loyalty to the crown versus sobriety and sedition. However, Oldham's poem was also a specifically Tory response to the Whig-led embargo of French wine. What mattered most to Oldham, in the poem at least, was the high cost and relative scarcity of claret: 'Yet oft in my Drink I can hardly forbear,/ To Curse 'em, for making my Claret so dear.' In this way Oldham uses claret – or its absence – to attack what he considers the political extremism, and the consequent dangers to liberty (as represented in the freedom to drink claret), posed by the Whigs. Thus, concludes Oldham, 'Ill

---

13 See chapters in this present volume by Angela McShane Jones ('Roaring Royalists and Ranting Brewers: The Politicisation of Drink and Drunkenness in Political Broadside Ballads from 1640 to 1689'), and Marika Keblusek ('Wine for Comfort: Drinking and the Royalist Exile Experience, 1642–1660').

drink in Defiance of Gibbet and Halter,/ This is the procession that will never alter.'[14]

The Wine-Cooper's Delight, a ballad published in 1681, attacks a different set of supposed Whig principles, but the embargo against French wine is the starting point and wine remains the central trope:

> The Delights of the Bottle are turn'd out of doors,
> By factious fanatical Sons of damn'd whores.
> French wines Prohibition meant no other thing,
> But to poyson the Subject, and beggar the K—.
> Good Nature's suggested with Dregs like to choak her,
> Of fulsom stum'd wine by the cursed Wine-Cooper.[15]

Having blamed the 'factious fanatical Sons of damn'd whores' (i.e. Whigs) for prohibiting French wines, and thereby promoting adulteration, the ballad goes on to describe a tavern scene in which an anarchic mob shouts down the king and asserts the nobility of its own members, all the while drinking a concocted invention of the 'Plaguy Wine Cooper.' Eventually, everyone but the wine cooper is drunk and sick and reeling on the floor. However, he too finally succumbs to his own toxic concoction, and falls down amid the spew and excrement of his customers.

The political allusions of this satirical song would have been clear to all but the most politically obtuse English listeners. Those who were against French wine were also against the monarchy; those who were against the monarchy were republicans, and disgusting, pathetic republicans at that. Drunkenness from wine and especially from claret was a sign of loyalty. And that was precisely the point, because those who approved the 'French wines Prohibition' could not be drunk on wine at all. They could only be drunk on the chemical creation of a dishonest wine *cooper*. This criticism was a strident Tory metaphor for the supposed impurity of Whig political ideology as well as a pun on the first Earl of Shaftesbury, the Whig leader whose surname, conveniently for his detractors, was Cooper.[16]

While claret was politically linked to the Tories from 1680 onward, it remained the most commonly consumed wine in England for at least another decade, and probably would have remained so for longer had not Europe-wide political events intervened. In 1688 William and Mary arrived in England from Holland, and James fled to France without a fight. Nevertheless, when a new embargo was placed on all French imports in 1689 – by a Whig-dominated Parliament – there were many within the loose-knit party who cried out for

---

[14] John Oldham, *The Claret Drinker's Song; or, The Good Fellows Design. By a person of Quality* (1680).

[15] *The Wine-Cooper's Delight, an anti-Republican song to the tune of 'The Delights of the Bottle'* (1681).

[16] See Angela McShane Jones, 'Roaring Royalists and Ranting Brewers', for more on the Earl of Shaftesbury.

their claret. The most conspicuous example of this cry came from Richard Ames, a forlorn claret lover, and somewhat ironically, a committed francophobe and staunch anti-Jacobite.[17] Ames's poem *The Search after Claret* and its three sequels[18] should be seen as part of a general attempt to neutralize the renewed political meaning of claret in the wake of the 1689 embargo, but even more overt was a poem he wrote in 1691, *A Dialogue between Claret and Darby-Ale*. In this latter poem, the anthropomorphized Claret proclaims himself to be 'the most immortal liquor . . . Sent down to be a Charm for mortal Cares, Son of the Sun, and brother to the stars.'[19] In contrast, Darby-Ale is down to earth, unpretentious, and, as the reader is to understand, a bit dull perhaps, but solidly English. Darby-Ale attacked Claret for being haughty, impure and foreign, but it was on this last count that Claret threw down the gauntlet with an insult, a rhetorical question and a bold assertion of claret's Englishness:

> You scoundrel Dog, am I not Naturaliz'd?
> The greatest part o' th' Nation own my Juice
> While they thy Justice Foggy-Ale refuse.[20]

Clearly, Ames was fighting an uphill battle. He was trying to protect claret against the charges of being elitist, adulterated, and most egregiously of all for his fellow Whigs, French. Latent within these charges were Whig critiques of Tories: they were essentially aristocratic; they espoused a new, impure form of government in which the king was absolute; and related to both of these, they were pro-French. Not so, said the straining author, claret had been 'Naturaliz'd' in England by its widespread and frequent use. Furthermore, the English preferred French claret to their own domestically produced ale.

Ames's doggerel was a valiant attempt by a claret-loving Whig to break the link between claret and the Tories, but poetry was not enough to undo what party rivalries and competing economic policies had wrought. By 1693, the last year of his life, Ames acknowledged that the taste for wine often split down party lines.

> The Red Wines together march decently all,
> like a Call of New Serjeants which go by Whitehall.

[17] Ames's known political works are: *The Character of a Bigoted Prince, and what England may expect from the return of such a one* (1691), which was republished the following year under the title, *Chuse which you will, liberty or Slavery; or, An impartial Representation of the Danger of being Subjected to a Popish Prince; The Jacobite Conventicle, a poem* (1692); *The Double Descent* (1692). Ames, a 'student at Lincoln's Inn,' died in 1693.

[18] Richard Ames, *The Search After Claret; or, a Visitation of the Vintners, a poem in two cantos* (1691); *A Farther Search after Claret; or, a Second visitation of the Vintners* (1691); *The last Search after Claret in Southwark: or a Visitation of the Vintners* (1692); *The Bacchanalian Sessions, or the Contention of Liquors, with a Farewell to Wine* (1693).

[19] Richard Ames, *A Dialogue between Claret and Darby-Ale, A Poem* (1691), p. 6.

[20] Ibid., p. 9.

In Coats party-colour'd, so these by Extraction,
Were half of them Spanish, and half the French Faction.[21]

In this instance, Ames's precise oenological divisions are rendered suspect by the requirements of rhyme, but what is notable is the absence of Portuguese wine. Import figures for London during the early 1690s suggest that there was nearly as much Portuguese wine as Spanish wine in England, while French wine was virtually nonexistent. And while we know now that these figures do not account for the vast amount of fraudulently declared wines and cannot be taken at face value, the evidence from Ames's poem correctly shows that port was not yet the solid symbol of the Whigs that it was to become. In the early 1690s Spanish wine was officially, and perhaps in reality, the most commonly imported wine into England;[22] and while it had no direct ties to Whig party commercial policy, it was not French, and hence, as a political symbol it was implicitly Whig. Nevertheless, as a party metaphor Spanish wine was not to last.

Claret as a symbol of the Tories, however, grew in strength throughout the 1689–96 embargo and in the years that followed. This overt connection can be seen in Ned Ward's periodical the *London Spy*, which was published between 1698 and 1700. Ward was a tavern-keeper, poet and self-described 'tippling philosopher'[23] in the City of London. His monthly serial was a bawdy satire on urban living, supposedly written to inform his country friends about the 'vanities and vices of the town.'[24] In Ward's view, London was debauched – a sort of giant Bartholomew Fair – but in an ironic twist that revealed Ward's High Church, Tory sentiments, the City's most dangerous inhabitants were not the drunken blackguards who roamed the streets looking for fights, but the self-righteous religious nonconformists, who according to Ward, would do away with all earthly enjoyment. Ward and his fellow Tory blades, however, enjoyed the pleasures of this world, which wherever they went in London included large amounts of politically (as well as socially and culturally) symbolic claret.

Of course, many urban and urbane Whigs wanted their claret too, but among the Whig middling sorts taste for French wine was not easily reconciled with hatred of the French. As Ames himself had written in one of his anti-Jacobite pamphlets: 'The FRENCH — Altho' indeed no Terrour lye/ in the Word *French*, yet there's a strange,/ and almost unaccountable Antipathy,/ Against 'em does in *English* Bosoms range.'[25] In itself, this hatred had little

21 Ames, *Bacchanalian Sessions*, p. 7.
22 Ludington, 'Politics and the Taste for Wine,' chap. 1.
23 Ward used this term in the title of a long poem he wrote, *Wine and Wisdom: or, the tipling Philosophers. A lyrick poem* (1710). The poem was a humorous account of wine drinking among ancient philosophers, and, Ward says in the preface, it was meant to be read aloud when wine was being consumed.
24 Edward Ward, *The London Spy*, vol. I, part 1 (1698), p. 3.
25 Ames, *Double Descent*, p. 24.

impact upon English love for claret. After all, one could hate the French but love French wine, which was precisely the case of Whigs like Ames. What was important, however, was the effect that Whig antipathy had upon foreign and commercial policy. Under Whig governments, wars, embargoes and tariff increases had made French wine hard to obtain legally, and when legal, more expensive than any other wine. As a result, it was increasingly difficult for all but a small class of wealthy and politically connected consumers, be they Whig or Tory, legally to purchase their favorite French wine.

A stellar example of just this sort of wealthy consumer, and a Whig, was John Hervey, the first Earl of Bristol (1665–1751). Hervey kept a meticulous book of expenses, which included wine, from 1688 until his death in 1751. True to form as a wealthy Englishman, he had cosmopolitan taste; his cellar was full of wines from Spain, the Canary Islands, Portugal, Madeira, Italy and Germany. But above all, he enjoyed wine from France. Even during the 1689–96 embargo he managed to purchase claret and hermitage (from the northern Rhône valley) and what he called 'Hermitage clarett,'[26] although under what import conditions it is not apparent. He also bought a suspicious amount of navarre and galicia (i.e. wines from northern Spain and, therefore, probably fraudulently declared claret), and less suspiciously sack, canary, rhenish and palm.[27] Between the Treaty of Ryswick in 1697 and the beginning of the next embargo against French goods in 1704, Hervey's choices were even more focused on France. For example, in 1698 he purchased a tierce (42 gallons) of burgundy; in 1699, three pipes (one pipe = 126 gallons) of navarre (again, probably claret at Spanish prices), a pipe and 36 bottles of wine from Languedoc, and 30 bottles of St Laurent (claret). In 1700 and 1701 he bought large amounts of champagne and burgundy from the merchant Michael La Roche, and in 1702 he bought four hogsheads (one hogshead = 63 gallons) of 'Obrian Wine' (Haut Brion), the prototype of first-growth claret, and another tierce of burgundy. Most tellingly of all, in December 1703, with another embargo about to come into effect, Hervey purchased a hogshead of 'Margoose Clarett' (Margaux).[28]

Clearly, for those who could afford them, French wines knew no party limits. Prominent Whigs like Hervey saw nothing wrong with drinking luxury

---

[26] 'Hermitage clarett' was probably hermitage from the Rhône valley near Tain. The term *clarett* may have been added by Hervey's wine merchant as a way to indicate a red wine from France, or as a way to make hermitage sound more familiar. It may also have been Hervey's own description. In any event, marketing terms were not yet agreed upon, to the occasional confusion of the historian.

[27] From Las Palmas in the Canary Islands, this was simply another name for canary wine, almost all of which was sweet malmsey.

[28] West Suffolk Record Office, Bury St Edmunds, 941/46/13/14, 'Expense Book of John Hervey, first Earl of Bristol.' Most of this information has been republished in *The Diary of John Hervey, first Earl of Bristol. With extracts from his book of expenses, 1688–1742*, ed. S.H.A. Hervey (Wells: Suffolk Green Books, 1894), 'Wine,' pp. 168–80.

claret and other French wines if they could afford them; the issue to them was whether regular claret should be widely available and generally affordable throughout all of England. They believed not, as this would mean giving large amounts of English gold and silver to France. It was this distinction between private preference and public policy that assuaged wealthy Whig consciences as they poured bottle after bottle of fancy French wine down their throats. It was also this distinction that facilitated the rise and politicization of port.

Claret was firmly Tory by the 1690s, but port was not yet Whig. Portuguese export wines, and in practice that usually meant port, first made inroads into the English market in the late 1670s, primarily as a result of an embargo against French wines. However, these wines at first were not popular and much of what was shipped as Portuguese wine was in fact fraudulently declared French wine.[29] Yet, despite this slow and inauspicious start, the volume of Portuguese wines in England increased over time, and by the late 1690s they were among the most frequently imported wines. In short, Portuguese wines were already on the rise when they got their biggest break of all, the beginning of another war between the Grand Alliance and France, this time with Spain allied to the latter. The result was that England looked to Portugal as never before to be a supplier of wines.

This next pan-European conflict began over the issue of the succession to the Spanish throne. Louis XIV claimed that the heir was his son, Philip of Anjou, while the Grand Alliance, led by William III, supported the more tenuous claim of Archduke Charles of Austria. Thus, when Louis concluded an alliance with Portugal in 1701, it was a severe blow to England, the Netherlands, and their ally the Holy Roman Emperor, because Portugal under French domination further isolated the Emperor's Italian possessions and increased the risk to English and Dutch ships on their way to the Levant or the West Indies.

As the mastermind of the struggle against a Bourbon universal monarchy William III believed it was imperative to win back the Portuguese. For this he called upon John Methuen, the son of a Bradford-on-Avon clothier who had lived in Lisbon from 1691 to 1696 as a member of the English legation. William died before his special envoy departed for Portugal, but in retrospect, he had initiated one of his most lasting diplomatic policies. With cash in hand, Methuen, along with the Dutch ambassador and the dissident Almirante of Spain, succeeded in convincing King Pedro of Portugal that his country's interests were not with a mighty Bourbon empire, but rather with the maritime powers and the Holy Roman Emperor.[30] The result was that two political treaties were signed in early 1703. The first asserted Archduke Charles's claim

---

[29] Ludington, 'Politics and the Taste for Wine,' chap. 1.
[30] A.D. Francis, *The Methuens and Portugal, 1691–1708* (Cambridge: Cambridge University Press, 1966), pp. 112–34.

to the Spanish throne, while the second cemented the military alliance between England, Portugal and the Netherlands.

After the two treaties were ratified by their respective governments, Methuen proposed a third treaty between England and Portugal uniquely, one that would reaffirm the two nations' longstanding commercial relationship. Methuen the government envoy was a merchant at heart, and with family and national interests in mind he had been seeking new outlets for English cloth in an age when national industries were jealously guarded against foreign competition. With bellicose France and Spain no longer possible trading partners, he sought to convince the more vulnerable and perhaps therefore more pliant Portuguese to open up their markets to English cloth. Without receiving permission from the Queen or her ministers, Methuen took it upon himself to promise a favorable market advantage for Portuguese wines if the Portuguese would end the prohibitive tariffs on English cloth. Famously brief, the Anglo-Portuguese commercial treaty stated that

> His Sacred Royal Majesty of Portugal promises, in his own Name, and in the Names of his Successors, that there shall be admitted at all times into Portugal, woolen cloths, and the other woolen manufactures of England, no otherwise than they used to be, before they were prohibited by Pragmatical Sanctions [i.e. sumptuary laws],

for which in return

> her sacred Royal Majesty of Great Britain be obliged in her own Name, and in the Name of her Successors, at all times to admit into England, Wines gathered from the Vineyards belonging to the Portugal Dominions, as that at no time . . . any more shall be demanded for such wines . . . than what shall, after deducting a third part of the Customs or Impost, be demanded from a like quantity of French Wine . . .'[31]

It was a risk for Methuen to offer these terms before consulting his government, but he felt confident that a Whig Parliament, so long as it was not barred from raising or lowering duties on all wines, would favor a treaty that hampered French wines on the English market. His gamble was correct, and Parliament quickly ratified the Anglo-Portuguese trade agreement.

G.M. Trevelyan called the three treaties negotiated by Methuen 'the most important group of diplomatic documents signed between the Grand Alliance

---

[31] *JHC*, XIV, 289–90, 20 Jan. 1704. The official English name for this treaty was 'The Treaty between England and Portugal, signed December 27th, 1703.' The 'Pragmatical Sanctions' were a series of laws enacted throughout the seventeenth century in Portugal that endeavored to restrict the consumption of luxury goods, especially of foreign manufacture, and to repair the Portuguese economy. These laws were deeply embedded in Counter-Reformation thought, so that austerity in dress had a spiritual underpinning as well. Most recently, a law prohibiting the use of English cloth had been decreed on 25 Jan. 1675. See Francis, *Wine Trade*, pp. 82–9; and Francis, *Methuens and Portugal*, pp. 184–218.

in 1701 and the Peace of Utrecht . . . They remained the basis of England's power in southern Europe till the days of Nelson and Wellington, and affected her commercial policy down to the era of the Great Reform Bill.'[32] Moreover, the Anglo-Portuguese commercial treaty of 1703, which came to be known incorrectly as *the* Methuen Treaty, had the effect of definitively linking the Whig party with the wine whose popularity increased as a result, port, and of solidifying port's role as the tavern wine of England.

Despite the fame of the Methuen Treaty among eighteenth- and nineteenth-century political economists, port devotees and port detractors, the effects of the Methuen Treaty were not immediate. In the immediate aftermath of the hastily passed treaty it remained to be argued whether, as the Whigs said, making port the Englishman's common draught was in the best interest of the nation because it deprived the French of English money while simultaneously guaranteeing the Portuguese market for English cloth. Tories like Charles Davenant thought that free trade with more populous and wealthier France would be more beneficial to England, and when the Tories returned to power in 1711 they quickly repealed the embargo on French wines that had been in place since 1704, saying: 'It hath been by experience found that the prohibition of French wines to be imported in to this Kingdom or Ireland, is injurious to your Majesty's revenue, and many ways prejudicial to your subjects.'[33] The end of the embargo against French wines was in line with Tory taste and politics, but the vast extent of fraud, smuggling[34] and adulteration[35] suggest that it was not only party politics to assert that prohibiting French wines was a dubious tool of fiscal and foreign policy.

Whigs, however, remained convinced that because France was the sworn

---

[32] G.M. Trevelyan, *England under Queen Anne*, 4 vols (London: Longmans Green, 1948), I, pp. 299–300.

[33] 9 Ann. c. 8 (1711).

[34] While most surviving evidence from the late Stuart era suggests that wine fraud was carried on to a greater extent than smuggling, the latter was nevertheless considered a problem. See also, *An Enquiry into the Causes of the Prohibition of Commerce with France, during the present War* (1708).

[35] Adulteration of wines in England was as old as the English wine trade itself. However, the high cost of French wine by the 1690s and throughout the eighteenth century increased merchants' incentive to create or 'lengthen' 'French' wine in particular with native ingredients. Witness Joseph Addison's comments in *The Tatler*, no. 131, 9 Feb. 1709: 'There is in this city a certain fraternity of chymical operators who work underground in holes, caverns, and dark retirements, to conceal their mysteries from the eyes and observation of mankind. These subterraneous philosophers are daily employed in the transmigration of liquors, and by the power of magical drugs and incantations, raise under the streets of London the choicest products of the hills and valleys of France. They can squeeze Bordeaux out of a slow, and draw Champagne from an apple.' *The Tatler*, ed. Donald F. Bond, 3 vols (Oxford: Clarendon Press, 1987), II, pp. 259–60. For a general discussion of wine adulteration in England and indeed throughout the world, see Rod Phillips, 'Wine and Adulteration,' *History Today* (July 2000), pp. 31–7; and Phillips, *A Short History of Wine* (London: Allen Lane, 2000). For a discussion of the adulteration of port, see Ludington, 'Politics and the Taste for Wine,' chap. 3.

enemy, an embargo against French goods was imperative for the prosperity of England. The Bishop of Salisbury, Gilbert Burnet, said that the 1711 act to repeal the prohibition against French wine passed, although 'not much to the honour of those who promoted it,' inasmuch as 'the interest of the nation lay against it so visibly, that nothing but the delicate palates of those who loved that liquor, could have carried such a motion through the two houses.'[36] Similarly, in *Spectator,* no. 43, Abraham Froth (Richard Steele), wrote regarding the same act:

> Verily, Mr. *Spectator*, we are much offended at the Act for Importing *French* Wines: A Bottle or two of good solid Edifying Port, at Honest *George*'s made a Night Cheerful, and threw off Reserve. But this plaguy *French* Claret, will not only cost us more Mony, but do us less good: Had we been aware of it before it had gone too far, I must tell you we would have petitioned to be heard on that subject.[37]

No one could deny that a bottle or two of port, a naturally strong wine and perhaps already fortified with a dash of brandy,[38] was better at 'throwing off reserve' (i.e. getting one drunk) than a similar amount of claret, which was said to be a 'cool' wine because of its relative lack of alcohol. But not all Whigs were swayed by this bacchic rationale. Indeed, in this instance Steele was merely playing to the crowd. Two years later, when a commercial treaty with France was a topic of popular and parliamentary discussion, Steele condemned the treaty on all but one ground, saying: 'Things that are of absolute Necessity cannot be reckoned prejudicial to a Nation; but *France* produces nothing that is necessary, or even convenient, or but which we had better be without, except claret.'[39] Indeed, in the debates surrounding the proposed commercial treaty with France in 1712–14, prominent Whigs like Steele acknowledged that they, and most English consumers, preferred claret to all other wines. However, they could not reconcile the importation of vast amounts of inexpensive claret, and therefore large amounts of money to France, with their fear of and antipathy for the French.

Some Whig propagandists responded to this tension within themselves by asserting that, as the Methuen Treaty with Portugal was the best possible commercial arrangement for England, consumers should be willing to pay more (as they already were) for their claret. As one Whig pamphleteer asked in an open letter in 1714 to the Tory trade commissioner Arthur Moore:

---

[36] Gilbert Burnet, *History of his own Time from the Restoration of Charles II to the Treaty of Peace at Utrecht, in the reign of Queen Anne*, 2 vols (London: W. Smith, 1840), II, p. 864.

[37] *The Spectator*, ed. Donald F. Bond, 5 vols (Oxford: Clarendon Press, 1965), no. 43, dated Oxford, 13 April 1711, I, pp. 181–2.

[38] For a discussion of the strength of eighteenth-century port, see Ludington, 'Politics and the Taste for Wine,' chap. 3.

[39] *The Guardian*, ed. John Calhoun Stephens (Lexington: University of Kentucky Press, 1982), no. 170, 25 Sept. 1713, 552–6.

I appeal to all the World, especially to you, Sir, if it is to be imagin'd, that any Body that can afford to drink Wine, will not sooner be at the extraordinary Expence of three half Pence for a bottle of French Wine, than confine themselves to drink Portugal Wine, for the sake of saving three half Pence, especially when French wine is so much more coveted than the other.[40]

Surely, price differences mattered to a majority of consumers, especially when the actual difference in cost between a standard quart bottle of claret and port could be a few shillings, not, as the author disingenuously claimed, a few half-pence. But the author of the pamphlet was correct to wonder whether cost alone was really enough to sway English wine drinkers when the central concession of almost every argument against trade with France was that the Methuen Treaty needed to be maintained because despite many years of drinking Spanish, Italian and most of all Portuguese wines, the English still preferred wine from France.[41]

In fact, for many consumers, added to the high cost of claret was fear and hatred of the French. This attitude, which found expression in innumerable pamphlets, broadsheets, sermons, essays and public debates of the time, was summarized by a Tory critic in a 1712 issue of *The Examiner*:

This nation has been so long engaged in War with the French, that some of our unthinking Britons have contracted a kind of personal Malice against them; never considering, that if our Country be ruined, it is perfectly indifferent to us, whether it be done by the French, the Dutch, the Germans, the Turk, the Devil or the Pope. But they think perhaps it is impossible with regard to the advantage of Britain, that the French should be to [sic] much crushed and confounded.[42]

Fear and hatred of France was so endemic in England that for many people the notion of a mutually beneficial commercial treaty was anathema. The prevalence of this idea in England gave the Whigs their tactical advantage in the commercial treaty debate because it allowed them to move smoothly from economic arguments to accusations of Tory treachery. For example, one anti-treaty pamphleteer was more than willing to question Daniel Defoe's national loyalty because of his open support for the treaty. 'How much soever he would be thought a Patriot of England,' opined the

---

40 *A letter to the Honourable A—r M–re, Com—ner of Trade and Plantations* (1714).

41 The examples here are numerous in pamphlet literature and journals, but see in particular, *The Consequences of a Law for reducing the dutys upon French wines, Brandy, Silks and Linen, to those of other nations. With remarks on the Mercator* (1713); *The British Merchant*, ed. King, I, pp. 346–52; *A Vindication of the late House of Commons, in rejecting the bill for Confirming the Eighth and Ninth articles of the Treaty of Navigation and Commerce between England and France* (1714). This last example stated quite plainly that French wines, 'being more agreeable to the generality of British Palates, . . . will be almost the only Wines in request, and become the Common Draught in every Tavern.' *A Vindication*, p. 17.

42 *The Examiner*, 7–14 Aug. 1712. The author of this article may have been Swift or Prior, both of whom wrote for the *The Examiner* at this time.

anonymous author, 'he will hardly be able to persuade thinking Men that he is not a hired factor for France.'[43] Another Whig propagandist responded with feigned disbelief to the pro-treaty argument that the duty on French wine should be lowered so that people may drink it more cheaply, since it was what they preferred, and with the help of illegal traders they were going to drink it anyway: 'But sure this Reason can never weigh with any thing that has the Name of a Gentleman, and far less with a PATRIOT, when he sees 'tis against the true interest of this Country.'[44] In this context of widespread and inveterate francophobia, it is easy to see how the Whigs had greater public credibility with their argument that the commercial treaty of France went against England's national interests.

Within this Whig conceptual framework – where the proposed commercial treaty with France was bad for England and the Methuen Treaty with Portugal was good – the act of drinking a Portuguese wine was overtly (if not also ironically) a symbol of one's English patriotism (as defined by the the Whigs). This connection is illustrated in an allegorical essay about the proposed commercial treaty at Utrecht written by Joseph Addison in 1713, wherein one Goodman Fact, plaintiff, is pitted against Count Tariff, defendant.[45] Goodman Fact, much like Darby-Ale before him and John Bull his contemporary, was

> a plain spoken person, and a man of very few words.[46] Tropes and figures are his aversion [explained Addison]. He affirms every thing roundly, without art, rhetorick, or circumlocution. He is a declared enemy to all kinds of ceremony and complaisance. He flatters no body.

If any reader did not get the point that Mr Fact was a solid (low church) Protestant Englishman, Addison went on:

> He appeared in a suit of *English* broad-cloth, very plain, but rich. Every thing he wore was substantial, honest, home-spun ware. His cane indeed came from the East-Indies, and two or three little superfluities from Turkey, and other parts. It is said that he encouraged himself with a bottle of neat *Port,* before he appeared at the tryal.

---

43 *The Consequences of a Law* (1713).

44 *The trade with France, Italy, Spain and Portugal, considered: with some observations on the Treaty of Commerce between Great Britain and France* (1713).

45 Joseph Addison, *The Late Tryal and Conviction of Count Tariff* (1713), in *The Miscellaneous Works of Joseph Addison*, 2 vols, ed. A.C. Guthkelch (London: G. Bell & Sons, 1914), II, pp. 265–72.

46 John Bull was invented in 1712 by Joseph Arbuthnot, also at the time of the Treaty of Utrecht. Addison seems to have plagiarized much from Arbuthnot's caricature and plot. The original John Bull was a cloth dealer involved in a lawsuit against Lewis Baboon (i.e. Louis Bourbon). Bull was 'an honest, plain dealing fellow, choleric, bold and of very unconstant temper.' Joseph Arbuthnot, *The History of John Bull* (London, 1712), p. 9. For a lengthy discussion of the career of John Bull, see Miles Taylor, 'John Bull and the Iconography of Public Opinion in England, 1712–1929,' *Past and Present*, 34 (1992), 93–128.

Needless to say, Count Tariff, as well as being an aristocrat – again a Whig attack on Tory stereotypes – was an eighteenth-century English caricature of a Frenchman:

> He was dressed in a fine brocade waistcoat, curiously embroidered with Flower-de-luces. He wore also a broad-brimmed hat, a shoulder knot, and a pair of silver-clocked stockings. He abounded in empty phrases, superficial flourishes, violent assertions and feeble proofs.[47]

Addison's intention was not to be subtle, and indeed his use of wine as a political symbol was quite clear: a *true* Englishman drinks port. This same point was even more succinctly stated in a bit of anonymous doggerel written around the time of the commercial treaty debate:

> Be sometimes to your country true,
> Have once the public good in view;
> Bravely despise champagne at court
> And choose to dine at home on port.[48]

A desperate Defoe responded to these attempts to link port and patriotism by alluding in the *Mercator* to one Herr Coopmanschap, 'The Dutch agent to Sir Poll, chairman of a certain club who meet behind the Exchange to drink Neat *Port*, and give up the English trade.'[49] But the old Tory bogeyman, the Dutch, no longer heated the blood of 'true-born' Englishmen the way the French did, and this was the bigotry against which French wine in England now had to struggle. In fact, when the Whigs returned to power in 1714, the very act of drinking claret could bring one's loyalty into question. That, at least, was the joke in Susannah Centlivre's comic play *The Wonder: A Woman Keeps a Secret* (1714): 'I have been drinking right French Claret, Sir,' says Don Felix to his prospective father-in-law Don Pedro, 'But I love my own Country for all that.' 'Ay, ay,' responds Don Pedro, 'who doubts it, Sir?'[50] Centlivre's

---

[47] Addison, *Late Tryal*, pp. 267, 269.

[48] Simon, *Bottlescrew Days*, p. 148, attributed this epigram to Jonathan Swift. However, the epigram is not included in Swift, *The Complete Poems*, ed. Pat Rogers (New Haven: Yale University Press, 1983). By 1712–13 Swift was a Tory, and therefore is unlikely to have penned these lines. In fact, in his *Journal to Stella* he records numerous occasions on which he drank champagne, but never port, with Bolingbroke. Consequently, I offer an alternative interpretation: these lines could have been a mild attack directed *at* Swift by one of his Whig acquaintances in London around the time of the Treaty of Utrecht, perhaps Addison or Steele, with whom he dined on occasion.

[49] *The Mercator*, 19 Dec. 1713.

[50] Susannah Centlivre, *The Works of the celebrated Mrs. Centlivre*, ed. J. Pearson, 3 vols (London: John Pearson, 1872), *The Wonder: A Woman Keeps a Secret*, III, p. 67. *The Wonder* was set in Lisbon, which makes the lines about French wine equally fitting; however, the lines were fully intended for an English audience, and Lisbon was understood to be London. The comedy is about the attitudes of English men toward English women. It may have been set in Portugal for

point was that Don Felix's loyalty to his country was considered doubtful by some, just as was Tory loyalty to the incoming House of Hanover.

In another play by Centlivre, *A Gotham Election*, written in 1715, she again uses the politicization of wine for comic effect. Friendly, an agent for the Tory grandee Sir Roger Trusty, is trying to ascertain the political leanings of Score-Double, an Innkeeper in Gotham, who is fully aware of the politics of wine: 'What do you please to drink, Sir?' asks Score-Double, a bit nervously.

> *Friendly*: Why, bring us the best your house affords.
>
> *Score-Double*: The best my house affords, ha, ha, ha, that is as you think it, Sir; – now most of our Gentry, for the last *vour* Years, d'ye mind, will touch nothing but *French* Claret – there are some that like your *Port* wines, but very few, and those of the poorer *Zort* too, as my barboard can witness.
>
> *Friendly*: Come, bring such as you like yourself.
>
> *Score-Double*: Why then, Master, we'll have a bottle of white lisbon.[51]

This was a clever evasion, because despite its Portuguese origins white lisbon was a politically neutral wine.[52] Claret, and its proposed substitute port, were the political give-aways.

Centlivre had a strong Whig bias in her plays and was an intimate of Farquhar and Steele.[53] Her own sentiments regarding the commercial treaty with France may have been summed up in another scene from *A Gotham Election*, which was a satire of the Tory party. In this scene, Tickup, a candidate for Gotham, is at a local tavern with Mallett, the son of Gotham's mayor, when the former commands a bottle of 'French Red' from the drawer at a local tavern. The drawer arrives with the bottle, they drink to Score-Double's health and then Tickup asks: 'Well, how do you like the Wine? I think 'tis pretty good.' To which Mallett replies, 'I think so too, Sir; – but second Thoughts is best.'[54] This last line is a direct allusion to Parliament's rejection of the proposed Treaty of Trade and Commerce with France on the third and final reading, and while it suggests Centlivre was an orthodox Whig, it does not tell us about her own taste for wine. This would be nice to know, because there is little evidence from this period as to what kind, when, where and in what manner women drank wine.[55] But as a playwright and social commentator Centlivre's evidence is

---

political reasons, or more likely to illustrate Centlivre's point that Englishmen were equally domineering (and foolish) as the southern European men whose attitudes they mocked.

51 Centlivre, *Works, A Gotham Election*, III, p. 158.

52 Francis, *Wine Trade*, p. 131.

53 *Dictionary of National Biography (DNB)*, III, pp. 1329–31.

54 Centlivre, *Works, A Gotham Election*, III, p. 165.

55 For discussions of drink and women, see chapters in this present volume by Karen Britland ('Circe's Cup: Wine and Women in Early Modern Drama') and Susan J. Owen ('Drink, Sex and Power in Restoration Comedy').

helpful. She perceived that wine had become a political language of its own and used that language to mock her party-divided society.

The political language of wine was closely tied to England's internal political debates and external economic policies. When the Whigs emerged politically victorious within England in 1714, so too did the wine that their party policies promoted. Similarly, when the Tories lost power, claret lost its chance to become once again the common draught of England's 'middle ranks.' First and foremost, this was the result of political decisions since the late 1670s that had made claret at times unavailable, and ultimately too expensive for most consumers. Second, English anti-Gallicanism became so virulent that it had the remarkable ability both to inform and transform the popular English palate. But the key word here is 'popular.' As Centlivre wrote, most of the 'Gotham' gentry in 1714 still drank claret, while only the poorer sort drank port. Indeed, we know already from the example of John Hervey that wealthy Whig gentlemen could be indifferent to the popular politics of wine, for which, to a very large degree, they had been responsible. Among the wealthy, fashionability and discernible quality, not party politics, dictated personal taste. This point is nicely illustrated in the personal preferences of John Churchill, the first Duke of Marlborough (1650–1722), who began the War of the Spanish Succession as a Tory but ended it as a Whig, and preferred French wine the entire time. Letters and receipts from wine merchants to Marlborough show that from the outset of the war until the Treaty of Utrecht, the field marshal known throughout Europe for humbling France's once-mighty army enjoyed champagne most of all, drinking the very best 'vin d'Ay,' 'vin de Sillery' and 'vin d'Aville' (d'Hautevillers). He also enjoyed large amounts of burgundy, hermitage and the most expensive claret.[56]

Marlborough's taste in wine was an outstanding example of the way that for those who could afford it, fancy French wines transcended party divisions. Such wines did not represent the enemy across the Channel; they represented fashion and good taste. A letter-cum-advertisement from the wine merchant Charles Fary to the anti-treaty journal *The Englishman* (the successor to *The Guardian*), shows precisely how Whig gentlemen contemplated and resolved the potential dilemma over their preference for French wine.

> But you are so warm in this latter Character, [i.e. being an 'Englishman'] that I fear you will have an Aversion to my Liquor because is it *French*; but I am an *English* Scholar, and read our Poets, and must therefore beg Leave to recite to you that of *Dryden*,
>
> > *Tho' at the mighty Monarch you repine,*
> > *You grant him still most Christian in his Wine.*

---

[56] BL, Add. Ms. 61349, f. 83, f. 68, f. 69, f. 108; Add. Ms. 61363, f. 48, f. 78, Wine bills and receipts of the first Duke of Marlborough.

'Thou jolly son of Nestor, be convinced that there is neither High nor Low, Whigg or Tory, against good Liquor. If the Bill of Commerce should pass, it will be all our Comfort; if it should not pass, we shall be able to pay for it, be it ever so dear.'[57]

By the end of Queen Anne's reign well-heeled English claret-lovers, whether Whig or Tory, believed that the national interest and personal taste for wine were entirely distinct. But as Fary readily acknowledged, they could afford to think that, come what may at Utrecht. We know that the Treaty of Trade and Commerce did not pass, and therefore that claret and other French wines remained expensive. As the history of the development of luxury claret reveals, this mattered little to the wealthy English consumers for whom the wine was created.[58] Indeed, evidence suggests that it mattered least of all to wealthy Whigs.[59] Nevertheless, as historians have long recognized, claret was politically affiliated with the Tories while port was politically affiliated with the Whigs. But, in the early eighteenth century at least, this was more a matter of what one considered best for the nation – and what one could afford – than it was an indication of personal preference. As for what wines people actually purchased and consumed, claret was a wine for the wealthy and port was a wine for the middling sorts.

---

57 *The Englishman*, ed. Rae Blanchard (Oxford: Clarendon Press, 1955), first ser. no. 8, 22 October 1713.

58 On this assertion see, Henri Enjalbert, 'Comment Naissent les Grands Crus: Bordeaux, Porto, Cognac,' *Annales: Economies, Sociétés, Civilisations*, 8 (1953), 315–28, 456–74; Enjalbert, 'L'Origine des Grands Vins,' in Charles Higounet (ed.), *La Seigneurie et le Vignoble de Château Latour: Histoire d'un grand cru du Médoc (XVIe–XXe siècle)* (Bordeaux: Fédération Historique du Sud-Ouest, 1974), pp. 3–18; René Pijassou, 'Le Vignoble Bordelais et la Naissance des Grands Crus,' in F.-G. Pariset (ed.), *Bordeaux au XVIIIe Siècle* (Bordeaux: Fédération Historique du Sud-Ouest, 1968), pp. 155–90; Pijassou, 'Le Marché de Londres et la Naissance des Grands Crus Médocains (fin 17ème Siècle–debut 18ème Siècle),' *Revue Historique de Bordeaux*, 23 (1974), 139–50; Pijassou, *Un Grand Vignoble de Qualité: Le Médoc*, 2 vols (Paris: Tallandier, 1980).

59 Ludington, 'Politics and the Taste for Wine,' chap. 3.

Drink and Gender

7

Circe's Cup: Wine and Women in Early Modern Drama

KAREN BRITLAND

> First, all you peers of Greece, go to my tent;
> There in the full convive we. Afterwards,
> As Hector's leisure and your bounties shall
> Concur together, severally entreat him.
> Beat loud the taborins, let the trumpets blow,
> That this great soldier may his welcome know.
>
> *Troilus and Cressida*, 4.5.271–6

IN *Troilus and Cressida*, conviviality occurs in a space between battles among a group of men whose martial exploits are the stuff of myth. Etymologically, convivial means 'living together with' (*OED*, con- + *vivere* live), and can be applied to members of a group who are fond of feasting and good company. In *Troilus and Cressida*, the group that assembles in Agamemnon's tent in Act 4 is defined, despite its apparent national differences, by a mutual regard for superlative soldiership and heroism.[1] Moreover, in the exchanges that precede the convivial invitation, it becomes evident that the national differences between the Trojan and Greek warriors are themselves blurred: Hector declines further battle with Ajax, the 'blended knight' (4.5.87) who is his 'father's sister's son, / A cousin-german to great Priam's seed' (4.5.121–2) precisely on the grounds of their shared heritage; and the aged Nestor greets Hector on similarly genealogical grounds, owning up to having known his grandsire and having 'once fought with him' (4.5.198) – the ambiguity of the phrase obscuring whether this was a battle against, or alongside the ancient warrior.

The notion of conviviality in the scene rapidly moves from a sense of feasting *with* to a sense of feeding *upon*, as Achilles encounters Hector and proclaims: 'Now Hector, I have fed mine eyes on thee . . . And quoted joint by

---

[1] See Laura Levine for a more detailed analysis of how the play produces a martial identity through the generation of rage; Levine, *Men in Women's Clothing: Antitheatricality and Effeminization, 1579–1642* (Cambridge: Cambridge University Press, 1994), pp. 26–43.

joint' (4.5.231–3).[2] This notion of consumption is mutual; in exchange, Hector requests to look upon Achilles, and is met with the rejoinder, 'Behold thy fill' (236). David Bevington has noted that the two warring sides in this play 'come increasingly to resemble one another . . . and speak in metaphors that elide the difference between martial and erotic conflict'.[3] The exchange between Achilles and Hector participates in this process, adapting a romantic discourse of scopic possession to one that is grounded in enmity. Achilles and Hector participate in a kind of visual cannibalism, particularising each other's bodies in an attempt to gain knowledge and mastery (Achilles' declaration that he will 'view [Hector] limb by limb' echoes, for example, his evident desire to hew him limb from limb). There is little distinction between being nourished and being wounded here; the synecdochic trope of dismemberment operating throughout the scene both fragments and reconstitutes the men's notions of themselves as warriors, and demonstrates that both of them require this confrontation with the enemy in order to constitute their own identities. There is a sense that the incorporation of a rival or double's strength into the self is a necessary part of the formation of that self, and it is consequently inter-esting that both Hector and Ajax promise that this process will be continuous (see 4.5.256 and 4.5.263): the warrior-identity is constantly in need of being reaffirmed. Furthermore, like Caesar's tale of Antony's ascetic martial diet in *Antony and Cleopatra*, this metaphorical feasting on strange flesh generates a notion of a community creating its martial identity through the expulsion of an alternative conceived as luxurious, effeminising and dangerous.

It is interesting to note, therefore, that this scene of male rivalry that ends with conviviality in *Troilus and Cressida* is bounded on both sides by the figure of Cressida: she is led on to the stage at 4.5.13 by Diomedes and greets the assembled Greeks with a kissing game in which she is passed from hand to hand distributing her favours; after Hector and the Greeks have left the scene for Agamemnon's tent, Troilus remains on stage to be informed by Ulysses that Diomedes will feast that night with Colchas, Cressida's father, and that he will pass the time bending his amorous looks on Troilus' beloved. What is excluded from the scene of conviviality is the presence of the woman, whose figure forms a troublesome parenthesis around it. If to be convivial is to live together *with*, then this necessarily implies a notion of living *without* (both in the sense of outside or beyond, and of lack). Cressida is kept outside the feasting in Agamemnon's tent, lacking the requisite martial attributes to participate in it. Her exclusion helps to define the community within the tent, but it also acts as a reminder that the original cause of the Greco-Trojan

---

2   The numerous references to feasting and drinking in this play have often been noted. For a short analysis of this theme, see *Troilus and Cressida*, ed. Kenneth Muir (Oxford: Oxford University Press, 1984), pp. 29–34.

3   David Bevington (ed.), *Troilus and Cressida* (Surrey: Nelson, 1998), p. 21. All references to the play are taken from this edition.

discord was a woman, that 'deadly theme', Menelaus' '*quondam* wife', Helen (4.5.180–2).

I want to investigate the ways in which the convivial is represented in a selection of early modern tragedies, considering how it relates to the notion of the feminine. One might imagine that women's close association with nurture and food preparation in the early modern family would make them central to ideas of conviviality and hospitality. However, time and again within these plays the figure of the woman delays or disrupts assemblies of men, acting as an impediment to the social. Woman inhabits a paradox: she is at once essential to the well-being and growth of a community, and yet her presence seems to threaten its integrity; she, like a Helen, a Cleopatra, or a Circe, can divert a man from his proper public role as a soldier and leader, and carry him into chaos. Meeting Cressida, for example, Ulysses, the famous Greek warrior, complains about the excesses of her body, representing it as a contaminating text that causes the undoing of 'every tickling reader': her tongue is glib, there's 'language in her eye' and even her 'foot speaks' (4.5.56–62). This uncontrollable oversignifying of Cressida's body is both bewitching and wanton. It poses a threat to masculine coherence, both personal and social.[4]

The figure of feasting in these plays is, similarly, at once healthful and destructive: taken in moderation it cements bonds; in superfluity, it destroys them. Wine is an especially resonant image in this context for it carries the additional connotations of sacramental redemption and sinful excess that leads to damnation. Joining the two notions of feasting and women is the idea of sensual appetite, calling to mind man's original sin and often deployed in a moralistic context as an aspect of the human condition. Frank Kermode has observed that the defeat of sensual temptation is frequently related in Renaissance literature to the Choice of Hercules, while the rejection of Pleasure takes the form of a refusal to drink of Circe's cup.[5] Indeed, in a version of such moralistic advice imparted by the neoplatonist Pico della Mirandola to his nephew, Gianfrancesco, an explicit analogy is made between the transformatory powers of Virgil's Circe and the dangers of the flesh. The flesh, Gianfrencesco is warned, could make us 'drunk with the wine of voluptuous pleasure, or make the soul leave the noble use of his reason and incline unto sensuality and affections of the body'. Similarly, Circe, he is told, 'used with a drink to turn as many men as received it into divers likeness and figures of sundry beasts'.[6]

---

4   Cf. the exchange between Achilles and Hector discussed above, in which the particularisation and reading of men's bodies helps to create identity. See also Laura Levine's slightly different reading of the scene in *Troilus and Cressida*, which ultimately insists on Cressida's unknowability; Levine, *Men*, p. 43.

5   Frank Kermode, *Shakespeare, Spenser, Donne* (London: Routledge, 1971), pp. 84–115, especially p. 85.

6   Sir Thomas More's translation of Pico della Mirandola's letter, in *The English Works of Sir Thomas More*, ed. W.E. Campbell (London: Eyre & Spottiswoode; New York: Lincoln

The figure of Circe stands behind much of the literature associated with drunken excess. She is, for example, depicted on the frontispiece of Thomas Heywood's anti-drinking tract, *Philocothonista* (1635), together with a verse that describes a crew of 'Calves, Goats, Swine, Asses, at a banquet set', and which informs the drunkard that he is no different from these animals, 'Since, like Cyrcean cups, Wine doth surprise / Thy sense, and thy reason stupifies'. Similarly, Patrick Hannay, in his poem *A Happy Husband*, advised his reader-ship that drunkenness gave rise to '*Contempt, disgrace,* and *shame*', adding that '*Cyrce* made swine / Of wise *Vlisses* fellowes, drunke with wine'.[7] Perhaps the most extended poetic treatment of this theme, however, occurs in Book 3 of Edmund Spenser's *The Faerie Queene* which, drawing on the Paris and Helen exchanges in Ovid's *Heroides*, describes how the lascivious Sir Paridell and Hellenore, the wife of Malbecco, his host, convey their lust for each other at a feast in words written in wine.[8] The discourse of wine, the poet informs us, is 'close' and 'secret'; Hellenore's cup is 'guilty', and the lines she reads on the table are 'a sacrament prophane in mistery of wine'. By presenting his readers with an inverted image of the redemptive power of wine, Spenser illustrates the choice at the heart of this book (and the Circe myth): one must decide to embrace moderation and moral virtue or fall to the sensual lure of the flesh.

Hellenore, Spenser continues, cast off by her lover Paridell, is later adopted by a group of satyrs who treat her as their housewife and handle her 'as commune good' with all the connotations of prostitution that this implies. The paradox that makes a woman both integral to and yet a potentially divisive member of society is apparently erased here by the communal activities of the satyrs who share both her body and her fruits of her domestic labour. None-theless, Hellenore's nightly activities with the half-animal satyrs clearly illus-trate her own descent towards the lustful bestiality they represent. Her husband, too, is reduced to the semblance of a beast in a manner that emphasises his status as a cuckold; unmanned by his wife's transgressions, he crawls on his hands and knees among her herd of goats, his beard and cuck-old's horns completing the effect of his transformation.

Spenser's articulation of the Ovidian myth locates women as central to

MacVeagh, The Dial Press, 1931), pp. 1, 10–11. This letter is also quoted by Meritt Y. Hughes in 'Spenser's Acrasia and the Circe of the Renaissance', *Journal of the History of Ideas*, 4 (1943), 381–99, 388. See Adam Smyth's chapter, below, for the use of the Circe myth in some accounts of drunkenness.

7 Patrick Hannay, *A Happy Husband* (1619), sig. B5r. The association of drunkenness with swinish bestiality is legion in Medieval and Renaissance literature. In *The Canterbury Tales*, for example, see 'The Man of Law's Tale', ll. 743–5, 'The Manciple's Prologue', ll. 40–5, 'The Pardoner's Tale', ll. 551–61; *The Riverside Chaucer*, 3rd edn (Boston, 1987). For the extension of the image to tobacco, see Joshua Sylvester, 'Tobacco Battered', in *Du Bartas his Diuine Weekes and Workes*, trans. Joshua Sylvester (1621), p. 1140.

8 Edmund Spenser, *The Faerie Queene*, ed. Thomas P. Roche (London, 1987), Book 3, canto 9.28ff.

hospitality and good housekeeping, yet demonstrates what happens if these notions are taken to excess. Not only are Sir Paridell and Hellenore danger-ously governed by their lusts, they push the notions of hospitality to an extreme when they force it to include not only the sharing of a host's food and shelter, but also his wife. This extreme notion is eventually illustrated by Hellenore's fate as the mistress of the group of satyrs to whom all goods are common. However, in a book whose subject is chastity and moderation, it is clearly not appropriate to indulge oneself with a beast who is able to 'come aloft' nine times in the night. Spenser demonstrates with admirable ease that sensual excess provokes a descent from heroic virtue to bestiality, and locates his 'second *Hellene*' as a lustful and intoxicating temptress who brings discord to society through her indulgence of the passions of weak, inconstant men.

The notion of bestial transformation has been described by Leonora Leet Brodwin as 'the *locus classicus* for the archetypal Circe'.[9] However, she percep-tively notes that this was not the only temptation offered by the sorceress and identifies three levels of temptation in the Homeric story, which give rise to three different states among Odysseus and his men.[10] The most debased of Circe's temptations is that which turns men's bodies into those of swine, leaving their minds intact. Odysseus' companions are welcomed to her island with a mixture of honey, cheese, and wine, into which is mixed a powerful drug. With a touch of her wand, she turns them into beasts, making them forget their native homes. Odysseus overcomes this temptation with the help of Hermes, who provides him with moly, the antidote to Circe's drug. To redeem his men, Hermes instructs Odysseus to threaten Circe with his sword and predicts that, held to ransom in this way, she will invite him into her bed. He must accede to her desires, but must protect himself by making her swear that such contact with her will not make him weak and unmanned. This, Brodwin observes, is the second of the temptations offered by the goddess: 'the degradation of masculinity through sexual enslavement' from which Odysseus protects himself by 'insisting that sexual experience be part of a sanctified rela-tionship devoted to higher ends'.[11]

Circe's final temptation occurs after Odysseus' men have been restored to their former appearance when she invites them all to rest on her island and recuperate. Odysseus remains on the island for a full year, feasting and carousing, until his men are forced to insist that they leave. Judith Yarnall comments on Homer's choice of vocabulary at this moment that the

> language here, highly unusual for subordinates addressing a leader, gives the measure of their exasperation. *Daimone*, they call him – an untranslatable term

---

9 Brodwin, 'Milton and the Renaissance Circe', *Milton Studies*, 6 (1974), 21–83. For a detailed examination of the sources of the story of Circe that were available to and popular in the sixteenth and seventeenth centuries, see Judith Yarnall, *Transformations of Circe: The History of an Enchantress* (Urbana: University of Illinois Press, 1994), espec. p. 54.

10 Brodwin, 'Milton', p. 23.

11 Ibid., pp. 24–5.

used for a person doing something so abnormal or incomprehensible as to imply a state of possession.[12]

Brodwin notes of this section of the story, that, 'the third temptation is the appeal of carefree happiness [that] only becomes vicious if it becomes habitual and the will grows inattentive to the voice of reproach'.[13] If Yarnall's observation about Homer's use of the word '*Daimonè*' is to be believed, then Odysseus comes very close at this point to succumbing to Circe's temptation.

The three levels of temptation identified by Brodwin in the Circe myth are, therefore, a fall into bestiality, effeminacy and idleness. I would add that all of these aspects of Circe's power are connected to a notion of hospitality: she welcomes Odysseus's men with food and wine; she accommodates Odysseus with her body; she feasts the restored Greeks abundantly for a year. As a female deity, her behaviour is appropriate; she provides nourishment and entertainment in a private space for men wearied from the public execution of their duties as warriors. Her island could be a comedic, pastoral space of retreat and recuperation. Instead, it offers a threat: the threat of luxury and idleness, enervation and effeminisation.[14]

Brodwin's observation that Odysseus controls Circe by insisting that sexual experience be part of a sanctified relationship is extremely apposite in this context, and comes to stand for his assertion of the concepts of mastery and control within the sphere of her household and island. Diane Purkiss has noted how Circe's island occupies a foreign liminal space within the Homeric text: the encounter with Circe, while it appears at first to be homely and familiar, turns out to be utterly unfamiliar; it is an encounter with a strangeness so powerful, in fact, that 'it overmasters the beholder'.[15] The drug offered to Odysseus' men by Circe strips them of their sense of origin; they lose their sense of nationhood and become tamed members of Circe's domestic community.[16] Overcoming Circe, asserting his mastery, Odysseus intervenes in this domestic arrangement, giving their former national identities back to his men. The apparently familiar space of Circe's island that proves to be utterly unfamiliar is relocated within a framework of mastery that seeks to give it back a familiar meaning.

---

[12] Yarnall, *Transformations*, p. 15.

[13] Brodwin, 'Milton', p. 25.

[14] Circe has long been recognised as the progenetrix of the seductive but enervating female characters in Renaissance literature, such as Spenser's Acrasia. For a discussion of this, see Meritt Y. Hughes, 'Spenser's Acrasia and the Circe of the Renaissance', *Journal of the History of Ideas*, 4 (1943), 381–99; see also Gareth Roberts, 'The descendants of Circe: witches and Renaissance fictions', *Witchcraft in Early Modern Europe*, ed. Jonathan Barry, Marianne Hester and Gareth Roberts (Cambridge: Cambridge University Press, 1996), pp. 183–206.

[15] Diane Purkiss, *The Witch in History: Early Modern and Twentieth-Century Representations* (London: Routledge, 1996), pp. 259–60.

[16] Purkiss says of this moment that Circe's drugging draught 'is a precise figure for going native'; ibid., p. 260.

Circe's hospitality to the Greeks is shown to be excessive. The idleness that she encourages in her guests strips them of volition and purpose, and they are swallowed up in a period of dilated time that prevents their forward progression on their journey. As a witchy marginal figure, Circe, like the troubling Cressida, inhabits an outside that disturbs masculine community and self-identity. She puts forward an appearance of welcoming domesticity, weaving, singing, preparing food, which turns out overwhelmingly to absorb the onward itineraries of her guests.[17] The kind of conviviality that she offers, while it most certainly implies a 'living together with', produces a situation in which her guests are forced to live without; beyond the bounds of their homeland, and thus outside their proper identities (where proper also carries the sense of 'property'). As a feminine figure, she encodes both the necessity of and anxieties about women's presence within a community; she is that which nurtures it and helps to define its boundaries, and that which must be rejected and expelled to maintain its health.

Laura Levine has demonstrated admirably how, in *Troilus and Cressida*, the Grecian Ulysses manipulates Cressida's unfaithfulness in order to generate rage in Troilus, thus bringing him out of Troy and into the war. Initially conceived as an overflowing of emotion that breaks down Troilus' sense of self, this rage ultimately helps to reinstate him within a community of warriors practising a martial masculinity. The figure of Cressida, in other words, which has kept Troilus out of the war, is now used as a means of bringing him into it. Similarly, Helen – whose 'white enchanting fingers' are employed to divest the heroic Hector of his armour in a manner that Levine reads as 'the perfect emblem for beauty's dangerous disorganising power' – is ultimately responsible for the creation of the warriors' heroic identities because she is the root cause of the Trojan war.[18] Both of these women enact a contradiction: they both help to construct masculine identity and to undermine it; they are health-giving at the same time as they are dangerously destructive, constituting the medium in which opposites are opposed.

As Levine indicates, the anxiety manifested in much Renaissance writing is not so much about the effeminising effects of women, but the manner in which their presence calls ontological categories into question. Shakespeare's play, to her mind, presents both its audience and, indeed, Troilus with two images of Cressida that cannot be reconciled, and ultimately renders problematic the possibility of 'making an interpretation based on either rational grounds or empirical ones'.[19] The conflict between empiricism and its other is, I think, most readily uncovered in Shakespeare's *Antony and Cleopatra*,

[17] As such, she might be said to prefigure Hegel's notion of womankind as 'the everlasting irony in [the life] of the community', who 'changes by intrigue the universal end of government into a private end'; G.J.F. Hegel, *Phenomenology of Spirit*, trans. A.V. Miller (Oxford: Clarendon Press, 1997), p. 288.

[18] Levine, *Men*, espec. p. 38.

[19] Ibid., pp. 39–43.

playing itself out between Roman and Egyptian modes of perception, between the characters of Octavius and Cleopatra. Just like the bewitching, but oversignifiying body of Cressida, the figure of Cleopatra in this play challenges both understanding and masculine coherence.

The first words uttered by Octavius when he enters on the stage make a claim for empirical evidence as the root of all truth and understanding. He declares:

> You may see, Lepidus, and henceforth know,
> It is not Caesar's natural vice to hate
> Our great competitor. (1.4.1–3)[20]

Not only does Octavius make a claim here that true knowledge of the physical world may be gained through the senses, he extends that claim to encompass the metaphysical; by looking at him, Lepidus will be able to perceive and understand his true nature. Octavius will not admit (at least, he will not allow himself to be *seen* to be admitting) that appearances can be deceptive. Where Cleopatra is a spectacle that, to the Romans, seems to transcend knowing, Octavius wants his followers to believe that he is an open book, that he is to be understood exactly as he appears to be. At the end of the play then, when Octavius confronts Cleopatra in her monument, what appears to occur is the triumph of empiricism over its other.

Arriving at Cleopatra's monument, Octavius' first act is to ask, 'Which is the Queen of Egypt?' (5.2.111). This statement demands specificity; it asks for Cleopatra to be identified so that she may be known. It is also a declaration that Octavius does not intend to engage with Cleopatra's own discourse of exotic display; in refusing to recognise the Queen through the clothes that differentiate her from her maids, he refuses to read her according to the Egyptian manner, and asks for her to be translated.

Next, Cleopatra, offering an inventory of her goods to Octavius, appeals to the authority of Seleucus, her treasurer, to confirm the truth that all her possessions are recorded. She exhorts him explicitly with the words, 'Speak the truth, Seleucus' (143), and Seleucus does speak the truth . . . only it is not an Egyptian truth. He replies in a manner that demonstrates that Cleopatra is duplicitous; she has kept back as much as she has made known to Octavius. On one level, this moment displays Cleopatra's loss of control over representation; Seleucus, her servant, refuses to tell her truth, and betrays her to Octavius. However, she then demonstrates a profound understanding of the position, and turns to the Roman leader with the words:

> See, Caesar! O behold
> How pomp is followed! Mine will now be yours
> And, should we shift estates, yours would be mine. (5.2.149–51)

---

20 All references are taken from *Antony and Cleopatra*, ed. John Wilders (London: Routledge, 1995).

She speaks to Octavius in a language that is his own, adoping his vocabulary of visual, empirical evidence. Nonetheless, her speech undermines the certainty of visual evidence, even as it seems to assert it. At first holding up the spectacle of Egyptian pomp, differentiated from and now fallen to Octavius' might, her words begin to blur the distinction, blending 'mine' into 'yours', 'yours' into 'mine' until Roman and Egyptian 'estates' and 'pomp' disappear into each other, threatening the integrity of 'Roman' and 'Egyptian' as differentiated categories.

Cleopatra, whose theatrical self-representations contribute to the impression that she defies categorisation, provides a radical disturbance to Octavius' empirical mode of knowledge, revealing the Machiavellian theatricality at the heart of his own self-representations. While he claims that his word is his bond, Cleopatra is under no illusions that that word is as slippery as her own, angrily declaring at his departure from her monument that 'he words me, girls, he words me' (5.2.190). What Octavius seeks is to tame Cleopatra's identity by reducing it to the same within the same. She realises that he will drag her to Rome as his hostage, where some squeaking actor will boy her greatness in the posture of a whore.[21] In Rome, she will undergo categorisation, defined against the matronly chastity of women like Octavia. If the fluidity of Egypt is to be seen as feminine, and Roman measure to be seen as a manifestation of masculine control, then categorised and rendered intelligible in Rome through the body of a Roman boy, she will no longer present a threat to Octavius or to Roman perceptions of the world.

Cleopatra is therefore well aware that the hospitality offered to her in Rome by Octavius means that she will be his hostage, held within his world vision and defined as he sees fit. Hospitality seems to hold within itself a notion of mastery, defining both appropriate behaviour (adherence to the rules of the house) as well as the expected roles and identities of host and guest.[22] However, within a system that seems to position femininity as the root of all trouble, what is the place of the woman? Cleopatra cannot be a guest in Rome on her own terms; the hospitality offered by Octavius is conditional. In contrast, that which Antony receives in Rome appears to overflow all measure; he is offered an abundance of food and drink, he is offered Cleopatra's body, and, as a metonymic result of this, it seems that he is also offered Egypt. This complete giving away of personal and national wealth is a fundamental challenge to Rome (an empire that amasses, rather than distributes wealth and property).

---

[21] In Shakespeare's play on the early modern stage, Cleopatra was, of course, already played by a boy. Levine makes a nice move when she identifies the notions of poetry and theatre within antitheatrical discourses as Circean and corrupting; Levine, *Men*, pp. 12ff. See also Jonathan Gil Harris on the subject of the boy actor in *Antony and Cleopatra*: Harris, ' "Narcissus in thy face": Roman desire and the difference it fakes', *Shakespeare Quarterly*, 45.4 (1994), 408–25, 423–5.

[22] See Jacques Derrida, 'Hostipitality', trans. Barry Stocker with Forbes Morlock, *Angelaki*, 5.3 (2000), 3–18, 9. See also Derrida, *Of Hospitality* (Stanford: Stanford University Press, 2000).

Furthermore, just as Hellenore's over-generosity with her favours brought Malbecco's household to ruin, it disturbs the notion of the good housekeeper within Renaissance society whose role is the preservation and increase of the family's wealth.[23]

Cleopatra, although she would appear to be the ultimate hostess, therefore becomes as dangerous as Circe. By not maintaining strict boundaries between host and guest, her form of hospitality takes away a man's desire for his homeland and encourages him to go native. To be a hostess like Cleopatra is, therefore, a kind of treachery that arrogates a man's purpose and that, consequently, weakens the sphere of public action to which he properly belongs. Once again, the notion of the convivial, when contemplated as the 'living together with' a woman, is hugely problematic, calling into question what it is to be hospitable.

From the Romans' perspective in the play, Egypt's exotic hospitality separates Antony from his public duties at home. Cleopatra and her land are represented as fecund, mutable and excessive. They are also somehow poisonous and fatal: the Nile breeds snakes and crocodiles at the same time as it nourishes the countryside; Cleopatra gives rise to a hunger that can never be satisfied. Excess in the play is feminised, becoming conflated with the corrupting influence that Cleopatra and her Egypt have over Antony.

Cleopatra, like Armida and Acrasia, is, in Janet Adelman's words, 'one of the daughters of Circe: charming and enchanting, but not safe company'.[24] Shakespeare's play, Adelman points out, makes a strong connection between the Egyptian queen and witchcraft: to Antony she is 'enchanting' (1.2.135), a 'grave charm' (4.12.25), and a 'witch' (4.12.47);[25] Pompey, too, fantasises about her powers of bewitchment when he invokes her to keep Antony seduced in Egypt:

> But all the charms of love,
> Salt Cleopatra, soften thy waned lip!
> Let witchcraft join with beauty, lust with both;
> Tie up the libertine in a field of feasts;
> Keep his brain fuming. Epicurean cooks
> Sharpen with cloyless sauce his appetite
> That sleep and feeding may prorogue his honour
> Even till a Lethe'd dullness –   (2.1.20–7)

The nexus of imagery employed here not only invokes the idea of sensual

---

23 On the economic threat posed by the 'leaky woman', see Gail Kern Paster, 'Leaky Vessels: the incontinent women of city comedy', *Renaissance Drama*, n.s. 18 (1987), 43–65, 59.

24 Janet Adelman, *The Common Liar: Essays on Antony and Cleopatra* (New Haven & London: Yale University Press, 1973), p. 65. Adelman usefully reminds us that Shakespeare's *Antony and Cleopatra* is a play of multiple perspectives that cannot be reduced to any one of them. However, the play does contain a forceful strand of Circean imagery.

25 See ibid., p. 28.

appetite, but participates in a wider play of imagery that associates Cleopatra with food: she is both the active agent that is to encourage Antony's feasting, and the passive object that he will consume; in other words, she is at once a daughter of Circe, *and* her cup of tainted wine. Cleopatra is imagined by Pompey to be lustful, she intoxicates, and, by way of his metaphor of a 'field of feasts', it is quite possible that she transforms men into beasts. However, most importantly, she threatens masculine honour and engenders a forgetfulness of home and duty. While it must be noted that Pompey's fantasy of Antony's degradation is immediately punctured in the play by news of the latter's arrival in Rome, other voices, including Antony's own, corroborate the fact that the Roman general is unmanned by his association with Cleopatra.[26] The Egyptian queen and her land (because metonymically she *is* 'Egypt') are associated with excesses so extreme that they lead both to moral and physical dissolution.

It is interesting, however, to note that the only scene in the play in which we actually witness excessive drinking occurs among Romans upon Pompey's ship. Like the convivial meeting of the Greeks and Trojans in Agamemnon's tent, this meeting takes place in an interlude between conflicts, providing us with an image of male fellowship among warriors who have been and will again become adversaries. In addition, Pompey's feast is constantly remarked upon by its participants as an imitation of Egyptian revelry, and we are made aware that the Romans are fascinated by their own fantastical notions of foreign exoticism. It is also notable that, unlike the Egyptian revels, there are no female participants at this feast. Women are excluded from such Roman social gatherings in a manner that both defines an arena of male sociability and that reinforces the equation made between corrupt Egyptian excess and femininity. Although the wine on Pompey's ship demonstrably erodes the Romans' reason, causing the men to stumble about and to slur their speech, any threat to them from these actions is averted. Despite the fact that during the feast Menas proposes treachery to Pompey, Pompey's sense of honour forestalls the plan and the drunken revels pass off safely, raising the question of whether it is not so much an excess of conviviality that produces danger in this play, but the combination of the convivial and the feminine. In this scenario, a feminised Egypt becomes that which Roman society must exclude in order to define its boundaries as a strongly martial nation; Egyptian extravagance is an expression of those aspects of Rome itself that it needs to disown and repress.

It was a woman who brought death into the world, fracturing wholeness and divorcing man from his privileged connection with God's creation, manifested in his ability to deploy a language stripped of metaphor and within which the name of a thing partook of the essence of the thing. Despite her role as the mother of humanity, Eve is figured as the bringer of death and corruption, a contaminating figure who threatens man's integrity, his language, and the coherence of his community. Therefore like wine, the symbol both of

---

[26] See, for example, 1.4.3–7; 2.5.18–23; 3.7.69–70; 3.10.19–24; 3.11.65–8.

sacramental redemption and dissolution, woman combines both a life-giving force integral to the health of the community as well being a corrupting and death-bearing presence that threatens its disintegration.

Elisabeth Bronfen has provided magnificent evidence to support her claim that 'the fear of death translates into a fear of Woman who, for a man, is death'. Desirable because distant, woman is, says Bronfen, 'absent or not quite there, a dream, a phantom, a mediatrix, a muse'. She, along with death, is considered to be unrepresentable, and yet is 'ubiquitously present "allegorically" in western representations as precisely such a limit and excess'.[27] In my last example of the association of wine and women in Renaissance drama, I want to turn to John Marston's *The Wonder of Women, or The Tragedie of Sophonisba* (1606) in order to investigate Bronfen's notion of the 'allegorical' connection between women and death.

Believing that Massinissa, her husband, has been killed in battle by Syphax, his rival, and begging for an hour in which to perform some mourning rites before surrendering herself to the conqueror, Sophonisba is left alone in her captor's bedchamber. Vangue, a slave, remains to guard her, and she is also accompanied by Zanthia, her maid, who has been bribed into Syphax's service. Completing her invocation to the gods, Sophonisba hands the unsuspecting Vangue a cup of wine, and proposes a toast to Syphax. Vangue drinks deeply, and draws Sophonisba's attention to the open mouth of a vault in, one imagines, the floor of Syphax's chamber. 'Close the vault's mouth', he urges, 'lest we do slip in drink' (3.1.148), and proceeds to describe the nature of this opening:

> This vault with hideous darkness and much length
> Stretcheth beneath the earth into a grove
> One league from Cirta – I am very sleepy –
> Through this, when Cirta hath been strong begirt
> With hostile siege the king hath safely 'scaped
> To, to –   (3.1.151–7)

With this he falls asleep, and Sophonisba admits that she had applied a potion of 'sleepy opium' to his drink (3.1.162). Vangue is laid in Syphax's bed as a substitute bride, and Sophonisba subsequently descends into the vault in an attempt to escape, leaving the scene with the words: 'Hark, gods, my breath / Scorns to crave life, grant but a well-famed death' (3.1.171–2).

This scene gives rise to a network of images that inaugurate a relationship between women, sexuality and dissolution. The situation has arisen in the first place because of Sophonisba's rejection of Syphax's suit, and his feelings of humiliation that she has chosen Massinissa over him. His passion for Sophonisba fills him with notions of revenge and he proclaims to Vangue:

---

[27] Elisabeth Bronfen, *Over Her Dead Body: Death, Femininity and the Aesthetic* (Manchester: Manchester University Press, 1992; repr. 1996), p. 205.

> I am disgraced in and by that which hath
> No reason – love, and woman. My revenge
> Shall therefore bear no argument of right:
> Passion is reason when it speaks from might.   (1.2.73–6)

Women and love do not possess reason; Syphax, contaminated by these things, is driven from rational argument to an emotive response that will lead to tyrannous excess and dissolution. His decision to renounce reasonable behaviour in favour of his passions has inevitable political consequences and draws attention to his deficiencies as a ruler. The play's opening scene locates it within a political milieu, demonstrating that love and alliance are to be conceived as public and political acts. Thwarted in his suit to Sophonisba, Syphax hopes to revenge himself on her father's city, calling down ruin on Carthage and hoping for its subjugation by Scipio's Roman forces. It is important here, I think, to note that his passion is conceived within a framework of male relations within which the presence of the woman sparks a rivalry that undermines both those relations and, concomitantly, the stability of the state.[28] In a way similar to that in which Levine reads the overflowing of Troilus' rage, this passion creates Syphax's martial identity, and shows it to be inhabited by its own destruction.

Sophonisba, as the play's self-avowedly chaste and steadfast virgin wife, might be said to encode the values that underpin the proper functioning of her society. For example, beset by Syphax and praying for deliverance to the gods Phoebe and Mercury (whom she characterises respectively as 'worthy chastity' and 'chaste wit'), she promises that all she craves from them 'Is but chaste life or an untainted grave' (3.1.130). Central to the play and acting as a benchmark of social virtue, she would appear to be the polar opposite of the witch, Erictho, to whom Syphax finally resorts to find a means to satisfy his passion. Peter Corbin and Douglas Sedge note that Erictho is marked as 'a figure of unconstrained appetite over against Sophonisba who can forgo the pleasures of the bridal-bed and maintain her virtue in the face of physical and moral pressures'.[29] Syphax, though, they observe, 'is linked with Erictho in her necrophilic practices by his threat to satisfy his lust on Sophonisba's corpse should she commit suicide'.[30] Similarly, Diane Purkiss, although she identifies Sophonisba as 'an unruly female who refuses to submit to [Syphax's] desire', notes that Sophonisba's 'chaste body emblematises the impenetrably virtuous

---

[28] It is therefore interesting to note, along with Gareth Roberts, and in the context of Syphax's desire for Sophonisba that 'the primary meaning of "seduce" is political rather than sexual: "to persuade (a vassal, servant, soldier etc.) to desert his allegiance or service" '; seduction, either of, or by a woman, is potentially a political act; Roberts, 'Descendants', p. 203.

[29] Peter Corbin and Douglas Sedge (eds), *Three Jacobean Witchcraft Plays* (Manchester: Manchester University Press, 1986), p. 13. All references to *Sophonisba* are taken from this edition.

[30] Ibid., p. 13.

state; the witch's theatricality confirms her power as the opposite of such clear bounds'.[31] In contrast, I think Sophonisba and Erictho are two sides of the same coin and participate in a discourse of disorder that returns to trouble the system from which it is expelled.

Syphax invokes Erictho after he has recovered Sophonisba and had her returned to his palace. In a manner that recalls the enervating effects that both Circe and Cleopatra have on their lovers, he complains that 'A wasting flame feeds on [his] amorous blood / Which [he] must cool or die' (4.1.90–1), and summons Erictho 'whose dismal brow / Contemns all roofs or civil coverture' (4.1.98–9). Existing beyond the bounds of civil society, Erictho is an outsider who is also a usurper, for she 'joys to inhabit' tombs from which she has forced out the ghosts (4.1.101). A tomb is a monument that localises the dead, providing a fixed place and time for mourning, and a means of historicising the past; one achieves knowledge of oneself by telling the story of one's ancestors, memorialising them in stone. Erictho fundamentally disrupts this process, displacing the ghosts from their proper locations, plundering and penetrating the male corpses with her fingers and tongue, and enforcing inanimate male bodies to bear her 'baneful secrets' (4.1.122). She lives near the ruins of a temple once sacred to Jove, now polluted with excrement and lewd graffitti, within a barren and dark cave whose mouth is choked with yew. Not only does she therefore appear to occupy a place on the outskirts of civil society, she also occupies a place between the living and the dead, at once delimiting a boundary and threatening it with collapse.[32] Significantly, her abode appears to be positioned near the exit of the tunnel that leads from Syphax's bedchamber, linking the two locations closely in the audience's imagination. This connection is reinforced by the fact that, not only does Syphax arrive behind Sophonisba in the wood having followed her from his chamber, he is 'heaved' back to his chamber from the wood after meeting Erictho, and subsequently lies with her (while she is disguised as Sophonisba) in his own bed.

This parallelism does reinforce Corbin and Sedge's notion that an equation should be drawn between the voracious Erictho and the equally excessive Syphax. However, the open maw of the vault into which Sophonisba descends after drugging the unsuspecting Vangue may be seen as symbolically connected to Erictho's cave, as well as to the plundered graves whose emptiness is emblematic of the disruptions to right order and the integrity of the state. This connection not only makes a link between Syphax's tyranny and Erictho's lust, it connects Sophonisba to Erictho through the notions of death, drugs and witchcraft.

---

[31] Purkiss, *Witch*, p. 261.

[32] I am resisting the temptation to pursue this image as a motif for the swallowing female womb, although Erictho's subsequent behaviour (in that she copulates with Syphax to ease her 'thirsty womb') would support the idea of the threat of the maternal irrupting within the play's symbolic order.

Sophonisba, the desire for whom has reduced Syphax to bestial lust (see 3.1.16–20), gives Vangue a potion of wine that produces a sleep so closely resembling death that Zanthia believes Sophonisba has poisoned him. Vangue had previously expressed an anxiety about the open maw of the vault, exhorting Sophonisba to close it, 'lest we do slip in drink' (3.1.148). The literal meaning of this phrase implies that Vangue is worried that he will fall into the hole while drunk. It might also be taken as an indication of his awareness that wine causes such a degeneration of the faculties that other, less literal, slips might occur (for example, he might slip in his duties to his master and permit Sophonisba to escape – 'we' at this point becoming a substitute for 'I').[33] Furthermore, there is an underlying connotation of sinfulness; the slip that began all slips and that opened the doors of death into the world. This combination of drunken sleep and the threatening mouth of the vault provide a symbol for the sleep of death and the open grave awaiting Vangue when his indiscretion is discovered and Syphax dispatches him to his final 'lasting sleep' (3.1.196).[34] Although Sophonisba admits to Zanthia that the hand that she used to adulterate the wine was 'fearful', with the implication that she did not have the courage to poison Vangue outright, there is again here an equation to be made between strong wine's potency and a woman such as Sophonisba who has the capacity, even against her own will, to undermine a man's reason. Suspended above this hideous, dark vault, open like the graves that Erictho has plundered, Sophonisba becomes the bearer of dissolution and, as such, she is quintessentially female.

Sophonisba, the chaste wife whose body, Purkiss suggests, 'emblematises the impenetrably virtuous state', nonetheless catalyses the disintegration of that state, unwittingly fuelling Syphax's lust, and then acting as an impediment to the bond of honour that binds Massinissa to his companion Scipio.[35] She disrupts the community of male–male relations, working, in counterpoint to Erictho, from within. The doubling that occurs when Erictho penetrates Syphax's bed disguised as Sophonisba serves more to emphasise the destructive potential carried by them both than to differentiate the lustful witch from the virginal wife.

Bronfen has argued that 'the feminine is associated with the polluting world of biology, with the time-bound individual, with corrupting flesh . . . with "bad" death'. An assault on the feminine body, she says, therefore 'serves to transcend these negative values, serves as triumph over the "bad" death as pollution and division'.[36] In Marston's play, as in *Antony and Cleopatra*, the

---

[33] A not unusual occurrence in this play; for example, compare Syphax at 4.1.96.

[34] There is also an equation to be made with the king's couch upon which Vangue sleeps and on which he is killed, and the same couch whereon Syphax consorts with the disguised Erictho, perhaps condemning his soul to damnation.

[35] Purkiss, *Witch*, p. 261.

[36] Bronfen, *Over Her Dead Body*, p. 199.

heroine's death is a cue for the reestablishment of homosocial bonds within a system based on masculine martial honour. Forbearing, like Cleopatra, to be enslaved as a symbol of the Roman victory, Sophonisba drinks poison prepared for her by Massinissa in a cup of wine and dies, she declares, 'happy in [her] husband's arms' (5.3.106). Coppélia Kahn has noted of Shakespeare's play that Cleopatra's death is conceived in terms of marriage.[37] Similarly here, Sophonisba's delayed marital night is translated into her ecstasy in death. The notion of drinking is, moreover, converted from a symbol of moral and physical dissolution to an expression of masculine self-identity. In the concluding speech of the play, Massinissa displays his victor's wreath upon Sophonisba's body, transforming it from a spoil of war to a funerary decoration and appropriating his wife's sacrifice into the economy of martial masculine relations. He also declares that he drinks 'deep of grief' and, in true Petrarchan fashion, makes Sophonisba's death the means through which he gains both voice and presence; although he comments upon the inexpressibility of his emotions, he bases his representation of himself upon the now-monumentalised and unquestionable virtue of his dead wife, 'Women's right wonder, and just shame of men' (5.1.59).

This monumentalising moment, just like the instant when Cleopatra turns herself into her own monument, becoming 'marble constant' as she fixes herself in death, renders Sophonisba's body comprehensible and therefore no longer contentious. However, in this moment her purified and beautiful corpse becomes the representative of something else. Bronfen has remarked of the nature of death that,

> because it is beyond any speaking subject's experiential realm, is always culturally contructed, always metaphorical; a signifier of lack which itself lacks a fixed signified in the symbolic register; a signifier of certainty against which all other cultural values are measured and confirmed, but which is itself unmeasurable, certain only in its negativity.[38]

The confrontation with death is the confrontation with the completely unknowable, with absolute otherness. In *Sophonisba*, as in *Antony and Cleopatra*, the play concludes with an image of death that is metaphorised and mastered as a pure female body. The social order, as Bronfen goes on to note, is reconstructed 'over the double rejection of the feminine body that occurs when it is firstly designated as liminal, polluted or excessively pure and secondly when it is symbolically reburied/reborn in the form of a masculine sign'.[39]

Woman is central to the good functioning of society through her roles as

---

[37] Coppélia Kahn, *Roman Shakespeare: Warriors, Wounds, and Women* (London: Routledge, 1997), p. 139.

[38] Bronfen, *Over Her Dead Body*, p. 72.

[39] Ibid., p. 200.

mother and housekeeper, and yet she a constant reminder of death and mutability. Like wine, she intoxicates and confounds the senses, leading one to a radical doubt that calls into question the reliability of empirical knowledge. Her dead body, however, serves as a place upon which the social order can be reestablished, restoring the purity of male–male relations by the effective banishment of sensual excess. Circe's cup holds both nourishment and poison, she is a health-giver and yet is also closely associated with death.[40] Most of all, she is that upon which conviviality is dependent, and yet she is that which it invariably pretends it functions without.

---

[40] In the Homeric story, Odysseus and his men are instructed by Circe to travel to the gates of the underworld in order to consult with the shade of the seer Tiresias.

8

Drink, Sex and Power in Restoration Comedy

SUSAN J. OWEN

THE theatre after 1660 was affected by significant social contradictions. Everyone has heard of the so-called merry monarch, Charles II, and of his mistresses of whom Nell Gwyn is the best known. Under Charles II there was a burgeoning of libertinism. If John Wilmot, Earl of Rochester was the best-known exponent, the chief practitioners were the Stuarts, Charles II and his brother and heir, James. The period after 1660 also saw the development of the sexual marketplace, ranging from prostitutes who catered for all tastes, to homosexual 'molly' houses, to a generalised fetishisation of sexual characteristics. There was also widespread moral disapproval of these developments. The king's promiscuity was often seen as a sign of political irresponsibility, as the arch-libertine Rochester himself noted: 'His sceptre and his prick are of a length, / And she may sway the one who plays with t'other / And make him little wiser than his brother.' When Rochester coined the designation 'merry Monarch' he was being sarcastic: Charles is 'A merry Monarch, scandalous and poor.'[1] In Andrew Marvell's poem *Last Instructions to a Painter* the Kingdom appears to the recumbent Charles in allegorical female form, and the king's response is to try to 'screw' it, literally and figuratively.

It is not surprising, therefore, that we encounter a contradictory attitude to libertinism in Restoration drama. Critics have debated extensively the question of how 'sexy' sex comedy is: how far does it promote or endorse the rakes' libertine values and how far does it anatomise them or hold them up to critical scrutiny or satire?[2] This issue is complicated by several factors. In the first

---

[1] *Rochester: Complete Poems and Plays*, ed. Paddy Lyons (London: J.M. Dent, 1993), p. 80, 'Verses For Which He Was Banished', line 21.

[2] An insight into issues in this debate may be gained from *Studies in the Literary Imagination*, 10 (1977), which contains several relevant articles. See especially Maximillian E. Novak, 'Margery Pinchwife's "London Disease": Restoration Comedy and the Libertine Offensive of the 1670s', pp. 1–23; and Robert D. Hume, 'The Myth of the Rake in Restoration Comedy', pp. 25–55. See also Dale Underwood, *Etherege and the Seventeenth-Century Comedy of Manners* (New Haven:

place, libertinism itself is not simply a philosophy of 'anything goes', sexually speaking, but propounds freedoms for the aristocratic rake that are not extended to women or to men outside the charmed circle. So a play might endorse libertinism in elite males but deride it in base imitators or women. Secondly, comedies may appear to endorse libertinism whilst actually depicting it with a satirical edge; or, more commonly perhaps, comedies may appear to condemn while actually titillating in the same way that violence against women may be ostensibly condemned but actually relished or fostered in Hollywood movies today. The matter is further complicated by the fact that what we know about the plays' reception tells us that a reaction of titillation and relish co-existed with moral disapproval, primarily from (some) women and from committed Christians.

The libertines dominate the action, but women play strong roles in the plays. How do the comedies explore power relations between the sexes? How far do particular plays promote male dominance and male bonds, and contain female transgression? How far do they open up a space for women's desire and female agency? For example, some critics argue that the humour of *The Country Wife* and *The Rover* is essentially at women's expense and that male control is firmly in place at the end.[3] Others see more sexual freedom for women.[4] There is broad agreement that marriage is a central theme, but how sceptically is the

Yale University Press, 1957); John Traugott, 'The Rake's Progress from Court to Comedy: a Study in Comic Form', *Studies in English Literature*, 6 (1966), 381–407; Harold Weber, *The Restoration Rake-Hero* (Madison: University of Wisconsin Press, 1986); and Warren Chernaik, *Sexual Freedom in Restoration Literature* (Cambridge: Cambridge University Press, 1995).

3   See, for example, Eve Kosofsky Sedgwick, *Between Men: English Literature and Male Homosocial Desire* (New York: Columbia University Press, 1985), chapter 3; and Pat Gill, *Interpreting Ladies: Women, Wit and Morality in the Restoration Comedy of Manners* (Athens & London: University of Georgia Press, 1994), who calls *The Country Wife* 'a nasty, gleeful misogynistic exploration of abasement' (p. 73). The strongest argument for the heroine of *The Rover* being entirely recuperated into the patriarchal economy she rebels against is made by Elin Diamond, '*Gestus* and Signature in Aphra Behn's *The Rover*', *Eighteenth-Century Literary History*, 56 (1989), reprinted in *Aphra Behn: New Casebook*, ed. Janet Todd (London: Macmillan, 1999), pp. 32–56.

4   On *The Country* Wife see, for example, Helen Burke, 'Wycherley's "Tendentious Joke": the Discourse of Alterity in *The Country Wife*', *The Eighteenth-Century: Theory and Interpretation*, 29 (1988), 227–41; Jon Lance Bacon, 'Wives, Widows, and Writings in Restoration Comedy', *Studies in English Literature*, 31 (1991), 427–43; and Douglas M. Young, *The Feminist Voices in Restoration Comedy: the Virtuous Women in the Play-Worlds of Etherege, Wycherley and Congreve* (Lanham, MD: University Press of America, 1997). James Ogden in the introduction to his edition of *The Country Wife* (London: A & C Black, New Mermaids, 1991) sees the play as critical of those who see women as objects (p. xxiii). On *The Rover* see, for example, Frederick M. Link's introduction to his edition of *The Rover* (Lincoln & London: University of Nebraska Press, 1967); Jones De Ritter, 'The Gypsy, *The Rover*, and the Wanderer: Aphra Behn's Revision of Thomas Killigrew', *Restoration*, 10 (1986), 82–92; Danielle Bobker, 'Behn: *Auth*-Whore or Writer? Authorship and Identity in *The Rover*', *Restoration and Eighteenth-Century Theatre Research*, 11 (1996), 32–9; Julie Nash, ' "The sight on't would beget a warm desire": Visual Pleasure in Aphra Behn's *The Rover*', *Restoration*, 18 (1994), 77–87.

institution treated? Different plays take different perspectives on abuses and inequalities within marriage, on women's economic and legal position, on incompatibility between love and social restrictions, and between freedom of choice and arranged marriage.[5] Moreover, we are now aware that 'sexual politics' goes beyond the treatment of women to include issues of masculinity and male sexuality.[6]

It is my contention that these issues may be illuminated by an exploration of the dramatists' treatment of drink. Drink is not a peripheral matter in Restoration comedies. On the contrary, it relates to themes, particularly of sex and power, which were central in Restoration society.[7] This essay focuses on sex comedy, which is not to say that that was the only type of Restoration comedy. However, it was a form of comedy that attracted disproportionate attention, both at the time and later. I want to argue that in Aphra Behn's *The Rover* the treatment of drink reveals Behn's ambiguity about libertinism. Then I want to show how in William Wycherley's *The Country Wife* drink becomes central in an altered balance of power between the sexes.

The central characters in Restoration sex comedies are libertines (also called rakes), such as Willmore in *The Rover* and Horner in *The Country Wife*. The libertines are ambiguous figures in two ways: predatory but also desirable; powerful, but always in danger of becoming the disempowered objects of desire. In Behn's play Willmore is the 'rover' of the title in two senses, as a wandering exiled Cavalier and sexually. He bears a resemblance to the libertine Earl of Rochester, to Behn's own lover John Hoyle, to Charles II and to Charles's brother James.[8] Yet Behn's avowed royalism does not prevent her

5   See G.S. Alleman, *Matrimonial Law and the Materials of Restoration Comedy* (Philadelphia: University of Pennsylvania Press, 1942); P.F. Vernon, 'Marriage of Convenience and the Moral Code of Restoration Comedy', *Essays in Criticism*, 12 (1962), 370–87; Robert D. Hume, 'Marital Discord in English Comedy From Dryden to Fielding', reprinted in *The Rakish Stage: Studies in English Drama, 1660–1800* (Carbondale: Southern Illinois University Press, 1983); Burke, 'Wycherley's "Tendentious Joke" '; Christopher Wheatley, 'Romantic Love and Social Necessities: Reconsidering Justifications for Marriage in Restoration Comedy', *Restoration*, 14 (1990), 58–70; Michael Cordner, introduction to *Four Restoration Marriage Plays* (Oxford: Oxford University Press), 1995.

6   See Weber, *Restoration Rake-Hero*, pp. 53–69, and 'Horner and his "Women of Honour": The Dinner Party in *The Country Wife*', *Modern Language Quarterly*, 43 (1982), 107–20; David M. Vieth, 'Wycherley's *The Country Wife*: An Anatomy of Masculinity', *Papers on Language and Literature*, 2 (1966), 335–50; William Freedman, 'Impotence and Self-Destruction in *The Country Wife*', *English Studies*, 53 (1972), 421–31; and Derek Cohen, '*The Country Wife* and Social Danger', *Restoration and Eighteenth-Century Theatre Research*, 10 (1995), 1–14.

7   For a fuller discussion of these contradictions see my *Restoration Theatre and Crisis* (Oxford: Clarendon Press, 1996), chapter 1 and *Perspectives on Restoration Drama* (Manchester: Manchester University Press, 2002), pp. 1–6.

8   See Angeline Goreau, *Reconstructing Aphra: a Social Biography of Aphra Behn* (Oxford: Oxford University Press, 1980), pp. 213, 226; and John Franceschina, 'Shadow and Substance in Aphra Behn's *The Rover*: The Semiotics of Restoration Performance', *Restoration*, 19 (1995), 29–42, 30. The likeness to James is made more explicit in the Dedication to the sequel, *The Second Part of the Rover* (1681).

from adopting a somewhat critical attitude to her Cavalier hero.[9] Willmore is an ambiguous figure, sexy and witty, but always in danger of becoming the mocked rather than the mocker. 'Love and Mirth! are my bus'ness in Naples' says Willmore, and he pursues both almost obsessively (I.ii.71).[10] 'Love' for Willmore means sex, to which he is addicted: 'there's but one way for a Woman to oblige me' (I.ii.243–4). Willmore enjoys the game of sexual conquest almost as much as the act itself and is averse to commitment: 'I am parlously afraid of being in Love' (V.i.393–4). Yet he is as eager in the pursuit of drink as of sex. It is no accident that 'Love and Mirth' are coupled in his statement of purpose. The signifier of mirth is the bottle.

Drink is also a marker of royalism in the play. The sexy Willmore is devoted to wine and women. For the royalist Behn drink is a signifier of Cavalier hedonism and liberating sexiness that can offer a social space for female as well as male desire. Her play is set in Naples at carnival time, and Willmore's drunkenness is part of the atmosphere of liberating festivity and freedom from social constraint. Willmore's bottle is specifically a wine bottle. The drinking of wine is a marker of good taste; an upper-class good taste that can encompass bawdy badinage and sexual antics, but not vulgarity or beer drinking.[11]

However, Willmore is not simply sexy and desirable. He is both predator and victim, damaging women but also tyrannised over by his own sex-addiction. Moreover, he shares some characteristics with Blunt, the play's comic butt, and with the fool Edwardo in Behn's source play, Killigrew's *Thomaso*. In particular, when drunk, Willmore can be a buffoon. Men's sexuality in the play is presented as dangerous, desirable and ridiculous all at the same time. Through her treatment of drink, Behn brings out the ambivalence of libertinism for women. In particular, she shows how drink brings out the dark side of male sexuality. Drunk, the rake becomes predator. In Act III,

---

9   On Behn's politics of *The Rover*, see Franceschina, 'Shadow and Substance'; Robert Markley, ' "Be impudent, be saucy, forward, bold, touzing, and leud": The Politics of Masculine Sexuality and Feminine Desire in Behn's Tory Comedies', in *Cultural Readings of Restoration and Eighteenth-Century Theater,* ed. Canfield and Payne, pp. 114–40; Arlen Feldwick, 'Wits, Whigs, and Women: Domestic Politics as Anti-Whig Rhetoric in Aphra Behn's Town Comedies' in Carole Levin and Patricia Sullivan (eds), *Political Rhetoric, Power, and Renaissance Women* (Albany: State University of New York Press, 1995); Meilinda Zook, 'Contextualizing Aphra Behn: Plays, Politics, and Party' in Hilda Smith (ed.), *Women Writers and the Early Modern British Political Tradition* (Cambridge: Cambridge University Press, 1998); and my own ' "Suspect my loyalty when I lose my virtue": Sexual Politics and Party in Aphra Behn's Plays of the Exclusion Crisis, 1678–83', *Restoration,* 18 (1994), 37–47; reprinted in *Aphra Behn: New Casebook,* ed. Todd (see n. 2), pp. 57–72.

10   All quotations from *The Works of Aphra Behn,* ed. Janet Todd (London: Pickering 1996), 7 vols, vol. 5: *The Plays 1671–1677.*

11   See my 'The Politics of Drink in Restoration Drama' in *A Babel of Bottles: Drink, Drinkers and Drinking Places in Literature,* ed. James Nicholls and Susan J. Owen (Sheffield: Sheffield Academic Press, 2000), pp. 41–51. Note also chapters in the present volume by Cedric C. Brown and Stella Achilleos.

Scene v, the drunken Willmore finds Florinda '*in an undress*' in the garden at night, waiting for Belvile. He tries to rape her, conducting his attempt as a grotesque mock-courtship in which he deploys various outrageous libertine arguments before resorting to force. For example, when Florinda calls him a 'Filthy Beast' (139) he says that they ought to lie together like animals in a state of nature because 'there will be no sin in't' (141). There is also the familiar libertine claim that her eyes 'gave the first blow' (150). Florinda is only saved by a fortuitous interruption. Anita Pacheco has argued that Behn exposes the play-world's rape-culture.[12] There is certainly some scope in the play for such a critique. Willmore's best friend Belvile is disgusted, and not only because the victim is his own girlfriend: 'if it had not been Florinda, must you be a Beast? – a Brute? a Senseless Swine' (III.vi.198–9).

Behn, then, is ambivalent. On the one hand, she uses drink as a marker of Cavalier sexiness and playfulness, as well as upper-class values. On the other, she uses it to expose the outrageousness of libertinism. However, there is a further level of ambiguity. This concerns Behn's own attitude to the darker side of rakishness. For there is no doubt that the drunkenness makes the rape scene comic. It may even seem to palliate the libertine's offence. Willmore's drunken fumblings are clearly meant to be funny. We may compare the disturbingly comic attempted rape scene in Costner's film *Robin Hood: Prince of Thieves*. True, some of the comedy is at Willmore's expense;[13] but there is also laughter at the floundering Florinda. While a reader might remain impervious to this, it would be hard for a spectator in the theatre (even a female one) to resist at least a temporary comic collusion with male values. Moreover, Act III, Scene v, follows a scene in which Blunt is humiliated by a prostitute, ending up stripped and thrown into a sewer. Behn offers little sympathy for this character, a parliamentarian, and encourages laughter at his discomfiture. So the audience is already in the mood to laugh at a victim's distress. If we laugh at Blunt's discomfiture, why not at Florinda's?

Blunt goes on the try to avenge himself on women for his humiliation by threatening to rape Florinda. This turns into a scene of threatened gang-rape as virtually all the men try to join in and Florinda is only saved by her (female)

---

[12] 'Rape and the Female Subject in Aphra Behn's *The Rover*', *ELH*, 65 (1998), 323–45; see also Ann Marie Stewart, 'Rape, Patriarchy, and the Libertine Ethos: The Function of Sexual Violence in Aphra Behn's "The Golden Age" and *The Rover, Part I*', *Restoration and Eighteenth-Century Theatre Research*, 12 (1997), 26–39; Dagny Boebel, 'In the Carnival World of Adam's Garden: Roving and Rape in Behn's *Rover*' in Katherine M. Quinsey (ed.), *Broken Boundaries: Women and Feminism in Restoration Drama* (Lexington: University Press of Kentucky, 1996), pp. 55–70; Jean I. Marsden, 'Rape, Voyeurism and the Restoration Stage' in *Broken Boundaries*, ed. Quinsey, pp. 185–200; Anthony Kaufman, ' "The Perils of Florinda": Aphra Behn, Rape and the Subversion of Libertinism in *The Rover, Part I*', *Restoration and Eighteenth-Century Theatre Research*, 11 (1996), 1–21.

[13] John Franceschina argues that after this scene Willmore changes from a Hobbesean rake to a 'fop'. The actor who played the part, William Smith, was also famous for Sir Fopling Flutter in Etherege's *The Man of Mode*. See 'Shadow and Substance in Aphra Behn's *The Rover*', p. 35.

cousin Valeria. Again, there are disturbing comic aspects, for example when the men decide to compare sword lengths to see which rapist should go first, forgetting that the Spaniard has the longest sword. No real outrage is expressed, nor is there any critique of male misbehaviour. The female point of view is not made prominent. Florinda voices her distress, but as soon as she is safe easily forgives everyone concerned. No moral is drawn, and the implication seems to be that if the woman concerned had not been Florinda, the gang-rape could have gone ahead. Even with skilful directing it would be hard to make an audience ashamed of their laughter and force them to question their collusion in oppressive values.[14] There are some (limited) gains for women at the end of this play, but Behn seems less concerned with anatomising a rape-culture than with depicting a drinking culture. In keeping with this, the play's ending celebrates conviviality and good nature.[15]

A similar ambivalence towards libertinism is apparent in *The Country Wife*, but in this play the treatment of drink is more complex. First I shall say what the issues of sex and power are in *The Country Wife*, then show how the treatment of drink in the play sheds light upon them. The first issue concerns the libertine hero and what type of man he is. Horner's name has a threefold significance, suggesting a cuckold-maker (the traditional symbol of the cuckold being horns), a wild beast with animalistic sexuality, and the horned devil. The play opens with a sensational ploy: Horner has employed Dr Quack to spread the rumour that a failed treatment for venereal disease has made him an eunuch. Quack wonders why Horner is not ashamed: 'I have been hired by young gallants to belie 'em t'other way, but you are the first would be thought a man unfit for women' (I.i.34–6).[16] This sets up a standard of normal male

---

[14] Susan Carlson's review of JoAnne Akalaitis's 1994 production (based on John Barton's 1986 RSC adaptation) says the audience (as well as the male characters) was implicated in the near gang-rape and not absolved from blame: 'Cannibalizing and Carnivalizing: Reviving Aphra Behn's *The Rover*', *Theatre Journal*, 47 (1995), 517–39.

[15] Critics who see the play as (with varying degrees of qualification) a celebration of the libertine masculinity that Willmore typifies include Maureen Duffy, *The Passionate Shepherdess: Aphra Behn, 1640–89* (London: Methuen, 1989); Katharine M. Rogers, *Feminism in Eighteenth-Century England* (Urbana: University of Illinois Press, 1982), p. 58; Nancy Cotton, 'Aphra Behn and the Pattern Hero' in Mary Anne Schofield and Cecilia Macheski (eds), *Curtain Calls: British and American Women and the Theater, 1660–1820* (Athens: University of Ohio Press, 1991); Laura Brown, *English Dramatic Form, 1660–1760* (New Haven: Yale University Press, 1981); and Markley, 'Be impudent', p. 121. For a darker view of Willmore and libertinism in the play, see De Ritter, 'The Gypsy, *The Rover*, and the Wanderer', pp. 85–91; Elaine Hobby, *Virtue of Necessity: English Women's Writing 1649–88* (London: Virago, 1988); Jacqueline Pearson, *The Prostituted Muse: Images of Women and Women Dramatists, 1642–1737* (London: Harvester, 1988), p. 153; Chernaik, *Sexual Freedom in Restoration Literature*, pp. 206–8; Pacheco, 'Rape and the Female Subject in Aphra Behn's *The Rover*', p. 341; and Kaufman, 'The Perils of Florinda'. Peggy Thompson sees Willmore as ambivalently depicted but ultimately salvaged as a (problematic) hero: 'Closure and Subversion in Behn's Comedies' in *Broken Boundaries*, ed. Quinsey. For a full analysis of the play, see my *Perspectives on Restoration Drama*.

[16] All quotations are taken from Ogden's edition (see n. 4).

behaviour and identity, as involving boasting of the sexual prowess upon which a man's pride depends. Such 'normal' men are mocked, the boasting being presented as often unfounded. It is therefore possible to see Horner as more truly a man in not caring about outward show: 'let vain rogues be contented only to be thought abler men than they are, generally 'tis all the pleasure they have; but mine lies another way' (I.i.37–9). Since his pretence makes him seem no threat to husbands and gives him access to wives, he can really enjoy the sexual pleasure that others merely boast of. Yet the question remains: in a society so much concerned with appearances, can he really be manly if he has lost the reputation of manhood? Critics have taken every conceivable perspective on Horner. Judgements of him have ranged from champion of sexual freedom to monster; from privileged trickster and true wit who exposes and satirises the vices and follies of others, to psychologically damaged individual.[17] In terms of 'sexual politics', they have ranged from seeing him as a supremely successful deployer of phallic power to a feminised object of women's desire and manipulation.[18]

Horner is the trickster whose ploys both exploit and expose the vices and

---

[17] Criticism has canvassed every shade and nuance. At one extreme are views of him as negative and destructive: for example, Bonamy Dobrée, *Restoration Comedy, 1660–1720* (Oxford: Oxford University Press, 1924); Norman N. Holland, *The First Modern Comedies: The Significance of Etherege, Wycherley, and Congreve* (Cambridge, MA: Harvard University Press, 1959); and Anne Righter, 'William Wycherley' in John Russell Brown and Bernard Harris (eds), *Restoration Theatre* (London: Arnold, 1965), pp. 70–91. Conversely, Virginia Ogden Birdsall views him as a wholly positive and creative comic hero: *Wild Civility: The English Comic Spirit on the Restoration Stage* (Bloomington: Indiana University Press, 1970). For other positive views, see: Thomas H. Fujimura, *The Restoration Comedy of Wit* (Princeton: Princeton University Press, 1952); and C.D. Cecil, 'Libertine and *Precieux* Elements in Restoration Comedy', *Essays in Criticism*, 9 (1959), 239–53. Laura Brown tries to marry positive and negative judgements, arguing that moral and aesthetic judgements remain separate as we applaud his ingenuity but deplore his actions: *English Dramatic Form*, pp. 49–55. Horner is seen as the instrument of social satire by T.W. Craik, 'Some Aspects of Satire in Wycherley's Plays', *English Studies*, 41 (1960), 168–79; and W.R. Chadwick, *The Four Plays of William Wycherley: A Study in the Development of a Dramatist* (The Hague: Mouton, 1975); and as a tainted or satirised satirist by Rose A. Zimbardo, *Wycherley's Drama: A Link in the Development of English Satire* (New Haven: Yale University Press, 1965), pp. 147–65; and Robert Markley, *Two Edg'd Weapons: Style and Ideology in the Comedies of Etherege, Wycherley, and Congreve* (Oxford: Clarendon Press, 1988), pp. 159–78. He is seen as neurotic or deranged by Anthony Kaufman, 'Wycherley's *The Country Wife* and the Don Juan Character', *Eighteenth Century Studies*, 9 (1975–6), 216–31; and W. Gerald Marshall, 'Wycherley's "Great Stage of Fools": Madness and Theatricality in *The Country Wife*', *Studies in English Literature*, 29 (1989), 409–29.

[18] Criticis disagree about whether he expresses sexual hostility and aggression towards women: see, for example, Kaufman, 'Wycherley's *The Country Wife* and the Don Juan Character', p. 216; or whether he recognises women's frustrations, appreciates their needs and ultimately recognises his kinship with them: see, for example, Weber, *The Restoration Rake-Hero*, pp. 62–5 and 'Horner and his "Women of Honour" '. Some see him as a successful male predator: for example, Sedgwick, *Between Men*, chapter 3; others as an ultimately disempowered object of female desire and agency: for example, Burke, 'Wycherley's "Tendentious Joke" '. Michael

follies of others. For example, his imposture immediately exposes the folly of Sir Jasper Fidget's, duped into forcing his womenfolk upon Horner in the belief that he is mocking the latter's impotence. Hypocrisy is also exposed, as Lady Fidget's very disgust at the idea of a eunuch reveals her hidden lust. As Horner is able to tell her under the guise of banter, 'your virtue is your greatest affectation, madam' (I.i.103). Horner's wit here and elsewhere is a marker of true manliness. False wit is consistently derided. As in *The Rover*, the man of true wit is a cavalier in both senses of the word, politically royalist and sexually free and easy.

He also loves wine – and specifically wine, not just any drink. Horner expresses the preference for wine that is typical of Cavaliers in comedies:

> Wine gives you liberty, love takes it away . . . Wine gives you joy; love, grief and tortures, besides the surgeon's.[19] Wine makes us witty; love only sots. Wine makes us sleep; love breaks it . . . for my part, I will have only those glorious, manly pleasures of being very drunk and very slovenly.
>
> (I.i.225–6, 228–10, 238–9)

Yet there is an irony here. Wine is usually seen as an aid to love rather than an alternative to it. As I have argued elsewhere, the trinity of love, wit and wine is repeatedly praised in Restoration poetry and drama.[20] Wine is by no means the least important of the three. In Rochester's libertine poem 'A Ramble in St. James's Park' wine comes first and the rakes then proceed to 'Drunkenness relieved by lechery'.[21] In Edward Ravenscroft's *The London Cuckolds* love and wit are no good without wine: one rake's response to another's telling him that he has been saying the love litany to his mistress is, 'Spoke like a cavalier, egad! If thy inclination did but lie a little more to the bottle, thou wouldst be an admirable honest fellow!'[22] By wittily exalting wine as against the love he is secretly pursuing, Horner thinks he is cocking a snook at his society, but the joke is partly on him as a man adopting the most stigmatised and ridiculous role in his society. Moreover, his plot is flawed from the start. Among the advantages of his imposture, Horner lists the ability to be rid of his creditors and his former mistresses, themselves creditors of a sort: 'of all old debts; love, when it comes to be so, is paid most unwillingly' (I.i.152–4). This marks the fact that Horner is chasing a futile and ever-vanishing goal: once won, women become a burden to be shed, an obligation to be evaded. Act I concludes with his cynical reference to jealousy and the pox as diseases inevitably bred by 'love and wenching' (I.i.505). So what becomes of his own devotion to the same?

In the exchange with his male friends in Act I, Scene i, Horner draws out his

---

Neill sees both possibilities present, as 'dichotomies collapse into semiotic perplexity': 'Horned Beasts and China Oranges: Reading the Signs in *The Country Wife*', *Eighteenth-Century Life*, 12 (1988), 3–17, 14.

[19] 'besides the surgeon's': i.e. in treatment for venereal disease.
[20] See my 'The Politics of Drink in Restoration Drama'.
[21] *Complete Poems and Plays*, p. 46.
[22] Edward Ravenscroft, *The London Cuckolds* (London, 1682), I.i, p. 45.

society's ideas of true and false manhood. The 'false men' the city husbands who are Horner's potential cuckolds, and old men in general, 'shadows of men' or 'Half-men' (I.i.199, 201) who run tame among the women because they have lost their sexual potency. The ageing Pinchwife is in the process of transition from libertine to potential cuckold, and his fear of being cuckolded brings about the dreaded event. Metaphorically linked to the cuckold is Sparkish, a blockhead who thinks he is a wit, but is despised by all the others for his ineptitude and self-deceiving pride: 'His company is as troublesome to us as a cuckold's when you have a mind to his wife's' (I.i.254–6). Pinchwife is knowing where Sir Jasper and Sparkish are credulous, but all are butts of the rakes' wit and trickery, and all in different ways procure their own sexual betrayal.

Yet the exchanges about true and false manhood in the play have a comic provisionality, for two reasons. Firstly, the false men are not that different from the others: Sparkish exhibits many qualities of the wits and 'the short-sighted world' sees no difference between him and them (I.i.253). In the second place, it is doubtful whether there are any 'true men'. All are to some extent mocked, including Horner himself. There is no moral difference between Pinchwife's scheme to ensure marital fidelity by marrying a simple wife and Horner's scheme to get close to wives and seduce them by pretending to be a eunuch. Horner is animalistic: his intimates frequently refer to him as 'beast' and 'toad'. Pinchwife, cuckolded, likens himself to 'a kind of a wild beast' (V.iv.308). Horner's friend Harcourt comes closest in the play to conforming to a heroic standard, but even he is not all that different from the other men. He can be as perfidious a friend as other men in this world. He aids Horner in tormenting Pinchwife in III.ii, and physically restrains Margery's would-be protectors as Horner leads her off. He seems to have a libertine reputation (II.i.134, 175), and in the opening scene he comes off the worst in an exchange in which he disreputably proclaims what might be called cavalier attitudes to women (I.i.214–21).

Wine is both the symbol and the literal solidifier of 'glorious, manly pleasures' (I.i.238–9). But what are such pleasures worth? The witty nature of the exchanges between men makes it hard to decide. Men enjoy their power-play up to a point, even if, like Sparkish, they are on the receiving end: it shows they are part of the gang. Male bonds seem strong in spite – or because – of the fact that relations between men are power relations. Humour, just as much as wine, greases the wheels of friendship and wit excuses much. Even Horner, supposedly shunning friends and laying aside his claim to manhood in the pursuit of sex, still enjoys the friendship of Dorilant and Harcourt just as before: the wits continue to include him as one of themselves. Yet wit excuses much that seems quite cruel, and no friendship is entirely innocent or wholesome. Horner's baiting of his friends in Act I, Scene i, mocks the way men talk, building upon one another's conceits, quick to follow a lead and to outdo one another in praising wine, and criticising women or fools. Horner is able to lead his friends on to adopt ridiculous and extreme positions.

Far from exalting male bonds over heterosexual ones, Wycherley shows men's pleasure in making fools of one another. Sir Jasper thinks he is rubbing salt in the wounds of the eunuch; while Horner feigns friendship to Sir Jasper in order to cuckold him, but later finds the burden of the loathsome friendship outweighs the rewards. Horner is devious even in his friendships with other wits: he enjoys drawing out his friends' views and secretly deriding them. The so-called friends delight in abusing and secretly mocking Sparkish who thinks he is one of them. They torment the already paranoid Pinchwife, revelling in playing upon his fear and jealousy. Indeed, one characteristic all the men in the play have in common is their delight in deriding and scoring points off one another. Such male friendship as exists has no future: the world of the play, in common with most Restoration comedies, is a world of young men. The young enjoy a barbed friendship, but the old have no chance. Old men are fools and cuckolds and Pinchwife, at forty-nine, illustrates the problem of the man becoming old, attempting to emancipate himself from the society of rakes and settle down. There is little real loyalty between men. Their witty discussions have a comic relativism as all perspectives interrogate one another. Both love and friendship – and the pursuit of them – are treated ironically. Drink becomes the appropriate signifier of values that are entirely fluid.

Are relations between the sexes privileged over male friendship, a site of greater truth and communication? Or are they also reducible to power-play? Power-play definitely comes into Horner's plots. Yet it is possible to see Horner as a man sensitive to women's needs, and Wycherley by implication as critical of his society's notions of sex and gender roles. Horner values wit in women, not just sexual availability: 'methinks wit is more necessary than beauty; and I think no young woman ugly that has it, and no handsome woman agreeable without it' (I.i.425–7). This does not prevent him seducing the witless Margery. Yet even this can be seen as a service to Margery, an awakening. Horner seems to have women's sexual interests at heart: 'women . . . are like soldiers, made constant and loyal by good pay rather than by oaths and covenants' (I.i.464–6).

This may be illustrated in a conversation that the men have about drink. Wycherley exalts drink, the marker of manliness, against love, as a prelude to other exchanges in which the meaning of the signifier is to shift. In Act III, Scene ii, the significance of drink shifts in the course of a witty exchange between Horner and his friends. At first drink enters the conversation simply as a jocular comparison, a reason for dining with rich fools, just as the supposed eunuch Horner needs a reason for frequenting the ladies. Harcourt then interrupts the repartee with a blunt question, 'But do the ladies drink?' (III.ii.30–1). Drink now becomes the subject of the conversation. Horner claims he will drink with the women because 'I shall have the pleasure at least of laying 'em flat with the bottle, and bring as much scandal that way upon 'em as formerly t'other' (32–4). Harcourt prophetically suggests 'you may prove as weak a brother amongst 'em that way as t'other' (35–6). Horner's friends are disgusted by the idea of his drinking with women, claiming that drinking with women is unnatural, that drink quenches love, and that 'Wine and women, good apart, together [are] as nauseous as sack and sugar' (49–50). Drink is supposedly a sign of manliness and a social adhesive of male bonding. The fact that women drink at all is a surprise to all but Horner:

> Quack: But do civil persons and women of honour drink and sing bawdy songs?
> Horner: Oh, amongst friends, amongst friends. (IV.iii.21)

Horner's knowledge of women's secret drinking seems at first to empower him, enabling him to expose their hypocrisy. However, women assert their own power. Lady Fidget professes to think the eunuch pretence entirely admirable and beneficial for women:

> But, poor gentleman, could you be so generous, so truly a man of honour, as for the sakes of us women of honour, to cause yourself to be reported no man? No man! And to suffer yourself the greatest shame that could fall upon a man, that none may fall upon us women by your conversation? (II.i.555–60)

What she does here is to co-opt his manoeuvre and turn it to her own advantage. What began as a way for Horner to seduce women and score over their husbands, becomes a device for women's benefit, and this is borne out as Horner becomes by the end the property of Lady Fidget and her 'virtuous gang, as they call themselves' (V.i.96).

Lady Fidget, Dainty Fidget and Mrs Squeamish may be circumscribed by social convention but they are certainly not powerless. They are somewhat grotesque as they prattle of honour while objecting to the fact that men of quality pursue actresses in preference to themselves (II.i.354–411). It is very hard to see how such hypocrisy could be presented as at all attractive, and their names suggest a ridiculous fastidiousness. But they are winners in the sexual game as they manipulate oppressive social codes for their own advantage and make the best of a bad world.

The most titillatingly outrageous example of Horner's chutzpah (or of any rake's in Restoration comedy) is his seduction of Lady Fidget in his china closet while her husband watches and comments from the next room with unwitting encouragement and unconscious double entendre: 'Wife! He is coming into you the back way!' (IV.iii.132). China becomes a metaphor for sex, but only Horner and the women know this. Wycherley invites us to delight in this but also, through the device of having the action observed by the Quack, to reflect upon Horner's position. At first sight, Horner's daring in the scene is breathtaking. He counters Lady Fidget's request to keep the 'dear secret' (IV.iii.65) of his potency from other women, for fear they will suspect her affair with him, by announcing his intention to sleep with them all:

> Nay, madam, rather than they shall prejudice your honour, I'll prejudice theirs; and to serve you, I'll lie with 'em all, make the secret their own, and then they'll keep it: I am a Machiavel in love, madam. (IV.iii.66)

The whole exchange appears to show Horner's power as he plays with his conquest. Yet the scene reveals, ultimately, the way in which Horner's power over women is open to question. The conversation also reveals the less obvious reality that it is women who have secret knowledge, as well as the power to destroy reputations.

Women take the sexual initiative: the idea of 'looking for china' in Horner's closet is Lady Fidget's. Moreover, the presence of other women alters the sexual balance of power. In the first place, they understand the secret language of 'china' where Sir Jasper does not, an instance of women's privileged relationship to language and communication in the play. And in the second place, they immediately assume that if 'china' is on offer, they can all have some:

> Mrs Squeamish: O Lord, I'll have some china too. Good Master
> Horner, don't think to give other people china, and
> me none. Come in with me too.   (IV.iii.190)

Horner becomes a purveyor of satisfaction for female consumers, a 'sex object'. It is a commonplace for the sex act to be described in terms of men stealing women's jewel. The dominant metaphor in the scene inverts this: the woman has stolen the man's china. As Horner says, 'Nay, she has been too hard for me, do what I could' (IV.iii.189). He, on the other hand, is no longer 'hard', no longer supremely potent, but depleted: 'Upon my honour I have none left now' (IV.iii.193). Lady Fidget, on the other hand, is still voracious: 'What, d'ye think is he had any left, I would not have had it too? For we women of quality never think we have china enough' (IV.iii.200). The remainder of the scene is taken up with Pinchwife's unwitting delivery of his wife's Margery's love letter to the astonished Horner, a further instance of women's ingenuity and sexual initiative.

However, it is women's relationship to drink that is really startling. Women's drinking is not merely a symbol or illustration of their wresting power from men. Their ability to drink really empowers them. Drink is a marker of manhood that women in this society assume for themselves. Far from being laid flat with the bottle, the women bring their own bottles to Horner's lodging, reveal that they are used to drinking two bottles each, and that they, like the men, equate drinking with 'honesty' (V.iv.19). They then carouse in a ritual that affirms both their power over Horner and their barbed and provisional union with one another, in an exact mirror-image of the men's relationships.

We may go further. There is a sense in which Horner and the whole sexual game come second to the drink itself. We see this in Lady Fidget's extraordinary drinking song:

> Why should our damned tyrants oblige us to live
> On the pittance of pleasure which they only give?
>   We must not rejoice

> With wine and with noise.
> In vain we must wake in a dull bed alone,
> Whilst to our warm rival, the bottle, they're gone.
> > Then lay aside charms
> > And take up these arms.
>
> 'Tis wine only gives 'em their courage and wit
> Because we live sober, to men we submit.
> > If for beauties you'd pass
> > Take a lick of the glass:
> 'Twill mend your complexions, and when they are gone
> The best red we have is the red of the grape.
> > Then, sister, lay't on,
> > And damn a good shape.   (V.iv.26)

Drink is a rival for their husbands' affections, but instead of competing with it they will possess it for themselves, a far more empowering paradigm than anything available in the sexual game. Drink is the agent of women's emancipation and self-expression. To describe taking up glasses as taking up arms locates drink explicitly within a gender battle. The word 'sister' reinforces this, as does the disdain for dieting and preserving the complexion. The other women affirm this: 'Dear brimmer', 'Lovely brimmer' (V.iv.42, 45).

Horner's knowledge of women's secret drinking, earlier a sign of his power, shifts to an awareness of his and all men's ultimate marginality. In V.iv we see the 'virtuous gang' triumphant in their possession of Horner. In the conventional cuckolding paradigm, the woman is a pawn in a power-play between men. Here the women affirm their power to drink and make a noise, assert their sexual needs, and order Horner to tell them the secrets of men's sexual behaviour. Horner has really become the women's plaything that he earlier pretended to be (to Sir Jasper's amusement and his own feigned disgust). His eunuch pretence has shifted from empowering ploy to a trap that places him in the power of the women who know the truth. The women resolve to become 'sister sharers' in Horner's services on their own terms (V.iv.169). Horner becomes 'Harry Common' (V.iv.177). That this is a move in a gender battle, reversing normal power relations, is suggested by the previous discussion of men's delight in sharing common women.[23]

It is typical of the ironic social reflexiveness of this play that drink actually plays a central role. It is both literally and metaphorically the key to understanding how the play's society is to be understood.

---

[23] In terms of female power, it should also be noted that Horner's cuckolding of Pinchwife eventually comes about through the contrivance of Lucy, who suggests that Margery disguise herself as Alithea, a drastic measure, which also has the benefit of showing Alithea Sparkish's true character. Horner has tried to employ Sparkish to disengage Margery from her husband, a singularly ineffective stratagem.

Improvement

9

'Health, Strength and Happiness': Medical Constructions of Wine and Beer in Early Modern England

LOUISE HILL CURTH AND TANYA M. CASSIDY

Water. . . . First, Wine, shall bee in most request among Courtiers, Gallants, Gentlemen, and Poeticall wits, *Qui melioris luti homines,* being of a refined mould, shall choose as a more nimble and active watering, to make their braines fruitfull, *Fecundi calices quem non*? but so as not confin'd to them, nor limitting them to you, more then to exhilerate their spirits, and acuate their inventions.

You Beere, shall be in most grace with the Citizens, as being a more stayed Liquor, fit for them that purpose retirement and gravitie, that with the Snaile carries the cares of a house and family with them, tyed to the attendance of an illiberall profession, that neither trot nor amble, but have a sure pase of their owne, *Bos Lassus fortius figit pedem*, The black Oxe has trod upon their foot: yet I bound you not with the Citie, though it bee the common entertainement, you may bee in credit with Gentlemens Sellars, and carry reputation before you from March to Christmas-tide I should say; that Water should forget his Tide.

You Ale I remit to the Countrie, as more fit to live where you were bred: your credit shall not be inferiour, for people of all sorts shall desire your acquaintance, specially in the morning, though you may be allowed all the day after: the Parson shall account you one of his best Parishioners, & the Churchwardens shall pay for your companie, and drawing their Bills all the yeere long, you shall bee loued and maintained at the Parish charge till you bee olde, bee allowed a *Robin-Hood*, or Mother *Red-Cap*, to hang at your doore, to beckon in Customers: and if you come into the Citie, you may bee drunke with pleasure, but never come into fashion. At all times you shall have respect, but with Winter Mornings without comparison. How doe you like my censure now?[1]

---

[1] *Wine, Beere, and Ale, together by the eares. A Dialogue, Written first in Dutch by Gallobelgicus, and faithfully translated out of the original Copie, by Mercurius Brittanicus, for the benefit of his Nation* (1629).

LTHOUGH tongue-in-cheek, this witty repartee provides a fitting introduction to the role of wine, beer and ale in seventeenth-century England. In this dialogue, each drink argues that the others should defer to 'him', as they each make claims of health, vigour and antiquity to assert their precedence: ale, for example, claims that there are many houses belonging to him whereas no one ever heard of a 'beerhouse'. The dialogue is concluded by the intervention of water (the basis for all drinks) who negotiates a peace settlement based on recognition of the province of each drink – the field and territory of supremacy that each drink enjoys: wine is for wits and scholars (improving mental health), beer is for the urban bourgeois (imparting a diet of strength and solidity), and ale is for the countryman (as an early morning pick-me-up). One drink that no one is intended to rely upon is water itself. Some form of alcoholic beverage is required within the daily diet of most everyone.

It is clear that wine, beer and ale were considered to be far more than simple beverages to quench thirst. Each played an important societal and cultural role in daily life, with each being perceived to suit particular socio-economic groups and particular bodily constitutions. In health terms, however, the main theme was that any type of alcohol, when taken in moderation, would help both to prevent and to treat illness.

ALCOHOL IN SEVENTEENTH-CENTURY ENGLAND

The relationship between drink (in many different forms) and the health of both the body and the body politic has a long history. In early modern England, wine and beer were widely used as tonics for preventing illness, and were also important components of therapeutic remedies. Alcohol was imbibed in various forms, sometimes by itself or as a vital ingredient in medicinal compounds. There was, however, a fine balance between consuming just enough and too much alcohol. People who regularly partook of excessive amounts were sure to suffer extensive moral and physical damage.

Alcohol also played an important part in the daily diet, with the choice of tipple reflecting socio-economic differences. Cheap wine was available to many, and cheap beer to virtually everyone, and was often considered more food than beverage. The prevalence of the use of small beer or new-brewed beverages within the household by all, especially at breakfast time, and even by young children, is widely recognised.[2] Most households and institutional

---

[2] Discussions regarding levels of consumption in the past are somewhat limited. Two exceptions are Josephine A. Spring and David H. Buss, 'Three Centuries of Alcohol in the British Diet', *Nature*, 270 (15) (1977), 567–72; and Peter Clark, *The English Alehouse: A Social History 1200–1830* (London: Longman, 1983). See also the Introduction to this present volume. Further discussion is available online, in a paper entitled 'How Much Did they Drink? The consumption of alcohol in traditional Europe', by A. Lynn Martin (Director of the

settings would produce some form of brewed beverage as part of their domestic routine. Alehouses were closer to being domestic settings than taverns or inns.[3] Wine, on the other hand, because it had to be imported and was therefore expensive, was often seen as a status symbol. Different wine varieties provided subtler class discriminations. In broader terms, wine was regarded as foreign, ale as domestic, while beer (hopped) underwent a controversial process of naturalisation in the period between 1500 and 1700.[4]

The specific types of wine that were available fluctuated in response to political events, and resulting market conditions.[5] Traditionally, the majority of wine consumed in England was imported from France. Over fifty-six varieties of French wines, compared to thirty of Italian, Spanish and Canarian, were available in London during the late Middle Ages.[6] By the beginning of the seventeenth century, French wines were clearly the market leaders.[7] The majority of these wines, as well as those from the Rhine and Moselle were imported in Dutch ships. This was not surprising, as Holland had the largest mercantile fleet yet known. In fact, as the first great commercial power, the Dutch dominated the European economy.[8] The passing of the Navigation Act of 1651 marked a major blow to Dutch–English trade. The act dictated that European vessels were only allowed to import goods from their own nations into England.[9] This helped to precipitate a series of naval wars with the Dutch in 1652–4, 1656–6 and 1672–3.[10] These wars dealt such a severe blow to the French wine trade, that it never fully recovered.[11]

Spain, Portugal, the Canaries and Maderia swiftly filled the gap in the wine market during the second half of the century. The terms sack, seck or secco were generically applied to wines from all these areas.[12] These types of wine

Research Centre for the History of Food and Drink), from January 2003 – posted at http://www.arts.adelaide.edu.au/CentreFoodDrink/Articles/HowMuchDrink.html. See also A. Lynn Martin, *Alcohol, sex, and gender in late medieval and early modern Europe* (New York: Palgrave, 2001).

3   Judith M. Bennett, *Ale, Beer and Brewsters in England: Women's Work in a Changing World, 1300–1600* (New York: Oxford University Press, 1996).

4   See Charlotte McBride's chapter in this volume, 'A Natural Drink for an English Man: National Stereotyping in Early Modern Culture'.

5   See Charles C. Ludington's chapter in this volume, ' "Be sometimes to your country true": The Politics of Wine in England, 1660–1714'.

6   M.P. Cosman, *Fabulous Feasts: Medieval Cookery and Ceremony* (New York: George Brasillier, 1976), p. 74.

7   A. Sim, *Food and Feast in Tudor England* (Stroud: Sutton, 1997), chapter 5.

8   M. Kishlansky, P. Geary and P. O'Brien, *Civilization in the West* (London: Addison Wesley/ Longman, 2001), vol. II, p. 593.

9   R. Davis, *The Rise of the English Shipping Industry in the Seventeenth and Eighteenth Centuries* (London: Macmillan, 1962), pp. 306–7.

10   J. Brewer, *The Sinews of Power* (London: Unwin Hyman, 1989), p. 11

11   J.C. Drummond and A. Wilbraham, *The Englishman's Food: Five Centuries of English Diet* (London: Pimlico, 1958), p. 113.

12   A.L. Simon, *History of the Wine Trade in England* (London: Holland Press, 1909), 3 vols, vol. 3, p. 323.

were readily available at modest cost, and so were widely served in both taverns and many homes. 'Canary' wine was considered superior to generic sack, and wine from Seres even better.[13] Although it became increasingly expensive in the second half of the century, French claret was still purchased by wealthier consumers.[14]

In political terms, both beer and wine connect with the politics of importation with all its invasive ramifications (ale as an entirely domestic produce is exempt). Anxieties about wine connect with anxieties about southern Catholic Europe, whereas concerns about beer are connected to northern Europe, overwhelmingly with Holland. Hopped brewed beverages are a Dutch innovation, and were slowly introduced into England from the beginning of the sixteenth century onwards. In 1599 the herbalist Henry Buttes praised hops as a desirable innovation, while humorously reminding his readers of what had become a familiar association between Protestantism or heresies and beer.

> Our forefathers knewe not the Hoppe: howbeit it is a most excellent hearbe, & exceedeth all other for good iuyce: for cleansing the blood, and scouring all the entrals, Besides the necessitie hereof in brewing of Beer is sufficiently knowne to *Germany* and *England*, and all these Northern parts of the worlde: yet I know not how it happened (as he merrily saith) that herisie and beere cam hopping into England both in yeere.[15]

Given Buttes' praise of hops it seems unlikely that he regarded either hops or Protestantism as heresy. Buttes acknowledges, however, that others did regard hopped 'protestant' beer as an evil innovation. Such attitudes persisted until the mid-seventeenth century, as evidenced by this extract from a conservative 'Catholic' poem in praise of ale:

> The naked complains not for want of a coat,
> Nor on the cold weather will once turn his taile:
> All the way as he goes, he cuts the wind with his Nose,
> If he be but well wrapt in a pot, &c.
> The hungry many takes no thought for his meat,
> Though his stomack would brook a ten-penny aile;
> He quite forgets hunger, thinks on it no longer,
> If he touch but the sparks of a pot, &c.
> [...]
> To the *Church* and *Religion* it is a good Friend
> Or else our Fore-Fathers their wisdome did faile,
> That at every mile, next to the *Church* stile,
> Set a *consecrate house* to a *pot*, &c.
> But now, as they say, *Beer* bears it away;

---

[13] G. Markham, *The English Housewife* (1615); reprint edited by Michael R. Best (Kingston: McGill-Queen's University Press, 1986), p. 137.

[14] Anon., *Country Almanac* (1676), sig. B1v.

[15] Henry Buttes, *Dyets Dry Dinner: Consisting of eight several Courses* (1599), sig. G4r.

> The more is the pity if right might prevail:
> For, with this same *Beer*, came up *Heresie* here,
>   The old *Catholick drink* is a *pot*, &c.
> And in very deed the *Hop*'s but a Weed
>   Brought o're against Law, and here set to sale:
> Would the Law were renew'd, and no more *Beer* brew'd
>   But all men betake them to a *pot*., &c.[16]

Published in the 1640s, this poem is (of course) anonymous, and the book-seller is indicated only with the initials 'J.R.' The author of the *Ex-Ale-Tation* would seem to be a Catholic who regards hopped beer as both a metaphor and a medium for protestant heresy. His poem begins with a very conventional series of compliments paid to ale – ale as meat medicine and muffler; ale the poor men's friend, and so on – before launching into an attack on beer. He associates beer with civil commotion (obviously referring to the Civil War) and even goes so far as to call hopped beer a kind of poison – beer will bring you to your 'bier'. There are other references, some of which we have noted, associating hopped beer with Protestantism since both innovations seemed to arrive in England round about the same time. Interestingly, Henry VIII, while still a loyal Catholic, had outlawed the use of hops in beer, whereas his strongly Protestant son, Edward VI, encouraged it. Hopping, of course had been imported as a practice from the Low Countries – which had themselves fought a Protestant war of independence against Catholic Spain.

Another, less doctrinally specific anti-beer discussion can be found in John Taylor's 1637 *Historie of the most part of Drinks, in use now in the Kingdomes of Great Brittaine and Ireland*, where he refers to beer as 'an Upstart and a foreigner or Alien'.[17] Antiquity is the key principle for Taylor, who is less specific regarding his political and religious affiliations. The longstanding authority of ale, according to Taylor, is evidenced by the fact that a vocabulary of ale has entered into the English language:

> *An* Beere house is ridiculous; but *An* Ale-Brewer or *An Alehouse* is good signifi-cant English; or to say *An* Beere brewer or *An* Beerehouse or (by your favour *An* Tavern) is but botching language in great Brittaine; but to say A *Alebrewer* or A *Alehouse* is more improper than to bud a childe.[18]

This linguistic defence of ale is intended to depict ale as fundamental to English identity itself. He quotes:

> a discreet Gentleman in a solemne Assembly, who by a politick observation, very aptly compares *Ale* and Cakes with Wine and Waters, neither doth he hold it fit

---

[16] *The Ex-Ale-Tation of Ale* (1668 [a reprint of the original 1646 edition]).
[17] John Taylor, *Drinke and Welcome: Or the Famous Historie of the most part of Drinks, in use now in the Kingdomes of Great Brittaine and Ireland* (1637), sig. B3r.
[18] Ibid.

that it should stand in the Competition with the meanest Wines, but with that most excellent Composition which the Prince of Physitians *Hippocrates* had so ingenously compounded for the preservation of mankinde, and which (to this day) speakes the Author by the name of *Hippocras,* so that you see for Antiquity, *Ale* was famous among the *Trojans, Brittaines, Romans, Saxons, Danes, Normans, Englishmen, Welch,* besides in *Scotland,* from the highest and Noblest Palace, to the poorest and meanest Cottage, *Ale* is universall, and for Vertue it stands allowable with the best receipts of the most Antientest Physitians; and for its singular force in expulsion of poison, is equall, if not exceeding that rare Antidote so seriously invented by the Pontique King, which from him (till the time) carries his name of *Mithridate,* And lastly, not onely approved by a National Assembly, but more exemplarily remonstrated by the frequent use of the most knowing Physitians, who for the wonderfull force that it hath against all the diseases of the Lungs, Justly allow the name of a *Pulmonist* to every *Alebrewer.*[19]

Taylor elides a moralised celebration of antiquity into a medicalised discussion of ale's nutritional and preservative qualities. For Taylor, however, medicinal issues are subordinated to a more general concern with 'ancient virtue'. However, other writers had, by the Caroline period, begun to subordinate descriptive dietary writing to a specifically medical agenda, an agenda that was, for the first time, tailored for a large English-speaking audience.

VERNACULAR MEDICAL BOOKS

Vernacular medical books were an important source for the dissemination of popular medical advice. There were many different types, ranging from specialised discourses on the benefits of coffee and tobacco to general handbooks meant for those of 'the meanest capacities'.[20] A variety of works were also available that bear a strong resemblance to 21st-century 'self-help' books. Our contemporary concept of drinking a glass or two of wine a day, for example, is strikingly similar to the advice found in seventeenth-century English language medical books.

Before the early seventeenth century the majority of printed medical works were in Latin.[21] Clearly, this would have made them accessible only to a small part of the population, mainly men who were university educated. The primary audience for Latin medical books was members of the College of Physicians whose classical education would have included Latin, and sometimes Greek.

---

[19] Ibid.

[20] W. Rumsey, *Organic salutis: An instrument to cleanse the stomach* (1659), sig. A1r, and T. Tryon, *The Way to Health, Long Life and Happiness: or, A Discourse of Happiness* (1697), sig. A1r.

[21] J. Henry, 'The Matter of Souls: Medical Theory and Theology in Seventeenth-Century England', in R. French and A. Wear (eds), *The Medical Revolution of the Seventeenth Century* (Cambridge: Cambridge University Press, 1989), pp. 48–112, p. 93.

This is not to suggest that there was no call for popular medical knowledge during earlier periods. During the late fourteenth century, there was a growing demand for the translation of medieval herb lore and other medical manuscripts written in Latin. By the early sixteenth century the genre of medical works written in English for laymen began to grow.[22] It was during the seventeenth century, however, that vernacular medical books became widely available, owing principally to the collapse of censorship and medical licensing.[23]

The greatest demand was for books that emphasised curing diseases with easily accessible remedies.[24] William Rondelet explained that instead of paying a 'Doctor or Physitian', the reader could purchase his 'short Books [which] tels what other may be administered instead'.[25] When Nicholas Culpeper translated the pharmacopoeia into English in 1649, he explained that he did this to enable the public to acquire commonly used medicines, without having to pay a physician. Given that the average London physician charged between 8s 8d and 10s per visit and a male day labourer made only 8d per day the market for such knowledge is easy to imagine.[26] Culpeper understandably antagonised the medical establishment by suggesting that everyday and easily available products might make medical expertise redundant. No product was more 'everyday' in the seventeenth century than ale or beer.[27]

Hops are 'under the dominion of Mars'. . . . open Obstructions of the Liver and Spleen to cleanse the Blood, to loosen the Belly, to cleanse the Reins from Gravel, and provoke Urine. The Decoction of the tops of Hops, as well of the tame as the wild, worketh the same effects. In cleansing the Blood they help to Cure the French Disease, and all manner of Scabs, Itch, and other breakings out of the Body; as also all Tetters, Ringworms, and Spreading Sores, the Morphew, and all Discolourings of the Skin. The Decoctions of the Flowers and Tops, do help to expel Poyson that any one hath drunk. Half a Dram of the Seed in Powder taken in drink, killeth Worms in the Body, bringeth down Womens Courses, and expelleth Urine. A syrup made of the Juice and Sugar, cureth the Yellow Jaundice, easeth the Head-ach that comes of Heat, and tempereth the heat of the Liver and Stomach, and is profitable given in long and hot Agues that rise in Choler and Blood. Both the wild, and the manured are of one property, and alike effectual in all the aforesaid Diseases.

---

22 P. Slack, 'Mirrors of Health and Treasures of Poor Men', in C. Webster (ed.), *Health, Medicine and Mortality in the Sixteenth Century* (Cambridge: Cambridge University Press, 1999), pp. 240–2.

23 D. Cressy, *Literacy and the Social Order: Reading and Writing in Tudor and Stuart England* (Cambridge: Cambridge University Press, 1980), p. 47.

24 A. Wear, 'The Popularisation of Medicine in Early Modern Europe', in R. Porter (ed.), *The Popularisation of Medicine, 1650–1850* (London & New York: Routledge, 1992), pp. 17–34.

25 W. Rondelet, *The Countrey-mans Apothecary* (1649), sig. A1v.

26 Andrea Cast, 'For Your Health: Medicinal Drinking in Seventeenth-Century England', in A. Lynn Martin and Barbara Santich (eds), *Culinary History* (forthcoming).

27 D. Nagy, *Popular Medicine in Seventeenth Century England* (Bowling Green, OH: Bowling Green State University, 1988), pp. 25–6.

By all these Testimonies, Beer appears to be better than Ale. *Mars* owns the Plant, and then Dr *Reason* will tell you how it performs these Actions.[28]

It must be remembered that early modern drinks are often confusingly labelled with names that 21st-century readers think they recognise. Unlike today, it was still common, especially in the first half of the century, to find unhopped brewed beverages, which as a result tasted very different from any brewed beverages available to the modern consumer. Unhopped ale was flavoured and preserved by 'gruit'. In England and northern Europe, gruit recipes varied but generally were produced from bitter herbs, which were chosen purportedly for medicinal reasons. It has been argued that the most popular herb was gale, and according to a recent article in the *Journal for the American Society of Brewing Chemists*: 'The decline of gruit was accelerated in the sixteenth and seventeenth centuries by the increasingly prevalent belief that bog myrtle (*Myrtica gale*), one of the principal ingredients, could harm the consumer's health.'[29]

Equally, popular medical writers regarded controlled wine drinking as a way of augmenting expensive medical treatments. One contemporary work by Tobias Whitaker, *The Tree of Humane Life*, focused exclusively on the medicinal usage of wine. Whitaker clearly believed that wine was a wonder drug whose use made it possible to maintain 'humane life from infancy to extreame old age without any sicknesse'.[30] As the following two sections will show, wine played an important role in both preventative and remedial medicine.

Wines such as claret would have tasted different from their modern counterparts as they were not clarified or matured before sale during the seventeenth century. It was therefore necessary to purchase and consume them while still young, whereas young beer was considered not an intoxicant but a food. As one contemporary author noted: 'no stale Drinks, whether Wine, Cyder, Beer or Ale, are so homogeneal and profitable to Nature as those that are Newer'.[31] Once again, there was a fine line, as very new wines were considered unfit to drink, causing 'the Stone and gravell, Obstruction the Liver, Reines and Ureters, and many times cause Dissenteries, Licentries, and other unnaturall fluxes'.[32]

Whether the wine was new or old, seventeenth-century consumers also needed to be wary of adulterated wines.[33] All wines were 'drunk from the

---

[28] Nicholas Culpeper, *The English Physitian Enlarged; with Three Hundred and Sixty Nine Medicines, made of English Herbs* (1695), pp. 129–30.

[29] Michael Moir, 'Hops – A Millennium Review', *The Journal of the American Society of Brewing Chemists*, 58(4) (2000), 131–46.

[30] T. Whitaker, *The Tree of Humane Life, or, The Bloud of the Grape* (1638), sig. A1r.

[31] Anon., *The Closet of the Eminently Learned Sir Kenelme Digbie Kt. Opened* (1669), p. 202.

[32] J. Booker, *Telescopium Uranicum* (1659), sig. B8r.

[33] As far as the adulteration of ale or beer is concerned opinion was divided as to what constituted adulteration or enhancement. For conservatives hops were themselves a form of adulteration.

wood', which meant that they were kept in wooden casks until just before serving time. The consequence of such storage was that, often, what arrived on the table tasted more like vinegar than wine.[34] If too much air leaked into the barrel, it could render the wine thick and undrinkable.[35] Similarly, if air was allowed to enter brewed beverages bacteria would form and spoil the product.[36] As contemporary reports illustrate, many unscrupulous vintners and alehouse keepers tampered with their wares that had gone off, and tried to pass them off as sound.[37] At the same time, there were many recipes to make both wine and ale or beer more palatable or interesting, some of which have carried down to the present day (mulled wine or 'Lamb's Wool' [spiced ale and apples], for example).[38] Some of these recipes made not only nutritional but medicinal claims.

Ale, beer and wine, even bad wine, could be used for a variety of medicinal purposes. For example, 'aqua vitae' was distilled from either wine lees or unsound wine.[39] This was thought to be such a powerful concoction that even tiny amounts would have noticeable medicinal effects.[40] A typical recipe might include four gallons of strong ale and one gallon of the lees of wine.[41] Various herbs would be added to the chosen liquid, which would be left for four days. At the end of that time it would be distilled in a 'limbeck' (alchemical drinking vessel).[42] For our purposes 'medicinal' encompasses both preventative and remedial discourses. Different drinks, associated with different people, become attached to either healthy regimes or curative treatments as appropriate.

PREVENTATIVE MEDICINE

The art of Physicke by the judgment of the learned hath two principall parts; the one declaring the order how health may be preserved: the other setting forth the meanes how sicknesse may bee remedied. Of these two parts (in mine opinion) that is more excellent, which preserveth health and preventeth sicknesse.[43]

The theme of it being easier to keep illness at bay than to drive it out was a regular feature in seventeenth-century vernacular medical books. *The Good housewife made a Doctor* reminded readers that it was 'one of the most

---

34 Drummond and Wilbraham, *Englishman's Food*, p. 113.

35 J. White, *A New Almanacke* (1643), sig. C1v.

36 P. Sambrook, *Country House Brewing in England 1500–1900* (London: Hambledon Press, 1996), chapter 3.

37 H. Platt, *The Jewel House of Art and Nature* (1594), p. 65.

38 K. Burton and H. Ripperger, *Feast Day Cookbook* (New York: David McKay, 1951).

39 Anon., *The Treasurie of Hidden Secrets* (1627), sig. B2v.

40 Sim, *Food and Feast*, p. 69.

41 Markham, *English Housewife*, pp. 126–7.

42 *Treasurie* (1627), sig. B2r.

43 T. Cogan, *The Haven of Health* (1612), sig. A3r.

important Businesses of this Life, to preserve our selves in Health'.[44] The almanac writer Richard Saunders explained that

> If we were careful to keep out diseases, we should not be troubled to drive them out: Reason tells us 'tis better to keep out an enemy, then to let him in, and afterwards to beat him out.[45]

Many popular medical books provided advice on ways in which people could protect their health. The majority of these revolved around leading a healthy lifestyle with an emphasis on moderation in all things. The astrologer and writer Thomas Langley urged his readers to 'take measure, and no more, for in measure resteth health and vertue'.[46] Alcohol, consumed in moderation, was thought to be an important ally in the fight against disease. Ale, beer and wine were all touted for their preservative properties. The almanac writer William White, for example, advised readers:

> For drinking Beer or Ale, thus we advise,
> Not to be sharp or sower in any wise.
> Let them be clear, well boyl'd, malt sound and good,
> Stale, and not new; all these cause healthful blood.[47]

According to Tobias Whitaker, 'the bloud of the grape' was 'neerest to the nature of the Gods and their nature is incorrupt'.[48] Furthermore, he thought that wine was the most nutritious beverage available, being 'more pure and better concocted then any other juyce, either of milke, egges, corne, fruits, or the like'. People who regularly drank wine could be expected to be 'faire, fresh, plumpe, and fat', rather than water or small-beer-drinkers, who 'look like Apes rather than men'.[49]

There is evidence also that strong beer was regarded not only as an intoxicant but as a more democratic alternative to water or small beer for those who could not afford wine:

> We shall not hear the Cry of the Poor complaining of Want, so long as, for a small Matter, they can send for so much good Bread and Beer, as will suffice their whole Families, which is not only a sustenance against Hunger, but a Preservative against Sickness.
>
> Then let not those, whose better Fare maketh them so insensible of poor Men's Wants, deny them that good Beer, which is so needful to their meaner Food, because that some abuse it.[50]

[44] P. Physiologus, *The Good housewife made a Doctor* (n.d.), sig. A2v.
[45] R. Saunders, *Apollo Anglicanus* (1681), sig. A7r.
[46] T. Langley, *A New Almanack and Prognostication* (1643), sig. B3r.
[47] W. White, *An Almanack* (1675), sig. B3r.
[48] Whitaker, *Tree of Humane Life*, p. 2.
[49] Ibid., pp. 29–31.
[50] Anon., *The Brewers Plea: Or, A Vindication of Strong Beer and Ale* (1647), p. 5.

Attempts by puritan authorities in the 1640s to regulate and control ale and beer consumption provoked this rejoinder, *The Brewer's Plea* (1647), which summarises many of the key arguments, not merely in favour of beer drinking, but in favour of *strong* beer drinking – strong beer being of better quality. The brewers' claim is that attacking beer is a species of class war, and that beer combines many nutrients and consolation that would otherwise be quite beyond the means of the mass of the population. In reply to those who warn of the dangers of alcohol, the brewers declare that one does not outlaw the use of fire, just because it can hurt people. Again, we see the range of functions beer and ale are expected to fulfil – the drink is a 'preservative', a 'salve', and an overcoat, as well as being a means to cheer and console.

A loose definition of 'moderation' was, however, intended to govern the consumption even of the good things of this world. Men, or women, who drank too much wine were asking for trouble. Whitaker's book warned that 'By the excessive quantity [of wine], you will adde so much oyle to the Lampe as shall extinguish it'.[51] Even if the wine didn't kill the drinker, it would 'penetrate into all the parts, and goes into the veins undigested, and prickes the nerves and brains'.[52] This would, in turn, 'inflameth the bloud, debilitateth the nerves [and] vexeth the head'.[53] Once the patient had been so affected, the way was clear for 'deadly diseases, as apoplexies, dropsies, palsies, the gout and many others' to strike.[54]

While too much alcohol could cause sickness, the same was said to be true of not drinking enough wine, ale or beer. As one author noted, many gentlemen believed the saying 'drinke wine & have the gowte, drink none & have the gowte'.[55] Samuel Pepys's physician diagnosed his kidney stones and decay of memory as the result of drinking too much wine (not to mention the copious consumption of ale of various strengths and qualities).[56] After abstaining from wine for several weeks, however, Pepys decided that he needed to drink wine 'upon necessity, being ill for want of it. And I find reason to fear that by my too sudden leaving off wine, I do contract many evils upon myself.'[57] At no point does Pepys mention feeling a need to give up ale or beer. Indeed, warm so-called 'buttered ale' seems to have been both a preventative and remedial cold remedy: 'So home late, and drank some buttered ale, and so to bed and to sleep.'[58] Warm drinks formed part of a larger symbolic system of

---

51 Whitaker, *Tree of Humane Life*, p. 50.
52 L. Lemnius, *The Secret Miracles of Nature* (1658), p. 121.
53 Whitaker, *Tree of Humane Life*, pp. 58–9.
54 H. Peachem, *The Complete Gentleman, The Truth of our Times, and The Art of Living in London* (1622), p. 238.
55 Cogan, *Haven of Health*, p. 4.
56 S. Pepys, *The Diary of Samuel Pepys*, ed. R. Latham and W. Matthews (London: Bell & Hyman, 1970–83), vol. 2, p. 17.
57 Pepys, *Diary*, vol. 3, p. 31.
58 Ibid., p. 275.

balance whereby cold phlegmatic complaints and constitutions were advised to absorb heat while warm choleric constitutions were given special drinks to cool them down.

Wine was considered an excellent tonic, which could maintain a healthy constitution, or 'strengthen the weakest temper'.[59] It was thought to be an extremely nourishing drink, particularly the sweeter varieties.[60] Brewed beverages were widely recognised for their nutritional as well as strengthening qualities. As such alcohol was often used as the core ingredient in a number of different drinks to preserve health. 'Gilly flower wine', for example, was said to be a 'great cordial'. This could be made at home, by combining gillyflowers, sugar candy and amber grease in 'a pottle of Sack'. After about a week or so it could be strained and used.[61]

Although many recipes were for cordials that were meant to protect the body in general, others claimed to be able to prevent specific illnesses, particularly the plague. One remedy contained sage, rue, brier or elder leaves, ginger and hot treacle mixed with a quart of white wine.[62] Another, said to be particularly good for preventing 'the danger of infectious air, plague and the pestilence', had a much longer list of ingredients. Based on a gallon and a half of white or rhenish wine, it included either the buds, husks or leaves of walnut, rue, balm, mugwort, celandine, angelica, agrimony, pimpernel and snapdragon.[63] Meanwhile, scurvy (in the seventeenth century a far vaguer and distinctly moralised term) could be prevented or treated with the help of 'purging ales'. These ales would facilitate the useful operation of vomiting but also contained vitamin-rich ingredients such as watercress, brooklime and 'scurvy grass'. The vagueness of 'scurvy' and the disease's association with 'lifestyle' as a whole meant that writers on this topic tended to obscure the distinction between prevention and treatment of a range of associated unhealthy symptoms and practices. The 'spring purge' was advocated as an annual treatment for scurvy, ridding the system of its effects and forestalling the next onset.[64]

---

[59] J. Friedman, *Miracles and the Pulp Press during the English Revolution: The Battle of the Frogs and Fairford's Flies* (London: University College Press, 1993), p. 172, and Whitaker, *Tree of Humane Life*, pp. 51 and 46.

[60] T. Tryon, *Healths grand preservative: or, the Womens best Doctor* (1692), p. 6 and Whitaker, *Tree of Humane Life*, p. 19.

[61] S. Jinner, *An Almanack or Prognostication* (1660), sig. B3v.

[62] G. Blunt, *An Almanack* (1657), sigs B5r and B5v.

[63] J. Shirley, *The Accomplished Ladies Rich Closet of Rarities* (1691), p. 10.

[64] See Cast, 'For Your Health' (forthcoming).

REMEDIAL MEDICINE

When illnesses inevitably struck, writers of popular medical books came to the rescue with advice on remedies. In general, these recommended 'a putting to' or 'a taking away' of excess humours.[65] The purpose of each method was to regain a state of humoral balance within the body. Whether there was a need to lessen certain humours, or perhaps to increase them, depended on the nature of the disease.

The first type of remedial medicine involved the introduction of substances into the body, which were meant to be retained in order to 'comforte . . . the chiefe officiall Members of the Body of Man'.[66] They were thought to be particularly effective when an illness was caused by a humour being 'any less . . . than it ought to be'.[67] Such imbalances could be rectified, it was thought, through a mixture of the proper diet, supplemented by medicinal potions.[68]

The second, and most common form of therapeutic treatment was concerned with 'taking away' or 'expelling' things from the body, such as blood, urine, faeces, mucus and sweat. Bloodletting, or phlebotomy, which comes from the Greek words 'phleps' or vein, and 'tome' or incision, was one of the most common ways to purge.[69] However, compound medications made up of various organic materials were also regularly used to purge the system. According to Tobias Whitaker, wine was one of the most important components in medicinal treatments meant to remove excess humours.[70] It was, in fact, called for in numerous remedies meant to provoke the body into emptying itself of unwanted humours.

Ale or beer and wine-based medicines were used to provoke vomiting or even 'neesing' [sneezing]. Gargarismes, or wine-based gargles, were another method used to clear imbalances in the upper body. An additional medicinal use for wine was to employ it to 'evacuate excrements of the body, or particularly purge bilious matter by urine'.[71]

In home-made remedies, the most common method was to use wine, ale or beer as the base to which other components were added. This generally involved the steeping, or dissolving of various organic and inorganic materials in the liquid. One recipe advised readers to rise early in the spring and drink a draught of wormwood beer before leaving the house.[72] Sarah Jinner's recipe

---

65   R. Allestree, *A New Almanacke and Prognostication* (1640), sig. C5r.
66   Ibid., sig. C5r and J. White, *A New Almanacke* (1651), sig. C2r.
67   D. LeClerc, *The History of Physick, or an Account of the Rise and Progress of the Art* (1699), p. 195.
68   T. Cocke, *Kitchin-Physick: or, Advice to the Poor, By Way of Dialogue* (1676), p. 9.
69   T.E. Crowl, 'Bloodletting in Veterinary Medicine', *Veterinary Heritage*, 1 (1996), p. 15.
70   Whitaker, *Tree of Humane Life*, p. 20.
71   Ibid., p. 27.
72   Nathaniel Culpeper, *Culpeper Revived* (Cambridge, 1698), sig. C4r.

for 'a snail-water for weak children and old people' specified a number of ingredients to be soaked in small beer:

> Take a pottle of Snails, and wash them well, in 2 or 3 Waters, and then in small Beer, bruise them shells and all, then put them into a gallon of Red cows milk Red rose leaves dryed, the whites cut off Rosemary, sweet Marjoram, of each one handful, and so distil them in a cold Still, and let it dry upon pouder or white Sugar candy, in the Receiver, drink of it first and last, and at 4 o'clock in the afternoon. A wine glass full at a time.[73]

Nicholas Culpeper, who was one of the best-known medical writers of his time, listed a number of what he called 'physical wines'.[74] All of these could be made at home from easily obtainable herbs. The patient was advised to 'drink a draught of them every morning'. Wormwood wine, for example, was made by soaking a handful of wormwood in a gallon of wine. Culpeper claimed that this 'helps cold stomachs, breaks wind, helps the wind cholic, strengthens the stomach, kils worms, and helps the green sickness'. Depending on the illness, the same method could be used employing other types of herbs.[75]

Remedies sometimes called for wine to be taken by itself. 'Red wine and claret' were reputed to cure children suffering from worms.[76] Another author suggested that 'a cup of good White-wine taken fasting' would purge choler and offensive humours from the stomach.[77] Presumably, the effects of alcohol on an empty stomach would also help to raise the spirits of the patient! This was, in fact, the aim of many remedies for treating lethargy or melancholia. One author suggested drinking a mixture of lavender, lemon, orange, sweet marjoram, oregano, sage, thyme, sugar and wine.[78] Married women suffering from 'melancholy' could try an infusion of sage, scolopendria, the flowers of borage, blueglose, roses and the roots of elencampe in wine.[79]

Wine was also 'good to recover your strength' after an illness.[80] One author suggested that the best way to 'restore the blood again' was to 'Take halfe a pinte of Muskadell, and a peniworth of sallet oyle, and put them together and drinke it in the morninge, and walke an houre after.'[81] If the patient had no appetite, simply drinking a pint of good wine would 'make thee have a

73 Jinner, *An Almanack* (1660), sig. B4r.
74 A. Johns, *The Nature of the Book: Print and Knowledge in the Making* (Chicago: University of Chicago Press, 1998), p. 228, and W.J. Bell, Jr, 'Medical Practice in Colonial America', *Bulletin of the History of Medicine*, 5 (1957), 447.
75 N. Culpeper, *Culpeper's Complete Herbal* (1653, reprint London: Wordsworth, 1995), pp. 414–15.
76 S. Rider, *Riders British Merlin* (1686), sig. 4r.
77 R. Saunders, *Apollo Anglicanus* (1656), sig. C4r.
78 W. Salmon, *The London Almanack* (1700), sig. A7r.
79 W. Sermon, *Select Physical and Chyrurgical Observations* (1687), p. 16.
80 A. Cowley, *The Cutter of Coleman Street* (1693), p. 12.
81 Anon., *The Widowes treasure* (1588), sig. C4r.

Stomach as sharp as the keenest Knife or Razour'.[82] When one was in a 'weak languishing state', it was important to consume 'Nourishing Meats and Drinks', including wines such as sack, malago or tent.[83] This was also thought to stimulate the action of the heart, thereby helping to hasten recovery.[84]

As many seventeenth-century medical texts make clear, however, readers needed to understand that what might be a 'fit' drink for treating one illness, might not be for another. All food and drink shared the characteristics of heat, cold, moisture and dryness with human beings.[85] This meant that the suitability of wine varied according to its own qualities, as well as the time of the year and the constitution of each individual.

To restore health, the patient was encouraged to consume food and drink with contrary qualities to their own complexion.[86] Wine was considered to be a 'hot food', which would heat and dry out human bodies.[87] As such, it was a particularly effective medicine for treating those of a cold, damp, phlegmatic nature.[88] People with a choleric constitution, who were already 'hot and dry' by nature, were warned to stay away from wine altogether.[89] As one writer explained, in the summertime,

> The natural heat is now dispersed abroad unto the outward parts of the body, and man is now not so hot within as in Winter . . . Yet are the smallest and coolest drinks most fitting for our health.[90]

CONCLUSION

The brief survey of the medicinal uses of alcohol in this chapter can only provide a starting point for further research on this topic. Nevertheless, it illustrates the many ways in which wine, beer and ale were consumed with the aim of preserving health, as well as in treating illnesses. It has also touched on the important societal and cultural roles played by drink in early modern England.

In the decades following the Restoration, traditional arguments regarding healthy drinking choices were reconfigured. Most significantly, we do not seem to find the same antagonistic relationship between beer and ale. The

82 Poor Robin, *Poor Robin's Almanack* (1680), sig. B5r.
83 Physiologus, *The Good Housewife made a Doctor* (n.d.), p. 5.
84 C. Wilson, *Food and Drink in Britain: From Stone Age to Recent Times* (London: Penguin, 1976), p. 363.
85 J. O'Hara-May, 'Food or Medicines?', *Transactions of the British Society for the History of Pharmacy*, 1 (1971), 65.
86 N. Siraisi, *The Clock and the Mirror: Girolamo Cardano and Renaissance Medicine* (Princeton: Princeton University Press, 1997), p. 72.
87 L. Mascall, *The Government of Cattel* (1662), pp. 303–4.
88 Whitaker, *Tree of Humane Life*, p. 26.
89 Dove, *Speculum Anni* (Cambridge, 1678), sig. C3r.
90 R. Healey, *A New Almanack and Prognostication* (1655), sig. B4r.

terms remain distinct, however, and, outside the metropolis, campaigns for real ale celebrate local traditions and achievements.

In the poem *A Tale of Bacchus Forsaking Wine in Favour of English Ale*, a Yorkshire representative at the court of the god Bacchus declares that, having tried every tipple under the sun, Ale, specifically Yorkshire Ale, carries the prize. According to this poem, there is absolutely nothing that Ale cannot accomplish. It is both medicine and intoxicant, life preserving and life affirming. The antagonism in this poem in not between ale and beer but ale and wine.

> It's pleasant to the Taste, strong and mellow,
> He that affects it not is no boon Fellow.
> He that in this drink doth let his Senses swim,
> There's neither wind nor storms will pierce on him.
> It warms in Winter, in Summer opes the Pores,
> 'Twil make a Sovereign Salve 'gainst cuts & sores
> It ripens Wit, exhillerates the Mind,
> Makes friends of foes, & foes of friends full kind:
> It's Physical for old Men, warms their Blood,
> Its Spirits makes the Coward's courage good:
> The Tatter'd Beggar being warm'd with Ale,
> Nor Rain, Hail, Frost, nor Snow can him Assail.
> He's a good man with him can then compare,
> It makes a Prentise great as the Lord Mayor:
> The Labouring Man, that toiles all day full fore,
> A Pot of Ale at Night, doth him Restore,
> And makes him all his Toil and paines forget,
> And for another day-work, hee's then fit.[91]

Following a fact-finding trip to Madame Bradley's Ale house in Northallerton, Bacchus first makes Madame Bradley countess of Stingo, and then forswears wine altogether, declaring that he will move to England and drink nothing but ale.[92]

It is a testimony to improved communications that by the end of the seventeenth century such a defiantly local drink could aspire to national celebrity. By the turn of the century, it has been argued by the historian Peter Mathias, pale ale brewers prospered in London 'supposedly on the increasing influx of gentry from the counties who brought better palates and bigger purses to city inns'.[93] At the same time common brewers increased in numbers in provincial towns, and with improved navigation on the Trent more and more highly prized ales, such as Nottingham or Darby ale, found their way to the city, as an imagined contest between claret and 'Darby' ale shows (although in this case

---

91 *The Praise of Yorkshire Ale, Wherein is enumerated several Sorts of Drinks, with a Discription of the Humors of most sorts of Drunkards* (York, 1685), pp. 4–5.
92 Interestingly, all the north Yorkshire alehouses celebrated in the poem are run by women.
93 P. Mathias, *The brewing industry in England 1700–1830* (Cambridge: Cambridge University Press, 1959), p. 6.

the claret seems to ultimately win out). In the 1691 *A Dialogue between Claret and Darby-Ale, A Poem. Considered in an accidental Conversation between two Gentlemen,* a countryman arrives in London hoping to enjoy a glass of claret with his metropolitan acquaintance, only to discover that his City friend prefers country beer.

> 1st Gent. Truly my ordinary Liquor is the product of our own country, good nappy well-brew'd Ale; but when I would regale my Sense, and treat my Palate, 'tis generally with a Pint or two of Nottingham or Darby.[94]

At the same time, this dialogue stages an interesting reversal, with the countryman singing the praises of claret, and the city man arguing for the supremacy of ale. As we have discussed, this division between the grape and the grain and the city versus the country dates back to at least the early part of the seventeenth century. The fact that this opposition can be reversed would tend to indicate the widespread availability of ale, beer and wine in both rural and urban settings.

The American sociologist and alcohologist Seldon Bacon in the early 1940s argued that drink fulfils a magical multi-faceted role in so-called 'primitive' societies, and a straightforward, comparatively marginal role in so-called 'modern' societies.[95] Renouncing such naïve developmentalism, we find the early modern period of beer and ale drinking, from the invasion of hops to the triumph of mass-produced porter, fascinating in terms of the various claims that are being made for this ubiquitous drinking experience. Ale and beer compete throughout the seventeenth century to claim the title of healthier drink, as well as competing with wine and (to a much lesser extent) water. It is important to note, however, that terms such as 'medicine', 'intoxicant' and 'social lubricant' lose something of their clarity in the context of a holistic 'humours'-based medical philosophy. Given that the mind and the body act on one another, the distinctions between 'life preserving', 'life affirming' and 'cheering' are hard to define.

Ultimately, the celebration of drink defies any narrowly medicinal justification while broadening access to the science of healthcare. A rich variety of drink-related texts in early modern England enabled more people than ever before to manage their liquid diet in an empoweringly responsible way. Throughout this period, such texts indicate a desire to champion a 'national drink', something that sums up the national character in terms of health and happiness, something that defines the people that consume it and makes them different – makes them, in short, 'better' people.

---

[94] *A Dialogue between Claret & Darby-Ale, A Poem. Considered in an accidental Conversation between two Gentlemen* (1692 [1691]). A contemporary reader has scribbled 'A good witty thing' on the title page of the British Library copy.

[95] S.D. Bacon, 'Sociology and the problems of alcohol: Foundations for a sociologic study of drinking behavior', *Quarterly Journal of Studies on Alcohol*, 4(3) (1943), 399–445.

10

Drinking Cider in Paradise:
Science, Improvement, and the Politics of Fruit Trees

VITTORIA DI PALMA

IN 1729, among the pages of Batty Langley's lavish *Pomona: Or the Fruit-Garden Illustrated. Containing Sure Methods for Improving all the Best Kinds of Fruits Now Extant in England,* was published the transcript of a letter entitled 'A Curious Account of the most Valuable Cyder-Fruits of Devonshire'.[1] This letter, written to Langley in 1727 by Hugh Stafford of Pynes, recounts the story of an apple tree. The tree was a wilding – that is, it grew from seed rather than being the product of grafting – and was to be found near Exeter, in the Parish of St Thomas. The tree came to notice because every other year it produced a large crop of apples, and in one of these years the Rector of the adjoining parish of Whitstone, the Reverend Mr Robert Woolcombe, took a graft of this tree to grow in his nursery. One day in March, a number of years later, 'a Person came there to him on some Business, and finding something roll under his Foot, took it up, and it proved an Apple of this precious Fruit.' Mr Woolcombe, noting that it was 'perfectly sound, after it had lain in the long Grass [. . .] of the Nursery, thro' all the Rain, Frost, and Snow of the foregoing Winter, thought it must be a Fruit of more than common Value'. Tasting it, he found that the juice of this apple 'seem'd to promise both the Body, Roughness, and Flavour that wise Cyder-Drinkers in Devon now begin to desire', and thus decided to cultivate this apple for himself. After the requisite number of years had passed, the grafts had produced enough fruit to make cider, and the resulting drink surpassed all expectations. Mr Woolcombe was so pleased with his discovery that he 'talked of it in all Conversations' and although his enthusiasm 'created Amusement at first, [. . .] when Time produced an Hoghead of it, from Raillery it came to Seriousness, and every one from Laughter fell to

---

[1] 'A Curious Account of the most Valuable Cyder-Fruits of Devonshire', in Batty Langley's *Pomona: Or the Fruit-Garden Illustrated. Containing Sure Methods for Improving all the Best Kinds of Fruits Now Extant in England* (London, 1729), pp. 135–50.

Admiration'. Accordingly, Woolcombe decided to give a name to honor the source of 'his British Wine', and since the original tree was wild, not grafted, 'he retained the name of Wilding; and, as he thought it superior to all others, so he gave a Title of Sovereignty to it; and hence the triumphant Royal Wilding.' The fruit formerly known as the Red-Hill Crab (the name deriving from the location of the original tree) became, through this act of baptism, an apple of note, a dignified crop. Illustrated in Langley's *Pomona*, the Royal Wilding became the pride of Devon, producing cider of such fine quality that it was held to be the finest cider fruit in all England. Crucial to this change in ascribed value was the act of naming. Stafford inveighed against those who might dare continue to call this apple by its former appellation, arguing that 'this name is injurious, because Crab (as yet) is used among us in a Sense of Diminution, at least, if not of Reproach'. Crabs were not only uncultivated, but thoroughly unappreciated, 'formerly suffer'd to fall and be eaten by the Hogs, when they would eat them, (which was not always because of their Harshness) or else to rot upon the Ground'.[2] The same fruit by a different name was not the same fruit at all.

A few years later, however, a contender arose to challenge the supremacy of the Royal Wilding. Stafford, experimenting in his orchard with growing apples from seed, found that, by 1724, some trees had borne enough fruit to make a quantity of cider. This cider, when distilled, 'ravish'd the Palm from the Royal Wilding. It had every one of the Qualities of that Cyder, and some of them to greater and manifest Degrees of Excellency; the Flavour of it in particular was finer and more delicate.' And, following the now established tradition, it was deemed necessary to name this hitherto unknown fruit:

> A Gentleman consulted on the important Occasion (was well acquainted with Mr. Woolcombe before-mention'd) had many Times, to promote Conversations, rallied him on the Subject of his new Discovery of the Royal Wilding, (of which, however, he was a great Admirer) and was now resolv'd to exceed him in the Name of this very Apple, and to leave no Room for him to go higher, should he find out any other Apple, or should he be minded to alter and raise the Appellation of the Royal Wilding.[3]

Thus, when asked to devise a suitable name, he

> first thought of Imperial Wilding; but finding Room yet left for Mr. Woolcombe, he proceeded to think of Celestial Wilding; and because he thought there might be yet an Ope left for Mr. Woolcombe to exceed that, he at last settled on Super-celestial, [. . .] and there rested secure.[4]

Stafford, in the spirit of friendly rivalry, was naturally highly pleased with this

---

[2] Ibid., pp. 139, 140.
[3] Ibid., p. 147.
[4] Ibid.

mark of general approbation, and made sure that his own apple was likewise illustrated in Langley's tome. And although 'Super-celestial Wilding' was by no means a modest name, Stafford did not feel that it was unmerited, asserting to Langley

> Nor are you to be surpriz'd if you think this Title set it above the celebrated Nectar which was in those upper Regions formerly drank by the Gods them-selves: for besides that, if the Truth was known, I am satisfied none of them ever drank a Drop of such Liquor in their lives,

making sure to add, however, that these were, of course, 'Heathen Gods, and therefore we did not make the least Scruple to affront them'.[5]

By the time this 'Curious Account' was published in Langley's *Pomona*, cider was more the stuff of amusing anecdotes than passionate pronounce-ments. However, the themes embedded in this letter – the adoption of a foundling, the act of naming as legitimation, and the link between cider and paradise – move the tenor of Stafford's narrative from report to fable, and reflect deep roots in an earlier period when cider had indeed been the focus of serious discourse and debate.

In the hopes of promoting a source of wine that would free England from a dependency on imports of canary, sack, and other foreign products, from the 1650s through the 1670s numerous tracts were published encouraging the widespread planting of orchards and the making of cider, perry, and other fruit wines.[6] The beginnings of these efforts are inextricably associated with the figure of Samuel Hartlib – the Protestant educational, agricultural, and religious reformer. The center of a wide circle of correspondents, Hartlib acted as a facilitator and publicizer, sharing and printing the activities and investiga-tions of a number of individuals who might otherwise have continued to work in isolation. In addition to circulating manuscripts among his many corre-spondents, he also rushed these missives into print, helping to generate an even wider dissemination of inventions and ideas. And in 1650, after more than ten years of publishing on spiritual, political, and educational matters, Hartlib turned his attention to agriculture. Of the numerous tracts relating to cultivation and the exploitation of natural resources published in the twelve years before his death, most famous was *Samuel Hartlib his Legacie*.[7] The *Legacie*, like most of Hartlib's publications, was a compendium of letters

---

5   Ibid.
6   Directions for making perry, cherry wine or damson wine were often subsumed in discussions of cider, the processes being understood as analogous, if not identical. Certainly many more pages were devoted to cider than to any other fruit-tree wine, and my chapter will follow this convention. The contemporaneous, if less successful movement to encourage vineyards and winemaking by such works as John Rose's *The English Vineyard Vindicated* could also be the subject of a very interesting discussion, but this lies beyond the scope of mine.
7   Samuel Hartlib, *Samuel Hartlib his Legacie: or An Enlargement of the Discourse of Husbandry used in Brabant and Flanders: wherein are bequeathed to the Common-Wealth of England more*

written by various authors, the longest and most influential of these being 'A Large letter concerning the Defects and Remedies of English Husbandry written to Samuel Hartlib' by Sir Richard Child. More an outline of subjects needing investigation than a series of directions or rules, Child's letter mapped the state of English agriculture and demonstrated how it could be improved by identifying twenty-two 'deficiencies': number five addressed the lack of orchard and fruit tree cultivation; number six the making of cider and perry.

With the publication of Child's letter, fruit tree cultivation and the production of fruit wines became central to the advancement of English husbandry. In the 1650s, Child's letter acted as a spur to other publications by members of Hartlib's circle; in the 1660s it was used as a blueprint for early scientific efforts to describe, understand, and exploit the English landscape by Fellows of the Royal Society. And although orchards and cider had only formed a small part of Child's enterprise, they soon became the subjects of a plethora of specialized publications, recognizable components of the seventeenth-century discourse of improvement.[8]

The books on fruit trees and cider of the 1650s all proclaim their links with Hartlib. Hartlib himself published an anonymous letter as *A Designe for Plentie, By an Universall Planting of Fruit-Trees* in 1652, and he encouraged Ralph Austen to put his knowledge and experience of orchards into print. *A Dialogue, or Familiar Discourse, and conference betweene the Husbandman, and Fruit-trees* appeared in 1651; *A Treatise of Fruit-Trees, Shewing The manner of Grafting, Planting, Pruning, and Ordering of them,* was published with *The*

Outlandish and Domestick Experiments and Secrets in reference of Universall Husbandry (London, 1651).

[8] The following list, arranged in chronological order, does not include all seventeenth-century texts that discuss orchards, but favors those that also treat cider: William Lawson, *A New Orchard and Garden* (London, 1618); John Parkinson, *Paradisi in Sole Paradisus Terrestris* (London, 1629); Samuel Hartlib, *A Designe for Plentie, By an Universall Planting of Fruit-Trees: Tendred by some Wel-wishers to the Publick* (London, n.d. [1652]; Ralph Austen, *A Dialogue, or Familiar Discourse, and conference betweene the Husbandman, and Fruit-trees* (Oxford, 1651) and *A Treatise of Fruit-Trees, Shewing The manner of Grafting, Planting, Pruning, and Ordering of them in all respects, according to new and easy Rules of Experience* (Oxford, 1653); John Beale, *Herefordshire Orchards* [written 1656] (Dublin, 1724); Ralph Austen, *Observations on some part of Sr. Francis Bacon's naturall history as it concernes, fruit-trees, fruits, and flowers: especially the fifth, sixth, and seaventh centuries* (Oxford, 1658); John Evelyn et al., *Pomona, or an Appendix Concerning Fruit-Trees, In relation to Cider* (London, 1664), contained in Evelyn's *Sylva, Or a Discourse of Forest-Trees, and the Propagation of Timber in His Majesties Dominions* (London, 1664); John Worlidge, *Vinetum Britannicum: Or A Treatise of Cider, And such other Wines and Drinks that are extracted from all manner of Fruits Growing in this Kingdom. Together with the Method of Propagating all sorts of Vinous Fruit-Trees. And a Description of the new-invented Ingenio or Mill, For the more expeditious and better making of Cider. And also the right Method of making Metheglin and Birch-Wine* (London, 1676); Moses Cook, *The Manner of Raising, Ordering, and Improving Forest and Fruit Trees* (London, 1676); John Beale and Anthony Lawrence, *Nurseries, Orchards, Profitable Gardens and Vineyards Encouraged* (London, 1677).

Spirituall Use of an Orchard in 1653; and 1658 saw *Observations on some part of Sr. Francis Bacon's naturall history as it concernes, fruit-trees, fruits, and flowers.* Hartlib used the preface of *A Designe for Plentie* to advertise Austen's forth-coming *A Treatise of Fruit-Trees,* and Austen subsequently dedicated his book to Hartlib.[9]

Also part of Hartlib's circle was John Beale, whose *Herefordshire Orchards* was written as a letter to Hartlib in 1656. It was through Hartlib that Beale was introduced to John Evelyn; the two men were to become great correspondents and almost kindred souls in their mutual enthusiasm for gardening and husbandry. And in this way the issue of cider passed, after Hartlib's death and with the institution of the Royal Society, into the orbit of early modern science. A number of articles in the Society's *Philosophical Transactions* were dedicated to methods for producing cider, and fruit tree planting was established as part of the agenda pursued by the Society's Georgical or Agricultural Committee, instituted in 1664.[10] Notable too was Ralph Austen's decision, in 1665, to rededicate his *Treatise of Fruit-Trees* to Royal Society Fellow Robert Boyle. His new dedicatory address lays stress on such Royal Society tenets as experience, experimentation, the use of plain language, the sharing of what had been closely guarded secrets. And – also in keeping with Royal Society dogma – the spiritual reform so central to Hartlib's concerns was downplayed. As an ecumenical and nonsectarian association, the Royal Society was wary of promoting a radical Protestant agenda. And Austen, clearly aware of the new parameters under which his treatise was appearing, not only claimed that his work would serve to increase the king's revenues, but that it was 'worthy the most serious Considerations and Endeavours of the Royal Society' because it was, in fact, 'a Royall Work'.[11]

But it was undoubtedly Evelyn's *Sylva, Or a Discourse of Forest-Trees, and the Propagation of Timber in His Majesties Dominions* that most effectively brought the issue of cider to a wide audience.[12] *Sylva,* although commissioned

---

9 'I am the more willing to divulge this brief Trace upon this Subject, because it will serve as a fore-runner to a larger Volume of Fruit-trees, which an experienced friend of mine, Mr. *Ralph Austin* hath in readinesse to put forth at *Oxford* [. . .] which now he is putting to the Presse, as by his own Letter written in November last 1652 he doth informe me: therefore I intend in this Preface and by this Treatise, as by a small taste of so good a matter, both to raise thine appetite and quicken thy desire to see that larger Work, and to stay thy stomack a little till it come forth [. . .].' Hartlib, *A Designe for Plentie.*

10 The minutes of the Georgical Committee meetings are in the Royal Society Archive, Domestic Manuscripts, vol. 5, nos 63, 64, and 65. For more on the Georgical Committee's activities, see Reginald Lennard, 'English Agriculture under Charles II: The Evidence of the Royal Society's "Enquiries" ', *The Economic History Review,* 4 (1932–4), 23–45, and Michael Hunter, *Establishing the New Science: The Experience of the Early Royal Society* (Woodbridge: Boydell Press, 1989), p. 86, nn. 37–40.

11 Austen, *A Treatise of Fruit-Trees,* 3rd edn (Oxford, 1665), n.p.

12 Evelyn also produced a number of translations of French works on orchards and fruit trees: *The Manner of Ordering Fruit-Trees,* by Le Gendre, in 1660; *The French Gardiner Instructing*

by the Officers of the Navy to encourage timber tree planting, included *Pomona, or an Appendix Concerning Fruit-Trees, in relation to Cider.*[13] Following the compositional structure used by Hartlib, it was a compendium of a number of short pieces by various contributors. Repeating information and at times even contradicting each other, they formed nothing like a coherent whole.[14] Evelyn, acknowledging this cacophonous character, explained that although 'some of the following Discourses seem less constant, or (upon occasion) repugnant to one another, they are to be consider'd as relating to the several gusts, and guizes of persons and Countries, and not to be looked upon as recommended Secrets'.[15] With *Pomona*, Evelyn sought to amass knowledge of regional, local, and variable practices; the overarching goals, in line with broader Royal Society aims, were to disseminate information, promote cultivation, and encourage experimentation.

Evelyn's *Sylva* established tree planting as a central component of land improvement, and its concerns were taken up by a host of later books on gardening. Moses Cook's *The Manner of Raising, Ordering, and Improving Forest and Fruit Trees* of 1676 acknowledged its inspiration from Evelyn, and included a long section on cider. In the same year John Worldige's *Vinetum Britannicum, or a Treatise of Cider* appeared, and in 1677 John Beale and Anthony Lawrence published *Nurseries, Orchards, Profitable Gardens and Vineyards Encouraged*. The influence of Evelyn's text was still to be felt in the following century, although treatises such as John Lawrence's *The Clergyman's Recreation* of 1715, Richard Bradley's *New Improvements in Planting and Gardening* of 1717, and Stephen Switzer's *Ichnographia Rustica* of 1718 evidenced more interest in orchards and espaliered fruit trees than in cider *per se*. Batty Langley's *Pomona* of 1729 – notwithstanding Stafford's letter – was in essence a very different kind of book: a luxurious folio volume of directions for raising apple trees with a large section of lavish plates illustrating varieties of apples. Although cider continued to be produced and consumed during the eighteenth century, its reign as an intoxicating subject was over.

In common with most seventeenth century husbandry manuals, these

---

How to Cultivate all sorts of Fruit-Trees, and Herbs for the Garden, by de Bonnefons, in 1669; Rene Rapin's *Of Gardens* in 1673; and De La Quintinye's *The Compleat Gard'ner; Or, Directions for Cultivating and Right Ordering of Fruit-Gardens and Kitchen-Gardens*, in 1693. However, none has any substantial discussion of cider.

13 It also contained the *Kalendarium Hortense*. As *Sylva* went through numerous editions over the years until Evelyn's death, it became the repository for various fragments of his writings on gardens that were originally intended to form his great unfinished work on gardening, the Elysium Britannicum. A transcript of this vast manuscript has recently been published as *Elysium Britannicum or The Royal Gardens*, ed. John E. Ingram (Philadelphia: University of Pennsylvania Press, 2001).

14 In addition to Evelyn's contribution, *Pomona* included Beale's 'Aphorisms concerning Cider'; Sir Paul Neil's 'Discourse of Cider'; John Newburgh's 'Observations Concerning the Making and Preserving of Cider'; Doctor Smith's 'Concerning Cider' and Captain Taylor's 'Of Cider'.

15 Evelyn, 'Animadversions', *Pomona*, n.p. (located between pp. 20 and 21).

works on cider emphasized practical application, and were made up, for the most part, of detailed directions for cultivating fruit trees and making cider. These recommendations – perhaps unsurprisingly – varied widely, according to the region, its particular crops, local habits of brewing, the predominance of an oral tradition, individual taste, and because the making of cider was apparently a delicate business: cider could be too sour, too sweet, full of particles, slimy and stringy,[16] off-colored, bitter, or rotten. Despite individual differences, however, most writers agreed that making cider required a six-step process: picking, resting, grinding, pressing, fermenting, and bottling.[17]

To begin with, a great quantity of apples was needed – it took between 18 and 24 bushels of apples to produce one hogshead of cider – and this fruit needed to be fully ripe.[18] According to Moses Cook, 'if you find the Kernels Brown, or the Seed rattle in the Apple, as in some they will or if you see them begin to fall much in still weather; or if you find them to handle like a drye piece of wood, sounding in your hand as you toss them up; then you may go to gathering as fast as you please [. . .]'.[19] While gathering, great care had to be taken to ensure that the fruit did not bruise, for a single bruise led inevitably to rot, and one rotten apple could spoil the entire harvest, making the fruit useless for cider. Some writers were so cautious they counselled picking each apple by hand and laying it in a basket cushioned with wool fabric; others, perhaps more aware of the enormous amount of time such a procedure would take, gave their readers permission to shake the fruit down from the tree, provided that the ground beneath was well cushioned by woollen blankets lying upon layers of barley straw.[20]

After the harvest, the apples were left to rest.[21] According to Beale, cider apples 'require full maturity, which is best known by their natural fragrancy; and then also, as ripe Grapes require a few mellowing days, so do all Apples'.[22] During this time it was essential that rot be prevented. All leaves and other

---

[16] Guards against 'roapy' cider and perry were frequently mentioned by writers. This was a condition that affected many drinks in the age before pasteurization: ale often became ropy, as did milk.

[17] This summary is based on the directions found in the following texts (see n. 8 above for full references): Austen, *A Treatise of Fruit-Trees*; Beale, *Herefordshire Orchards*; Beale and Lawrence, *Nurseries, Orchards, Profitable Gardens and Vineyards Encouraged*; Cook, *The Manner of Raising, Ordering, and Improving Forest and Fruit Trees* (1679); Evelyn, *Pomona*, contained in *Sylva, Or a Discourse of Forest-Trees*; Parkinson, *Paradisi in Sole Paradisus Terrestris*. Exceptions will be noted individually.

[18] Cook, *The Manner*, p. 200. Taylor recommends 20–22 bushels in his 'Of Cider', *Pomona*, p. 48.

[19] Cook, *The Manner*, p. 200.

[20] Hand picking is recommended by Austen in *A Treatise of Fruit-Trees*, p. 151; shaking by Cook, *The Manner*, p. 200.

[21] Dr Smith says they should be ground immediately and not hoarded: see his 'Concerning Cider', *Pomona*, p. 46.

[22] Beale, 'Aphorisms', *Pomona*, p. 23. Newburgh, however, thinks that adding some rotten apples assists fermentation and produces a clearer cider. 'Observations', *Pomona*, p. 43.

Fig. 10.1: An apple press and, in the background, hedgerows planted with fruit trees. Frontispiece, J.W. Gent, *The Second Part of Systima Agricuturæ, or yᵉ Mistery of Husbandry & Vinetum Britanicum or Treatise of Cider, &ct.* (1689). By permission of The British Library, BL 1490.s.21.

extraneous matter were to be removed, and although most writers assumed that the apples would lie in piles, they also cautioned of the potential for bruising, 'which soon turns to rottenness; and better sound from the Tree then rotten from the heap'.[23] In order to insulate the fruit from any damp, clay or earth floors would be covered with straw, reeds, or boards.[24] The apples would then lie for a week to ten days if they were ripe when gathered, three weeks to a month if they were winter fruit or very green.[25] When the apples began to sweat it was time to press.

Extracting juice from the fruit could be accomplished in a number of ways: 'Some have cider-Mills on purpose, wherein they grind the Apples, as Tanners do their bark, and then bring them to the Press; others Pownd them in Troughs, till they be small; it comes all to one' (see Fig. 10.1).[26] Improvements to cider mills continued throughout the century, and writers such as Beale and Worlidge used their texts to publicize new machines. Beale wrote that he 'saw a Mill in Somersetshire which grinds half a Hogshead at a grist, and so much the better ground for the frequent rolling',[27] while Worlidge used the title page of the second edition of his *Vinetum Britannicum* to publicize a 'New-Invented Ingenio or Mill, for the more expeditious making of Cider' (see Fig. 10.2).[28] After standing overnight, the ground-up apples were pressed, and the resulting juice was immediately put into barrels, clean and specially prepared for fermentation (see Fig. 10.3).[29]

Fermentation seems to have been a somewhat mysterious process.[30] Disagreements are evident in the texts between those writers who recommended that barrels have a vent hole, and those who feared that allowing air into and out of the barrel impeded fermentation. Beale's instructions for this stage of the process exude a sense of urgency: 'Soon after grinding it should be prest, and immediately be put into the Vessel, that it may ferment before the spirits be dissipated; and then also in fermenting time the Vent-hole should not be so wide as to allow a prodigal waste of the spirits; and as soon as the ferment begins to allay, the Vessels should be filled of the same, and well stopped.'[31] The liquor was to stay in the barrels until fermentation was complete, something that often occurred around the end of March.[32] Finally, 'When Cider is setl'd, and altogether, or almost clarifi'd, then to make it

---

23 Beale, 'Aphorisms', *Pomona*, p. 23.

24 Newburgh, 'Observations'; Taylor, 'Of Cider', *Pomona*, pp. 41, 48.

25 Cook, *The Manner*, p. 201.

26 See Austen, *A Treatise of Fruit-Trees*, p. 145.

27 Beale, 'Aphorisms', *Pomona*, p. 23.

28 Worlidge, *Vinetum Britannicum: Or A Treatise of Cider*.

29 On barrels, see Newburgh, *Pomona*, p. 42, and Taylor, who includes an image, *Pomona*, p. 49.

30 Thomas Willis's *De fermentatione* (London, 1660), is mentioned by Sir Paul Neile as a source of information.

31 Beale, 'Aphorisms', *Pomona*, p. 23.

32 Ibid., p. 24; Smith, 'Concerning Cider', *Pomona*, p. 46; Neile says the beginning of April, 'Discourse', *Pomona*, p. 38.

Fig. 10.2: Technical advances in cider making. Frontispiece, John Worlidge, *Vinetum Britannicum: Or A Treatise of Cider, And such other Wines and Drinks that are extracted from all manner of Fruits Growing in this Kingdom* (2nd edn, 1678). By permission of The British Library, BL Eve.a.47.

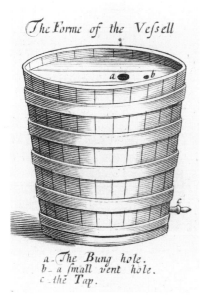

Fig. 10.3: A barrel. John Worlidge, *Vinetum Britannicum: Or A Treatise of Cider, And such other Wines and Drinks that are extracted from all manner of Fruits Growing in this Kingdom* (2nd edn, 1678), p. 100. By permission of The British Library, BL Eve.a.47.

spriteful and winy, it should be drawn into well cork'd and well bound bottles,'[33] and various ingredients could be added to improve the taste. A bit of sugar (lump sugar was preferred to loose, as the latter tended to be 'sophisticated with Lime, Allome, and other things'[34]) or a few raisins could mitigate any tendency toward asperity,[35] while other recommendations included juniper, ginger, rosemary, bay, wheat, eggs, figs, mustard, syrup of raspberries, or even rotten apples.[36] Finally, 'the liquor being thus well Botled, may be kept in several places, either in Gravel or Sand, in a Celler up to the neck, and some may be sunk down into water, in some secure, convenient place; or otherwise to keep them cool, and exclude the Aire, especially in the heat of Sommer'.[37] Made, bottled, and stored, the cider could last for a variable amount of time, but most writers agreed that it should be consumed within the year.

The types of apples and pears recommended for cider varied by region and by period, but in general, the harder, sourer, and, in general, more unpleasant to eat the fruit was, the better it tended to be for making drink.[38] As early as

---

[33] Beale, 'Aphorisms', *Pomona*, p. 29; for more on bottling, see Taylor, 'Of Cider', *Pomona*, p. 50.

[34] Austen, *A Treatise of Fruit-Trees*, p. 147.

[35] Cook, *The Manner of Raising*, p. 202; Beale, 'Aphorisms', *Pomona*, p. 24; Neile, 'Discourse', *Pomona*, p. 36.

[36] Beale, 'Aphorisms', *Pomona*, p. 28; Newburgh, 'Observations', *Pomona*, p. 42. Taylor doesn't approve of adding spices, but allows for syrup of raspberries: 'Of Cider', *Pomona*, pp. 50, 47.

[37] Austen, *A Treatise of Fruit-Trees*, p. 147.

[38] This, however, is contradicted by Neile, who explicitly sets out to prove that cider made from eating apples is superior to that made from 'hard apples' or crabs: see his 'Discourse', *Pomona*, p. 31.

1629 the apothecary John Parkinson asserted in his *Paradisi in Sole* that 'it is usually seene that those fruits that are neither fit to eate raw, roasted, nor baked, are fittest for Cider, and make the best'.[39] Likewise, 'the Perry made of Choke Peares, notwithstanding the harshenesse, and evill taste, both of the fruit when it is greene, as also of the iuyce when it is new made, doth yet after a few moneths become as milde and pleasant as new made, and will hardly bee knowne by the sight or taste from it'.[40] This property of wild, bitter fruits to produce good cider and perry was one much commented on in the seventeenth century, as it was thought by some to show 'the goodnesse of God, that hath given such facility to so wilde fruits, altogether thought uselesse, to become useful, and apply the benefit thereof both to the comfort of our soules and bodies'.[41]

However, for Parkinson there was no point in discussing crabs or wild apples at any length because 'Wildings and Crabs are without number or use in our Orchard, being to be had out of the woods, fields, and hedges rather then any where else'.[42] Being wild plants, they were outside the realm of cultivation, and thus had no place in the refined, enclosed space of the orchard. However, as educated men began to turn their attention to fruit tree cultivation, and books on orchards began to multiply, it began to be clear that crab apples were worthy of more considered attention. As with pears, where the hardest and most bitter fruits made the best perry, so too it was confirmed that crab apples and 'wildings' made the best cider. Particular success was had with one type of fruit originally known as the Skidmore Crab, which, sometime in the 1630s or 1640s, was rebaptized the Redstreak or Redstrake Apple.[43] In Austen's curious *A Dialogue, or Familiar Discourse, and conference betweene the Husbandman, and Fruit-trees* – a treatise in the form of a question-and-answer session between the farmer and his trees – when the husbandman asks why the Redstrake Apple, which makes the 'rare Cider of Herefordshire' was formerly known as the Skidmore Crab, the fruit trees answer: 'It's true, we grew, and bore Fruits for many yeares; and our Fruits were called Skidmore Crabs, and were very much undervalued; and in disparagement for many yeares; but when our Natures were considered, and tryed and men had Experience of us, our Fruit was found to be better then any other sort of Fruit for Cider; and now are we every where cryed up, and in great esteeme amongst all men.'[44] By the time of *Pomona*'s publication, the esteem accorded the Redstrake Apple was well established: Beale writes that the use of Redstrakes ''Tis lately spread all

---

[39] Parkinson, *Paradisi*, p. 589.

[40] Ibid., p. 594.

[41] Ibid.

[42] Ibid., p. 588.

[43] This date is an estimate. Parkinson, writing in 1629, clearly has little interest in crab apples, while Austen, in his *A Dialogue, or Familiar Discourse* of 1651, and in his 1653 *A Treatise of Fruit-Trees* speaks about the recent esteem that Redstreak apples have attained.

[44] Austen, *A Dialogue, or Familiar Discourse*, p. 58.

over Herefordshire; and he that computes speedy return, and true Wine, will think of no other Cider-apple, till a better be found';[45] Dr Smith names the 'Red-Strake' as one of the best fruits for cider used in Gloucestershire,[46] and Capt. Taylor writes that cider from pepins and other varieties cannot compare to 'the Cider drawn from the Cider-apple, among which the Red-strakes bear the Bell; a Fruit in it self scarce edible'.[47] And in Worlidge's *Vinetum Britannicum*, the Redstrake's preeminence is proclaimed by the frontispiece, where the illustration of a cider press names the Redstreak as the generic fruit of choice (see Fig. 10.2). From crab to apple, weed to crop, the case of the Skidmore Crab brings up larger issues about attitudes toward wild nature and the reciprocal role of cultivation.[48]

The Skidmore Crab, like the Red-Hill Crab discussed earlier, had no need of a name when it grew wild in hedgerows, so inedible that even pigs would turn their snouts up at it. However, once its use was discovered, it was allowed to enter the space of cultivation and civilization: it became an apple. Its move from wild, useless and unnamed, to useful and domesticated required an act of naming, and this name ensured that it could be recognized and therefore cultivated. The process of domesticating the wild, of using human ingenuity to make fertile or productive what had been seen as barren or useless, illustrated by the case of the Skidmore Crab, introduces what is perhaps the central term of the seventeenth-century discourse of husbandry: improvement.

Improvement was a word whose significance lay on many levels. The ideology of improvement was used both in tracts advocating a general enrichment of the land through husbandry – the conversion of waste lands into fertile fields – and in those whose focus was apple-tree planting and cider.[49] Beginning in 1652 with Hartlib's *A Designe for Plentie*, a multifaceted argument was set forth whose main tenets would be repeated, with little variation, throughout the period's literature on cider, notwithstanding the shift in patronage from the Protestant and parliamentarian Hartlib to the royalist and ecumenical Royal Society. Arguing for the planting of fruit trees of identifiably English provenance – apple, pear, walnut, and quince – the anonymous author proposed that a law be made to encourage their propagation both on privately held lands, and on 'all Wastes and Commons'.[50] The promotion of fruit tree

---

45 Beale, 'Aphorisms', *Pomona*, p. 24.
46 Smith, 'Concerning Cider', *Pomona*, p. 46.
47 Taylor, 'Of Cider', *Pomona*, p. 47.
48 This process is, of course, an earlier parallel to the story of the Royal Wilding. It is perhaps significant that not until the eighteenth century does the wild origin of the tree receive emphasis in the formulation of the new name.
49 Ralph Austen, in his dedicatory address to Samuel Hartlib in *A Treatise of Fruit-Trees*, cites his precursors in Hartlib's publication program, including Blith's *The English Improver Improved*; Child's letter in *Samuel Hartlib his Legacie*, 1651; and the anonymous *A Designe for Plentie* of 1652.
50 Hartlib, *A Designe For Plentie*, p. 6.

planting thus went beyond encouraging landowners to plant orchards in their gardens, but extended to all kinds of land, both cultivated and uncultivated. The proposal called for two types of additional planting: mixing fruit trees with hedgerows in banks and along the edges of fields (see Fig. 10.1), and placing single trees in the middle of arable fields at a considerable distance from one another.[51] Behind this scheme was the ideal of making the waste fruitful, of taking scraps of land commonly thought to be unusable, or uncultivatable – commons, wastes, banks, hedgerows – and making them productive. Fruit trees were particularly suitable for this as they tended not to require very fertile soil to flourish: 'Fat land is not best for Cider fruit, but common arable,'[52] wrote Beale, and others commented on the ability of the pear tree, in particular, to flourish in hard, stony, unpromising ground. This call for the planting of fruit trees outside of the traditional space of the orchard can be seen as part of a larger ongoing process of extending the aesthetic vision formerly reserved for the enclosed spaces of pleasure grounds to the landscape as a whole – making all of England, in effect, into one vast garden. The benefits of this proposal were seen to be manifold.

First, it was argued that this scheme would benefit the poor. Using arguments similar to those used to justify the enclosure of commons, these writers claimed not only that fruit tree planting would provide employment, but also that the fruit produced could serve as food and drink to nourish the destitute.[53] The increase in cider production would, it was argued, lessen the need for other drinks such as ale and beer, and this would mean that that land currently used for the cultivation of barley and hops could be used for wheat instead. Finally, the wood of the fruit trees would provide timber for fuel, and, with the decrease in beer production, more wood could be saved in order to be used for carpentry. The positive effects of fruit tree planting would strengthen the nation, increase its self-sufficiency and economy, and result in greater plenty and a better quality of life for all.

The nationalism of these arguments is pronounced, and appeared in various guises. Apples and pears and their wines were, these authors claim, suitable to the English climate and thus tailored to English constitutions. Arguing that climate and taste went hand in hand, Evelyn wrote that 'we English [are] generally more for insipid, luscious, and gross Diet, then for the spicy, poignant, oylie, and highly relish'd (witness our universal hatred of Oyls, French-wine, or Rhenish without Sugar, our Doating on Currans, Figgs, Plum-pottage, Pies, Pudding, and Cake)', implying that an English constitution should, by rights,

---

[51] Stephen Switzer's *Ichnographia Rustica* of 1718 illustrates the longevity of some of these ideas. Switzer advocated a rural style of gardening that mingled garden and plantation, and his engraving of Paston (an idealization of his work at Grimsthorp) clearly shows individual trees planted in the middle of arable plots.

[52] Beale, 'Aphorisms', *Pomona*, p. 25.

[53] The enclosure movement did not, of course, end up having such unmitigated benefits for the poorest classes as these tracts optimistically envisioned.

be bred on English products.[54] Beale, too, looked forward to the day when 'good Ale, good Beer d'Angleterre, good Cider, and Brandies drawn from English wines, which are all of English growth, and English Manufacturers, shall raise a greater profit, both at home and by exporation, than hath sometimes been gained by our Staple-trade'.[55] The wholesome self-sufficiency that would supposedly result from large-scale cultivation of apple and pear trees would result in England relying less on foreign imports of wines, and perhaps also be able to tip the balance in favor of exports over imports.

The local and rural connotations of cider, however, needed to be combated before the drink could become prized by the nation's gentry. Evelyn aimed to give cider a royal pedigree by stressing 'how much this beverage was esteemed by His late Majesty, and Court',[56] and further attempted to undermine the aristocratic associations of wine by noting that few could bear to drink it without adding sugar or other substances. Punning on the dual connotations of the term sophisticated, he dubbed wine 'the Cheat' and drew attention to the 'Transformations, Transmutations, Adulterations, Basterdizings, Brewings, Trickings, and Compassings of this Sophisticated God'.[57] Not artificial and aristocratic wine, but genuine and natural cider was to be the drink of choice for the nation's landowners.

Given the promotional tenor of these texts, it is hardly surprising that the potential negative effects of cider are barely mentioned. Drunkenness, for example, makes only one appearance, when Beale remonstrates against the difficulty of exporting cider from its place of origin: 'And by defect of transportation, our Store of Cyder is become a Snare to many, who turn God's Blessing into wantonness and drunkenness.'[58] Instead, it is beer, ale, and wine that are targeted as the source of unseemly conduct, with 'the multiplicity of men practicing Brewing, and Malting' characterized as 'rather a bane than a benefit to this Common-wealth; ministring occasion to thousands of blinde and unnecessary Tipling-houses, whereby drunkennesse, disorder, and dangerous plots are fomented and nourished to the great dishonour of God, and disturbance of the State and Commonwealth'.[59] Cider, instead, will provide the 'deliverance of multitudes' from the rapid and perilous sequence of 'Idlenesse, Beggery, Shame, and consequently, Theft, Murther, and (at last) the Gallowes'.[60] The only negative attribute of cider and perry commonly mentioned – discussed by Austen in a chapter entitled 'Windiness of Cider, only at first' – is dismissed as a side effect that soon disappears once one becomes accustomed to drinking fruit-based beverages on a regular

[54] Evelyn, *Pomona*, p. 3.
[55] Beale and Lawrence, *Nurseries, Orchards, Profitable Gardens and Vineyards Encouraged*, p. 18.
[56] Evelyn, *Pomona*, p. 4.
[57] Ibid.
[58] Beale, *Herefordshire Orchards*, p. 16.
[59] Hartlib, *A Designe For Plentie*, p. 15.
[60] Austen, 'Dedication', *A Treatise of Fruit Trees*, n.p.

basis.[61] Instead, what was extolled were cider's health benefits – cider was said to be particularly good for stomach ailments, for promoting long life, and for banishing that English malady, melancholy.

But finally, and most importantly, the issue of improvement had spiritual, as well as material consequences. Austen linked religious and horticultural aims explicitly by employing biblical arguments to justify his promotion of fruit tree cultivation: 'God planted a Fruit-garden; That is, He caused a parcell of ground to bring forth Plants and Trees most exquisite and usefull for man, and enriched that place with more fruit-fulnesse and beauty, then any other part of the Earth, and called it Eden, that is, a place of Pleasures.'[62] And if an orchard was like Eden, so the husbandman was like Adam: God 'saw that a Garden of Fruit-trees was the meetest place upon all the Earth, for Adam to dwell in, even in his state of perfection'[63] and gave to Adam 'in his innocency' the task 'to keepe and order the Garden of Fruit-Trees [. . .] for his greater delight and pleasure: so that his imployment, as it is ancient, so it is honourable'.[64]

However apples, in particular, were also invested with a dubious moral charge. Often identified as the fruit used by Eve to tempt Adam, the apple in these treatises has a rather ambivalent position. The speaking trees of Austen's *Dialogue* state that they 'were present, & stood by, when thou, and thy wife, did both of you, transgresse the Command of our Creator, in the Garden of Eden, in that yee did eate of the Forbidden Fruit',[65] and caution the husbandman that he not take too much pleasure in the sensual delights of an orchard for 'a serpent may be hid even amongst pleasant, and beautiful flowers; the old Serpent is still alive; that bitt, and stung thy first Parents; in the Garden of Eden they setting their minds too much upon the beauty, and excellency of the Fruits that they saw'.[66] Rather than being simply a recitation of Scripture, this parable illuminates what was likewise, for many seventeenth-century writers, a present danger, for, as the trees aver, 'thou maiest be sure he hath not lost any of his Malice, Power, or Policy; but is watchful day, and night, to do thee, and others mischiefe'.[67] Both original fruit and vehicle of original sin; equally the means by which to regain Eden, and bearing responsibility for its loss, the apple was a fruit whose cultivation crystallized a contemporary tension between science and spirituality, an uneasy balance between the need to know, and the mortal temptation to know too much.

And it is in this dual sense that the discourse of improvement attains its most significant implications. By tilling the soil, by taming the wild, by making

---

[61] Ibid. (1665 edn), p. 229.
[62] Ibid., p. 24.
[63] Ibid., p. 22.
[64] Ibid.
[65] Austen, *A Dialogue, or Familiar Discourse*, pp. 2–3.
[66] Ibid., p. 14.
[67] Ibid.

the sterile fertile, humans were following God's decree to Adam and Eve after they were banished from the Garden of Eden. Sent out into a wilderness of weeds and thorns to mix their labor with the soil, the first humans thus provided the pattern for salvation. And in this identification of improvement of the soil with improvement of the soul, apple tree cultivation held a privileged place. If England were to be planted so that it abounded 'with goodly Fruit-trees, and other Profits, where now are barren Wasts: Might it not then be called another Canaan, flowing with Milke and Hony, of which it is recorded, that there were Fruit-trees in abundance'?[68] This vision of 'the waste and wilde places all abounding with fruitfull trees (*like the Garden of God*) keeping their order, and distance: each one offering the weary traveller some little collation to quench his thirst, and refresh his spirits; inviting him to rest under their shadow, and to taste of their delicates, and to spare his purse' (a benefit, the author adds, 'well known in the Western Counties of this our *England*[69]) was that of England as Eden. The widespread cultivation of apple trees would mean, in effect, recreating paradise in England, redeeming the country's sins, and populating it with moral, healthy, and wealthy denizens, drinking cider in their very own Elysium Britannicum. Not merely fit for Adam and Eve, or the heathen gods for that matter, through the discourse of improvement cider was proclaimed the tipple of choice for the English citizen.

[68] Austen, *A Treatise of Fruit Trees* (1657 edn), dedication, n.p.
[69] Ibid., p. 9.

Excess

11

A Natural Drink for an English Man:
National Stereotyping in Early Modern Culture

CHARLOTTE McBRIDE

THE practical difficulties of eating and drinking on stage are well known to any actor, and so it is not surprising that there are relatively few occasions in early modern drama when a character is required to carouse or to tuck in. An association with drink or food, however, does emerge in the plays of the period as a technique of characterisation, and close consideration of some of these attributions reveals not just an equation between excessive consumption and lack of moral control but also some links between certain beverages and foods as specific stereotypes of national identity. John Fletcher's play *The Pilgrim* (1621) is set in Spain, and the 'Persons Represented in the Play' are nominally Spanish.[1] There is, however, one exception. For the man who enters with the rousing cry, 'Give me some drink', identification is immediate: 'O, there's the Englishman' agree those already on the stage (3.7.16). The comic timing emphasises the rueful recognition by a London audience in the early seventeenth century that the Englishman abroad is characterised by his consumption of alcohol. Not only that: it at once becomes clear that only a particular drink will do. Before the Englishman's entrance there has been talk of 'Aquavite', but his thirst is for something heartier:

> Fill me a thousand pots, and froth 'em, froth 'em.   (3.7.17)

The Englishman's drink is evidently the foaming tankard of beer. Beneath the comedy lie notions about national stereotyping and, I suggest in this chapter, a political discourse that casts excessive consumption of beer as a threat to the social well-being of the English nation state.

The characterisation of the Englishman as a beer-drinker reflects a growing sense of national identity and racial stereotyping. A brief history of the

---

[1] John Fletcher, *The Pilgrim*, in *The Dramatic Works in the Beaumont and Fletcher Canon*, ed. Cyrus Hoy (Cambridge: Cambridge University Press, 1985), 10 vols, vol. 6, pp. 111–224.

production and consumption of beer in England reveals a shift during the sixteenth century from perceptions of beer as a new and foreign product to its status as the defining English drink.

The commonplace drink in medieval England had been ale, a brew of fermented malt, water and spices. In a society without reliable access to safe, clean water (which was becoming increasingly polluted as the urban population increased), ale offered the health advantages of filtration, but its instability and poor keeping qualities necessitated frequent production in small quantities. On the other hand, ale-making required little specialised equipment or capital outlay; it therefore constituted an ideal domestic product and, as Judith Bennett has established in her study of women's involvement in the brewing trade, the making of ale was principally regarded as women's work.[2] Beer, produced from fermented malt, water and hops, had been made in continental Europe since at least the eleventh century and imported into England since at least 1400. As Peter Clark observes in his social history of the alehouse, beer was a more appealing product than ale, being more alcoholic but no more expensive.[3] Its bitterness compared with ale might have been a taste acquired by medieval English soldiers on campaign in Europe.[4] By the beginning of the sixteenth century, beer was being brewed in England.

The brewing of beer lent itself to commercial enterprise, as it requires considerable capital expenditure on equipment, is well-suited to mass production and can be stored and transported without spoiling. Although great households had the resources to switch domestic production over to beer-brewing, for most drinkers beer was only available commercially in alehouses.[5] Early seventeenth-century England saw the emergence of two distinct drinking cultures: a home-based, home-brewed activity for women in their newly defined role as homemakers, and a public activity for men to strengthen their social and economic bonds. As the manufacture of beer threatened the livelihood of the small-scale ale-producers, opposition began to coalesce around perceptions of beer as a foreign product destroying a staple of English culture, and ale began to be invested with notions of tradition, which can perhaps still be observed today in the tendency of multinational breweries

---

[2] Judith M. Bennett, *Ale, Beer, and Brewsters in England: Women's Work in a Changing World, 1300–1600* (New York & Oxford: Oxford University Press, 1996), pp. 3–13.

[3] Peter Clark, 'The Alehouse and the Alternative Society', in *Puritans and Revolutionaries. Essays in Seventeenth-Century History presented to Christopher Hill*, ed. Donald Pennington and Keith Thomas (Oxford: Clarendon Press, 1978), pp. 47–72, p. 51. The advantages of seething the wort with hops are that the beer produced 'although more bitter [than ale] to the taste, drew more alcoholic content from less grain, carried much more easily, and lasted longer' (Bennett, *Brewsters*, p. 79). 'Small beer' was made by 'pouring a fresh volume of water over the wort in the vat after the strong ale had been drawn off' (Peter Clark, *The English Alehouse: A Social History 1200–1830* (London: Longman, 1983), p. 97: 'ale' here meaning 'beer').

[4] Richard Boston, *Beer and Skittles* (London: Collins, 1976), p. 22.

[5] See Bennett, *Brewsters*, p. 81, on the production of beer in the households of gentry and the nobility.

to brand their premium products as ales rather than beers.[6] A protectionist stance towards the manufacture and sale of ale led initially to the conception of beer-drinking as un-English and unpatriotic. As Bennett has commented, 'beer was an alien drink, produced by aliens and drunk by aliens'.[7] Andrew Boorde, comparing beer unfavourably with ale in 1542, states that 'Ale for an englysshe man is a naturall drynke' whereas 'Bere [. . .] is a naturall drynke for a dutche man'.[8] The association with the Dutch arose primarily from the establishment of Flemish refugee communities in Kent in the sixteenth century, bringing with them the technology and knowledge of the hop-growing and beer-brewing industry. By the end of the century, when beer had begun to dominate the London market for alcohol, much of it was being produced by English brewers, although foreign workers, whether as employees or as independent brewers, continued to feature strongly in the public perception of the trade.[9]

But beer, also known as 'Flemish ale', was familiar from the English campaigns in the Low Countries. English involvement in the struggles of the Netherlands against the Spanish army of occupation had led to a series of military losses entailing heavy casualties and great hardship for the expeditionary forces commanded by the Earl of Leicester. The connotations of 'Flemish' were further complicated for the English by the tales of the refugees. The Spanish troops suppressed opposition in the Low Countries with a brutality that appalled Protestant communities and states across Europe. This was the army that supporters of a forcible return to Catholicism, with Mary Queen of Scots replacing Elizabeth, conspired to bring over to England in the 1570s and 1580s: these were the troops that the Armada aimed to collect and transport across the North Sea. The sufferings of the Flemish people made the English sensitive to the proximity of the Spanish troops and the reality of the threat which they presented to an English Protestant state. In this context, a doubly

---

6 The term 'ale' in this context has lost its meaning of differentiation from beer. Modern ales usually contain hops and are, technically, beers. Calling them 'ale', usually associated with labelling that employs 'olde-worlde' signifiers such as woodcut illustrations and a black-letter typeface such as 'Old English', attempts to market these brands as artisan products providing a cultural link with an imagined past.

7 Bennett, *Brewsters*, p. 79.

8 Andrew Boorde, *A Compendyous Regyment or a Dyetary of Helth* (1542), sig. F2r–v. Water, on the other hand, 'is not holsome by it selfe for an englysshe man, consyderynge the contrary usage, whiche is not concurraunt with nature, water is colde, slowe, and slacke of dygestyon' (sig. E4r–v). Boorde's objections to water are not framed in terms of its pollution but its contra-indication in humoral theory. The malign effects of Dutch liquor reassert themselves in Hogarth's 'Gin Lane' engraving (1751). It is noticeable that its counterpoint, 'Beer Street', valorises beer, indicating that by the mid-eighteenth century, beer had become naturalised and ale has disappeared. See Jenny Uglow, *Hogarth: A Life and a World* (London: Faber, 1997), pp. 493–500.

9 See Bennett, *Brewsters*, p. 80.

uneasy sense of 'Flemish', to mean both tortured and torturer, pervades the power of the term in early modern understanding.

By the second half of the sixteenth century, a taste for beer was widely established in England and the need to import hops, its vital ingredient, began to be seen as an economic drain on the country. In what we might perhaps read as an early exhortation to 'dig for victory', a number of publications of the period advance the argument for anglicising the production of hops for economic and political reasons. William Bulleyn's strictures that 'many rotten Hoppes, or Hoppes dried like dust, [. . .] cometh from beyonde sea', and his approving account of 'the goodly fieldes, and fruitfull groundes of Englande [that] doe bryng foorthe to mannes use, as good Hoppes as groweth in any place of the worlde',[10] draw upon a strongly confident credo, which not only sets up as comparators 'Englande' on the one hand and the rest of the world on the other, but asserts the natural superiority of the English product in any field. The publication in 1574 of Reginald Scot's *The Perfect Platform of a Hop-Garden*, the first manual of hop culture in England, advances the same agenda. Urging his readers to follow his advice and grow hops, Scot criticises purchasing hops abroad as 'a publicke despyte unto the common wealth' and castigates the failure to produce enough home-grown hops as:

> [making] roume for straungers to depryve us of our commodities, who maytaine ignoraunce in our bosomes, and beggerie in our Purses, while we nourish disdayne in our hearts, and sloth in our hands, and hereby we set our shame uppon a stage for all the worlds to gaze uppon, and make our folly so palpable, that Strangers from beyonde the Seas, (which neither heare nor see us) can grabbe it out, for we can be content uppon our Alebench, to entytle our Countrie to the name of fertilitie, and yet deprave the same with our peevishnesse, and slaunder it with our sloth, expounding and excusing our negligence by our ignoraunce, and covering the one with the others weedes.[11]

Scot's language utilises a complex interplay of imagery from economic, moral and xenophobic vocabularies to bring the production of beer within a patriotic discourse. He casts foreign producers as 'strangers', an emotive classification that excludes any notion of co-operation or familiarity and rejects any possibility of beneficial interchange, whether economic or cultural. The association of 'ignoraunce' with 'beggerie' constructs knowledge as a commercial tool, disregarding the humanist notion of the moral value of education. Ideas about moral value are present in the passage, however, in its catalogue of vices. To fail to plant hops, according to Scot, is not only to impoverish one's country but to demean it. The shame 'set [. . .] uppon a stage for all the worlds to gaze uppon' is attributed to the whole nation, in a manoeuvre that raises the stakes

---

10 William Bulleyn, *Bullein's Bulwarke of Defence* (1562), p. xiib.
11 Reginald Scot, *The Perfect Platform of a Hop-Garden* (1574; reprinted in facsimile, Amsterdam: Theatrum Orbis Terrarum; and New York: Da Capo Press, 1973), pp. 53–4.

from a revelation of individual apathy to an exposure of collective culpability. What hurts, Scot argues, is not so much the cost of importing commodities, but the invitation given to the suppliers to sneer at the English for their feck-lessness. Above all, the notion of display intrinsic to his image of 'set[ting] our shame uppon a stage for all the worlds to gaze uppon' provides a salutary reminder that the display of stereotyped figures of deviance on the early modern stage functions partly if not wholly as a shaming device that denigrates certain behaviours or allegiances for a moral and political purpose.

The Spaniard John [*sic*] Huarte fails to differentiate between the Low Countries and England, picturing them both as irredeemably northern, and therefore 'hav[ing] all of them want of understanding', citing Aristotle as his witness that 'such as inhabit verie cold regions partake less understanding than those who are born in the hotter' and determining consequently that 'the Flemmish, Dutch, English, and French [. . .] their wits are like those of drunk-ards'.[12] Huarte's equation between mental vacuity and drunkenness stigma-tises the English (and his other targeted nations), being less interested in the cause than the symptoms of stupidity. In this context of inter-national mud-slinging, the emergence of an intra-national irritation at individuals who conform to such expectations becomes clearly explicable.

The early seventeenth century saw a steady rise in the publication of treatises and pamphlets excoriating drunkenness. They reflect a Puritan distaste for personal loss of control: they develop a rhetoric that introduces drunkenness into the political debate, increasingly framing it as a characteristic vice of the court and the Protestant ruling classes. Thomas Young stigmatised drunken-ness as 'Englands Bane' in his pamphlet of the same name: 'this vice of drunkennes, (which indeede is the Metropolitane citie of all the province of vices) which Reason made me intitle my Booke, *Englands Bane*: because no Nation is more polluted with this capitall sinne, then ours'.[13] Young's meta-phor of political order, constructing a topography of transgression, echoes concerns observable in contemporary treatises on syphilis, casting the disor-dered behaviour of the individual as a threat to the social fabric of the nation. He goes on to lament that 'Our Nation [. . .] should ape-like imitate Forraigne countries in their vices' rather than their virtues. This is despite what he regards as the natural propensity of the English to virtue, aided by 'God [who] of his especiall goodnes to our Nation, hath indued us with singularities of apprehen-sion, dexteritie of invention, and meanes for discipline, exceeding all the bordering countries of the world'.[14] Young's language at this point, recruiting

---

[12] John Huarte, *The Examination of Mens Wits, translated by R.C., Esquire* (1594), p. 116. Spain, on the other hand, is ideally geographically located to conform to Galen's dictum that 'those who are seated between the North and the burned Zone, are of great wisedome' (Huarte, *Examination*, p. 116).

[13] Thomas Young, *Englands Bane: or, the Description of Drunkennesse* (1617), sig. A2v.

[14] Ibid., sig. A4r.

the reader into a shared 'us' that presumes Englishness, explicitly opposes 'our Nation' against all others. The threat to national standing coalesces into a protest that 'all Christians have just cause to complaine, and to crie out that we have received by the Low Countries the most irreperable damadge that ever fell on the Kingdom of England'.[15] Again, the use of 'we' as synonymous with 'the Kingdom of England' imposes English concerns and loyalties upon the nations of Britain, while the hyperbolic assessment of 'most irreparable [. . .] ever' sets an agenda in which drunkards are both victims and perpetrators of crime. Subsumed within a representational status as an Englishman, the drunkenness of the individual degrades the whole nation.

The supremacy of beer over ale that came into effect during the second half of the sixteenth century fostered the emergence of a masculine drinking culture in which men drank together in the public arena of the inn and the alehouse. A growing cultural concern about drunkenness became inseparable from anxieties about the alehouses, which increasingly were perceived as fostering excessive drinking and encouraging social disorder by hosting gatherings of men, especially those of the middling and lower classes. Drink, the places where it could be procured, and the people who drink it, take on an aura of at the least unrespectability and at worst dissidence and sedition. Clearly ways had to be found to discourage, contain and control what were increasingly being seen as deviant behaviours.

The social historian Peter Clark proposes a hierarchy of public places for drinking in early modern England. As has been noted elsewhere in the present volume, the inn was the highest class, providing decent accommodation and food and serving ale, beer and wine (these were the establishments that later in their history evolved into hotels).[16] The tavern was licensed only to serve wine. In London, taverns, situated on major thoroughfares, provided an affordable meeting place for men with interests in common.[17] The alehouse stood at the bottom of the social ladder, selling ale and beer, cider and rough spirits for consumption on or off the premises. London alehouses, principally located in

---

15 Ibid., sig. D2r.
16 See, in particular, the Introduction.
17 Famously, writers drank and talked together at the Mermaid in Cheapside, the Sun, the Half Moon in Aldersgate Street, the Feathers in Cheapside, the Dog and the Triple Tun, and the Devil Tavern (fully the Devil and St Dunstan) between Middle Temple Lane and Temple Bar, where the upstairs 'Apollo room' was adorned with Ben Jonson's welcoming verse. See Rosalind Miles, *Ben Jonson: His Life and Work* (London & New York: Routledge & Kegan Paul, 1986), pp. 135, 207–9. Jonson numbered Beaumont and Fletcher among his drinking companions, as well as, famously if apocryphally, Shakespeare on his last and indirectly fatal binge. One of the most persistent biographical legends of the Jacobean period is Jonson's capacity for alcohol. His work makes many references, often self-deprecating, to his drinking, and there are stories that he suffered for it. When he wrote a long, vitriolic and libellous epigram about Cecilia Bulstrode, the poem was allegedly stolen from him while he was drunk and given to the lady, with deleterious effects upon his standing at Court (Miles, *Jonson*, pp. 91–2).

back-alleys and minor streets of the City, also sold a very limited range of food and offered basic accommodation – sometimes no more than a bed in the kitchen.[18]

Because they catered for the poorest sections of the community, alehouses were the fastest-growing sector of the drink-selling trade during the economically troubled late sixteenth and early seventeenth century. They were subject to licensing by the City authorities, but the law seems to have been haphazardly and laxly enforced. Alehouse-keeping seems often to have been taken up as an economically necessary sideline by low-paid working men such as shoemakers and tailors. Women, who in medieval society performed low-skill, low-status, low-reward work brewing ale and selling it, tended to become the sellers of beer in alehouses, with no improvement in skills, status or pay, while men took on the 'high-tech' work of brewing beer and supplying the alehouses.[19] William Clowes' identification of 'lewd alehouses' as 'the very nests and harbourers' of 'rogues, and vagabondes: [. . .] many lewd and idell persons, both men and women'[20] exemplifies the suspicion with which the alehouses are regarded in bourgeois writing of the period. As a social focus for the growing classes of itinerant unemployed or casually employed men and women, the alehouses provided a metonym for the varied and multiple threats to good order for which these out-classes were feared by the middling sort. Clark comments on the correlation between population expansion and the increase in drinking, noting that alehouse-keeping provided a source of income, albeit at subsistence level. For consumers, ale and beer offered a cheap energy source – prices rose more slowly than those for bread and other staples – and a narcotic reprieve from the day-to-day miseries of existence.[21] William Vaughan echoes Clowes in declaring that 'Tavernes are the causes of licentiousnes', describing them as 'these paltry Cottages' in which 'a man shall meete at all times, day or night, yea, in the dawning, twilight and midnight with drunken dissolutes'.[22]

The low-life clientele of the alehouse features in early modern plays as an inversion of the social order, representing a world turned upside down. Clark observes that plays represent the alehouse as 'the trysting-place of an under-world populated by gulls and vagabonds, robbers and whores, a world which though parasitical is also a mirror image of the moral sham, the trickery and hypocrisy of respectable society'.[23] Mistress Quickly is described in the list

18 See Clark, 'Alehouse', p. 49.
19 Bennett compares the marginalisation of women in the brewing industry as new technology appeared with the emergence of exclusively male medical societies and colleges as male medical practitioners basing their expertise of new theories communicated by publication ousted the traditional wisdom of women healers, handed down orally.
20 William Clowes, *A Short and Profitable Treatise touching the cure of the disease called (Morbus Gallicus) by Unctions* (1579), sigs B1v–2r.
21 Clark, 'Alehouse', pp. 52–4.
22 William Vaughan, *The Spirit of Detraction* (1611), pp. 127, 129.
23 Clark, 'Alehouse', p. 48.

of characters in *2 Henry IV* as 'hostess of a tavern', The Boar's Head at Eastcheap, from which Doll Tearsheet works as a whore.[24] Representing herself as 'a poor widow of Eastcheap' and 'a poor lone woman' (2.1.71, 32), Quickly appears to occupy a slightly higher degree of economic security than subsistence alehouse-keepers; she refers to 'mine own house' (2.1.15) suggesting property ownership and 'my Dolphin chamber' (89), indicating furnishings and décor with pretensions to a comfortable or bourgeois standard. Her reference to dining-chambers, complete with plate and tapestry (143) also raise the economic and social position of The Boar's Head above that of the alehouse: perhaps unsurprisingly for a house that numbers knights (and the heir to the throne) among its clientele.[25] Her tavern, however, also functions as a brothel, over which she presides as a bawd, offering Doll's services to Falstaff (2.1.165).

The play's concerns with moral and financial degradation and corruption do not particularly focus on the tavern's function as a marketplace for alcohol consumption. The low-life characters in *Measure for Measure* have been described as inhabiting 'a diseased world of brothels and prisons',[26] but Mistress Overdone's brothel appears also to function as an alehouse, in which Pompey serves as tapster as well as 'parcel bawd' (1.2.100, 2.1.60). Even more than in *2 Henry IV*, the play takes for granted that public drinking houses primarily function as brothels. The association between the two forms a commonplace of early seventeenth-century citizen comedies. The low-life sub-plot in Jonson's *The New Inn* (1629), which, as Michael Hattaway notes, offers 'a realist and neutrally presented slice of tavern life',[27] provides a late example of the conventional representation of the public drinking-den as a hotbed of iniquity.

As Clark has summarised, alehouses were:

> a new and increasingly dangerous force in popular society; [...] they were run by the poor for the poor, victualling and harbouring the destitute and vagrant, breeding crime, disorder, and drunkenness, fostering promiscuity and other breaches of orthodox morality; and [...] they served as the stronghold of popular opposition to the established religious and political order.[28]

[24] All references to Shakespeare are to *The Oxford Complete Works Compact Edition*, ed. Stanley Wells and Gary Taylor (Oxford: The Clarendon Press, 1988).

[25] There was a Boar's Head tavern in Eastcheap at the time. The name and character of the hostess, and the nature of the business conducted there, must be a matter of speculation, but its representation in the play afforded the pleasure of recognition and reinforced the notion of the play as 'real', allowing the credentials of the noble and regal figures in the play as historical entities to seep over into the low-life scenes. The Braun and Hogenberg map of London (1572) distinguishes only two 'Beere Houses' east of London Bridge. Their particular significance is lost to us.

[26] *Oxford Complete Works*, ed. Wells and Taylor, p. 789.

[27] Ben Jonson, *The New Inn*, ed. Michael Hattaway (Manchester: Manchester University Press, 1984), p. 3.

[28] Clark, 'Alehouse', p. 48.

Additionally, the brewing and selling of beer was perceived as an economic threat to indigenous English production, threatening the livelihood of the small-scale ale-producers. Thirdly, the rise of an alehouse culture, encouraged by the commercial production of beer, contributed to divisive social change, as drinking – at least for men – moved out of the domestic sphere into an exclusively male social activity taking place in spaces that were also associated with gambling, lawlessness, prostitution and social disorder. But as time went by, and English brewers became established, and English hop fields began to supply the market, beer prevailed as the most commonly available drink. By the time *The Pilgrim* was written in 1621, beer had effectively usurped the symbolic position of ale as a definitively English drink. The depiction of the Englishman in the play reveals a social anxiety about drunkenness rather than the specific drink.

A letter from the Lord Mayor and Court of Aldermen betrays considerable concern that London's brewing industry 'so replenished the tippling-houses with headstrong Beer, that great scarcity of bread corn was occasioned'.[29] Richard Rawlidge also narrows the patriotic focus, acknowledging that 'the glory of the Land is pretious, and the disgrace thereof odious' but declaring his concern to be the abuse of 'this most famous, and praise-deserving Citty' of London by 'Drunkennesse, needlesse drinking, and Gaming permitted in Ale-houses'.[30] He laments that

> Whereas there are within and about the Citties Liberties but an hundred twenty two Churches for the service and worshipp of God: there are I dare say above thirty hundred Ale-Houses, Typling-houses, Tobacco-shops, &c in London, and the skirts thereof, wherein the Divell is daily served and honoured.[31]

The unequal arithmetic had been noticed previously, when it had been claimed that there were 'ten Tavernes for one Church, ten divels for one Saint, ten tospots for one temperate'.[32] Rawlidge's tract also paints a vivid picture of the economic consequences of drunkenness, complaining that the brewers' customers satisfy their craving 'even in these hard times, where all men complaine of such hardnesse, and yet they will not leave their good liquor, although they starve for want of clothes and firing'.[33] Considered in the light of these anxieties, which clearly express a concern that the excessive consumption of beer undermines the social, religious and economic fabric of the state, the Englishman in *The Pilgrim* earns his place in bedlam by his surrender to his

---

[29] *Analytical Index to the series of Records known as the Remembrancia preserved among the archives of the City of London A.D. 1579–1664* (London: E.J. Francis, 1878), p. 28.

[30] Richard Rawlidge, *A Monster Late Found Out and Discovered* (Amsterdam, 1628), Epistle Dedicatorie, p. 1.

[31] Ibid., p. 3.

[32] William Vaughan, *The Spirit of Detraction* (1611), p. 129.

[33] Rawlidge, *Monster*, p. 4.

uncontrollable desire for beer, which betrays his country even as it destroys his self-government.

Because Bedlam – the madhouse – is where we find him. Fletcher's English beer-drinker is one of the five inmates encountered by the play's hero when he visits bedlam. *The Pilgrim* is one of four early seventeenth-century plays that set some scenes in the madhouse, where an array of inmates are encountered, usually for the moral reflective benefit of the hero and, by implication, the audience.[34] *The Pilgrim* features a scholar, a parson, a Welshman and a 'She-Fool' as well as the Englishman. These vignettes do not present an inter-changeable series of all-purpose comic – or exotic – madness, but represent distinct aspects of contemporary political and social contention, contributing to the play's exposition of a social, political and religious agenda. The repre-sentation of the Englishman as a beer-swilling drunkard not only reveals a key concern, but also draws on a long tradition of association between drunken-ness and madness in popular perception.

Drunkenness registers as a social concern in medieval culture, being remarked upon as analogous with madness in its setting aside of reason.[35] Chaucer's admonition against gluttony in 'The Parson's Tale' warns that 'whan a man is dronken, he hath lost his resoun; and this is deedly synne'[36]; 'The Pardoner's Tale' points out the indistinguishability of madness and drunkenness, 'But that woodnesse [madness], y-fallen in a shrewe, Persevereth lenger than doth dronkenesse'.[37] Paul Hentzner records in his *A Journey to England* (1598) 'the general drink is beer, which is prepared from barley, and is excellently well tasted, but strong and what soon fuddles'.[38] Early seven-teenth-century society perceived drunkenness to be increasing, and consider-able anxiety can be traced in early modern writings. The Puritan pamphleteer William Prynne, seeking to prove 'the drinking and pledging of Healthes, to be sinfull, and utterly Unlawful unto Christians',[39] incorporates a swingeing attack on King Charles and his court, vilifying the company kept by the king as 'the very scouring dreggs, and scum of men' who by association 'make the great Defendor of the Faith, the ground, the Patron, and grand Protector of all intemperance; as if Drunkennesse were the sole and onely Faith that Kings defend'.[40] Prynne distinguishes between Puritans and Protestants, praising

---

34 The other plays are Thomas Dekker's *The Honest Whore (Part 1)* (1604), Dekker and John Webster's *Northward Ho* (1607) and Thomas Middleton and William Rowley's *The Change-ling* (1622). Additionally, Webster's *The Duchess of Malfi* (1613–14) adopts the bedlam sub-genre and creates a madhouse in the Duchess' chamber.

35 See Adam Smyth's chapter, below, for further discussion of the perceived links between drunkenness and a loss of reason.

36 Geoffrey Chaucer, *Complete Works*, ed. Walter W. Skeat (London: Oxford University Press, 1912, 1973), p. 705.

37 Ibid., p. 558.

38 Quoted in Boston, *Beer and Skittles*, p. 26.

39 William Prynne, *Healthes Sicknesse* (1628), title-page.

40 Ibid., sig. A2v.

Puritans for making 'a conscience of praying constantly and privatly' and mocking Protestants for making 'no conscience of drinking openly and howerly, even beyond excesse it selfe'.[41] Such a context allows the possibility that the English madman's drunkenness allocates him to Protestantism, and brings the bedlam scene in *The Pilgrim* into contemporary political friction between contesting religious factions in the run-up to the revolutionary decades of the seventeenth century.

The display of the drunken Englishman in *The Pilgrim*'s bedlam provides a satisfying spectacle of retribution to a London culture increasingly ready to interpret individual behaviour as communally representative. He may also embody xenophobic fears that imported customs and commodities were undermining national sanity: it is notable that John Webster's caricature of a 'drunken Dutch-man resident in England' complains that 'his new Trade of brewing Strong-waters makes a number of mad-men'.[42]

While the comic performance of the bedlam figures, presumably by popular actors with a personal following, might contribute to the attractiveness of the dissident behaviour they represent, the very fact of their demonstrated incarceration in the madhouse insists on the power of the state to quench such behaviour. *The Pilgrim*'s English beer-drinker might be a recognisable fellow-citizen, but, by installing him in bedlam, the play judges such behaviour to be anti-social. It seems, therefore, that the bedlam figures inevitably collude with the State's need to contain dissidence and stigmatise difference. This is not to adopt the choice proposed by Ania Loomba and Martin Orkin between an ideological reading (of Shakespeare) as either subverting or reinforcing 'cultural [. . .] hierarchies'.[43] The bedlam scenes register a potential for subversion by recognising the existence of dissidence, even though they do not celebrate it. As Stephen Greenblatt appreciated, 'There is subversion, no end of subversion, only not for us'.[44]

41 Ibid., ¶4r.

42 John Webster (?), 'New Characters (Drawne to the life) of severall persons, in severall qualities', in *The Complete Works of John Webster*, ed. F.L. Lucas (London: Chatto & Windus, 1927), 4 vols, vol. 4, p. 32.

43 Ania Loomba and Martin Orkin (eds), *Post-Colonial Shakespeares* (London & New York: Routledge, 1998), p. 1.

44 Stephen Greenblatt, 'Invisible Bullets: Renaissance authority and its subversion, *Henry IV* and *Henry V*', in Jonathan Dollimore and Alan Sinfield (eds), *Political Shakespeare: New Essays in Cultural Materialism* (Manchester: Manchester University Press, 1985), pp. 18–47, p. 45.

12

'It were far better be a *Toad,* or a *Serpant,* then a Drunkard': Writing About Drunkenness

ADAM SMYTH

IN this chapter I would like to take a broad look at several seventeenth-century texts that describe drinking and, in particular, at texts that discuss the state of being drunk. My concern is with textual constructions of drunkenness, rather than the physiological condition: I am interested in the vocabularies, references, arguments – in the discourses – employed in early modern accounts of drunkenness. In these texts, what happened to men and women when they drank to excess? How was drunkenness represented by the early modern writer?

Naturally, my treatment is not exhaustive. There are different traditions of writing about drunkenness: as chapters in this volume have shown, the 'sons' of Ben Jonson, for instance, celebrated drunkenness in manuscript (and later printed) poetry as a marker of social exclusivity, and drew a connection between hard drinking and an elite poetic wit;[1] disenfranchised royalists lauded drunkenness, textually, to signal defiance, royalism and a counter-puritan political agenda.[2] But my focus, here, is generally on writings designed for a more popular audience: cheap printed works that address an unspecified reader. Most of the texts I discuss seek to condemn drunkenness – many of them vituperatively – but I also want to consider one printed book, which sought to celebrate and indeed encourage drunkenness, to examine how this pro-drink text picked up and responded to established condemnations of drunkenness.

---

[1] Stella Achilleos, 'The *Anacreontea* and a Tradition of Refined Male Sociability', above; Joshua Scodel, *Excess and the Mean in Early Modern English Literature* (Princeton & Oxford: Princeton University Press, 2002), chapter 7: 'Drinking and the Politics of Poetic Identity from Jonson to Herrick', pp. 199–224.

[2] Marika Keblusek, 'Wine for Comfort: Drinking and the Royalist Exile Experience, 1642–1660', above.

*

One feature that unites the books I discuss is, paradoxically, the drunkard's absence from the text. Rather than a drunkard's account, we are offered the words of a narrator describing drunkenness: the drunkard has no direct voice, and his (or, more rarely, her) experience is constructed by a conspicuously detached narrator. There certainly are theatrical representations of drunkards – Sir John Falstaff, 'fat-witted with drinking sack',[3] speaks for himself; but in most writing about drink, and certainly in the texts I examine here, the drunk's voice is a never present, and the state of being drunk is always mediated – filtered; distilled – through sobriety. Even mid-century royalist poetry that defiantly celebrates drink does not generally depict drunkenness, but rather declares an intention to drink to excess. Drunkenness is an extra-textual experience, something about to happen, after the pen has been put down.

The need to assert this detachment – to introduce this gap between subject and narrator – is a feature of Charles Darby's poem *Bacchanalia: or a Description of a Drunken Club* (1680). The verse opens with a description of the narrator's position in relation to the coterie of drinkers he portrays.

> It was my hap Spectator once to be,
> As I unseen, in secret Angle, sate,
>   Of that unmanly Crowd,
> Who, with Wits low, and Voices loud,
>   Were met to Celebrate,
>   In Evening late,
> The *Bacchanalian* Solemnity.[4]

The poem begins, paradoxically, with the narrator's attempt to distance himself from his subject. He artfully positions himself as an outsider, observing from afar – emphasising his chance happening upon the scene, rather than any planned encounter; his role as 'Spectator', not participant; and his detached position, 'unseen, in secret Angle'. Indeed, not only does the narrator dissociate himself from the drinking group; he also shifts responsibility for this poetical vignette on to the drinkers themselves: drinkers who with 'Voices loud' make it impossible not to overhear their '*Bacchanalian* Solemnity'. Rather than initiating this account, the narrator is merely a transcriber of words made public by the drinkers' 'babbling':

> That previous Tribe would their own Acts reveal,
> Since Wine (transparent thing!) no secret can retain.[5]

---

3 William Shakespeare, *Henry IV, Part One*, I.2.2–3, in *The Riverside Shakespeare* (2nd edn), ed. G. Blakemore Evans (Boston: Houghton Mifflin, 1997). See also Charlotte McBride, 'A Natural Drink for an English Man: National Stereotyping in Early Modern Culture', above.

4 Charles Darby, *Bacchanalia: or a Description of a Drunken Club* (1680), sig. A2.

5 Ibid.

The narrator is only a cipher for an inexorably self-publishing account. Drinkers reveal themselves, and the narrator, and Darby, recede.

If the opening to Darby's text suggests a fear of being implicated in the subject denounced, this nervousness characterises many seventeenth-century condemnations of drinking. Thomas Heywood's *Philocothonista, or, the Drunkard, Opened, Dissected, and Anatomized* (1635) is, like Darby's poem, a vivid condemnation of drink and drinkers. In order to convince the reader 'Of the most horrid effects of Drunkennesse, and [to exhort] a Christian like . . . Sobriety and Temperance',[6] Heywood presents Biblical, classical and contemporary substantiations, including a celebration of the 'Sober age' before the flood, and a survey of the different drinking habits of contemporary nations ('The *Italians* are something moderate . . . The *French* . . . love the best of their own grapes so well, that they keepe the choyce and chiefe wines to themselves, and send the smallest and refuse into *England*').[7] To clinch the argument, Heywood presents 'Divers stories of such whom immoderate drinking hath been most ridiculous' – including tales of 'A drunken Servingman', 'A swaggering Miler', 'A sleepie drunkard', 'A drunken Malt-man', and 'A drunkard in a Well'.[8]

As these brief headings indicate, the book is written with a verve that suggests a dangerous familiarity with the drunkenness being condemned. As a consequence, Heywood is careful to mark his text out as a corrective to, not an endorsement of, excess drinking. He stresses that the book is intended only for 'the sober and discreet Reader', and in his opening 'The Author to the Booke', Heywood notes that while the subject of the book is the drunkard, the book itself is untainted through association. In a verse that recalls Ben Jonson's second epigram and its anxious description of what the book does – and does not – represent, Heywood assures his book that

> Thou are none such: Then Booke, away, begon,
> And tell the World, Ebrietas quid non.[9]

A similar anxiety defines denunciations of other pursuits associated with convivial company. Charles Cotton's *The Compleat Gamester* (1674) is a detailed description of 'How to play at Billiards, Trucks, Bowls, and Chess. Together with all manner of usual and most Gentile Games either on cards or dice.' But like Darby's narrator, Cotton is anxious not to be tainted with his chosen theme. 'Mistake me not,' he (disingenuously?) pleads,

> it is not my intention to make Gamesters by this Collection, but to inform all in part how to avoid being cheated by them: If I am imperfect in my discoveries,

---

6 Thomas Heywood's *Philocothonista, or, the Drunkard, Opened, Dissected, and Anatomized* (1635), p. 78.
7 Ibid., pp. 1, 29.
8 Ibid., pp. 69–78.
9 Ibid., sig. A2.

impute it to my being no profest Gamester, and the hatred I bear that Hellish society . . . I might sooner by my study come to be Nature's Secretary, and unriddle all her *Arcana*'s, than collect from them any new unpractised secret, by which they bubble ignorant credulity, and purchase money and good apparel with everlasting shame and infamy.[10]

Cotton finds himself in a difficult position that requires artful extrication. His book is a detailed explanation of gaming, but the low status of such pursuits – the 'everlasting shame and infamy' they induce; the 'ignorant credulity' that characterises participants – forces him into the comically unconvincing claim that his text will function as a warning away from gaming. The thesis has its benefits: most notably, flaws in the text become signs of the author's virtuous disengagement. But the dextrous manoeuvring leaves an unsettling impression of anxiety. 'Mistake me not,' Cotton pleads.

If authors such as Darby and Cotton felt a little too close to the flame, what were the connotations surrounding drunkenness that forced Darby's extrications? How was drunkenness understood? Perhaps the most consistently noted characteristic of drunkenness – particularly in condemnations – was that it induced a loss of rationalism and, in particular, a loss of control over words: 'as . . . [the drunk] can ill rule his hand, so worse his tongue',[11] so 'when the Wine is in a man, hee is as a running Coach without a Coachman'.[12] We have already seen how Darby's *Bacchanalia* depicts drinkers being unable to limit and order their language: as a result of wine ('transparent thing!'), drinkers reveal their 'Acts' and denounce themselves. Michel de Montaigne considers a similar point in his essay 'On drunkenness':

> just as the must fermenting in the wine-jars stirs up all the lees at the bottom, so too does wine unbung the most intimate secrets of those who have drunk beyond measure.[13]

In some mid-century royalist poetry, declaring 'intimate secrets' was celebrated as virtuous candour, in opposition to secrecy and deceit. But more commonly, and certainly in explicit condemnations of drink, this loss of control over language was denounced. The loss of linguistic autonomy led to notions of drunkenness as a self-condemning sin, and drinking as a self-destructive act – a vice that turns back on itself, in Jonsonian fashion. The drunkard 'is led like the Oxe to the slaughter, as his owne executioner';[14] is

---

10 Charles Cotton, *The Compleat Gamester: or, How to play at Billiards, Trucks, Bowls, and Chess. Together with all manner of usual and most Gentile Games either on cards or dice* (1674), 'The Epistle to the Reader', sigs A6v–A7.

11 Robert Harris ('late Pastor of Hanwell, Doctor of Divinity, and President of Trinity College in Oxon'), 'The Drunkards Cup', in *The Works of Robert Harris* (1654), pp. 283–308, p. 297.

12 Thomas Young, *Englands Bane: or, The Description of Drunkennesse* (1617), sig. E2.

13 Michel de Montaigne, *The Essays of Michel de Montaigne*, trans. and ed. M.A. Screech (London: Penguin Press, 1991), pp. 381–91, p. 382.

14 *Characters, or Wit in the World in their proper colours* (1663), sig. E12v.

'drowned in his owne orbe;'[15] 'is the greatest enemy to himselfe';[16] shall 'drink the very blood of their wives and children'.[17]

Darby's poem presents drinking as the process of gradually drowning a personified and noble Reason (the quality 'by which Mortals are / Most like their Maker, and do bear / Their Great Creator's Superscription'):

> See! The Waves rise, and Billows foam;
> And washing first her [i.e. Reason's] Foot, and Shin,
> Then Wast, and Shoulders, Neck and Chin,
> At last quite stopt her mouth, surround her piercing Eye,
> Yea swallowed Head and Brain,
> Till nought of her doth visible remain.

Drinkers move from a pre-drink rationalism, through a mad 'babbling' of speech, to a disordered but silent slumber, when – in Heywood's words – 'thou shalt be as one that sleepeth on the top of the Mast'.[18] At the end of the evening, wordless bodies – ugly parodies of their former ordered selves – lie strewn across the chamber:

> Some down into their Seats do shrink,
> As snuffs in Sockets sink;
> Some throw themselves upon the Bed,
> Some at Feet, and some at Head,
> Some Cross, some Slope-wise, as they can;
> Like Hogs in straw, or Herrings in a pan.[19]

A preacher in 1638 painted a similar picture of a community after heavy drinking:

---

[15] Ibid., sig. E12.

[16] John Earle, *Micro-cosmographie: Or, a Peece of the World Discovered; In Essayes, and Characters* (1628) (1669 edn), pp. 38–9.

[17] R[ichard] Younge, *The Blemish of Government, the Shame of Religion, the Disgrace of Mankinde; or, a Charge drawn up against Drunkards, and presented to his Highness the Lord PROTECTOR, in the name of all the Sober Partie in the three Nations. Humbly craving, that they may be kept alone by themselves from infecting others; compelled to work and earn what they consume: And that none may be suffered to sell Drink, who shall either Swear, or be Drunk themselves, or suffer Others within their walls* (1656), p. 8.

This notion that the drunkard will turn on and destroy his own family is surprisingly common. Heywood, *Philocothonista*, pp. 78–91 relates '*the most horrid effects of Drunkennesse*' through notionally factual accounts of, among other things, a '*Wiltshire . . . yong gentleman well borne, but riotously conditioned,* [who] *ran his sword through his owne mothers body, and slew her when shee came with her grave and Matron like advice, to counsell and diswade him from ryotising and lewd company. Nay, have not some Husbands slaine their Wives, when they have come home from swilling? And Wives cut their husbands throats, after they have beene tipling? The Father hath flung his knife at the Mother, and missing her, kill'd the Child; one Brother hath slaine the other in the Taverne: and one man stab'd his deare friend in the Ale-house*' (pp. 79–80).

[18] Heywood, *Philocothonista*, p. 81.

[19] Darby, *Bacchanalia*, sigs D–Dv.

Go but to the town's end where a fair is kept, and there they lie, as if some field had been fought; here lies one man, there another.[20]

In Richard Younge's *The Blemish of Government, the Shame of Religion, the Disgrace of Mankinde; or, a Charge drawn up against Drunkards* (1656), not only does alcohol lead to a cacophonous loss of control over words (hence the common seventeenth-century phrase 'roaring boys': 'one Drunkard hath tongue enough for twentie men . . . as if all the *thirtie bells in Antwerpe steeple* were *rung* at once'),[21] but drink also enables the Devil's words to displace the drunkards'. Drinkers become mere ciphers for Satan:

> Drunkards are the *Divels captives*, at his command, and ready to do his will; and . . . he rules over, and workes in them his pleasure . . . opens their mouths, speaks in and by them . . . stretcheth out their hands, and they act as he will have them.[22]

In a depiction of drunkards in *The Character of a Tavern* (1675) – an unattributed and expanded version of part of John Earle's *Micro-cosmographie: Or, a Peece of the World Discovered; In Essayes, and Characters* (1628) – the defining trait of drinkers is a lack of their own language, and a consequent borrowing of words from other sources. To be drunk is to quote, ceaselessly: to reissue another's words. Thus there is one drunkard who is

> breaking a Jest . . . another repeating scraps of old Plays, or some Bawdy Song, this speaking *Latine*, and a fourth *Nonsense*, whilst all with loud hooting and laughing confound the noise of *Fidlers*.[23]

The drunkard is dependent on recycling the words of others – and that word 'repeating' ('repeating scraps of old Plays') is particularly potent: suggesting a speaker endlessly rehearsing tired quotations, and effacing himself with each repetition. There is an interesting connection to be made, I think, between these kinds of often puritan criticisms of drunkenness – drinkers only recite others' lines – and puritan criticisms of theatrical performance, where actors similarly become ciphers for someone else's language. The tavern is often depicted as a stage, and drinkers as players.

Predictably enough, a loss of control over language is often presented as a process of feminization. Darby's *Bacchanalia* describes 'that unmanly Crowd' – unmanly with their 'Wits low, and Voices loud', and with their 'babbling Privacy'. And in a condemnation of gaming by John Philpot, 'A Gamester' – similarly robbed of his autonomy – is 'troubled and perplext in his minde; his eyes are still effeminate'.[24]

---

20 Quoted in Keith Thomas, *Religion and the Decline of Magic* (London: Penguin, 1973), p. 21.
21 Younge, *The Blemish of Government* (1656), p. 6.
22 Ibid., p. 3.
23 *The Character of a Tavern. With a brief draught of a Drawer* (1675), p. 2.
24 John Philpot, *A prospective-glasse for gamesters: or, a short treatise against gameing* (1646), p. 9.

Darby's description of drunkards as 'Hogs in straw, or Herrings in a pan' is striking but entirely representative among condemnations of drink. When Richard Younge declared 'it were far better be a *Toad*, or a *Serpant*, then a Drunkard',[25] he was constructing a distinction that most texts dramatically collapsed: to be a drunkard *was* to be a toad, or a serpent. And this was a predictable extension of the notion of drunkards as men devoid of both reason and an ordered language. A drunkard – 'gross and brutish . . . all body and earthy'[26] – is 'a picture of a Beast, a Monster of a man';[27] 'a strange Monster, halfe man, halfe beast, swimming in the Ocean of *Bacchus*, and like the Whale belching and foming out of his mouth and nostrils abundance of that frothy and unsavoury Element he so lately ingurgitated.'[28]

Some texts detail the transformation with more precision, suggesting that particular kinds of drunkards become particular kinds of beasts. *Englands Bane: or, The Description of Drunkennesse* (1617) by Thomas Young – tutor to the young John Milton – identifies

> of *Drunkards* nine sorts. The first is Lyon drunke, which breakes glasse windowes, cals the Hostesse Whoore, strikes, fights or quarrels, with either Brother, Friend or Father. The second is Ape-drunke, who dances, capers, and leapes about the house, sings and reioyces, and is wholly rauisht into iests, mirth and melodie. The third is sheepe drunke, who is very kind and liberall, and sayes, by God captaine I loue you? . . . The fourth is Sow drunke, who vomits, spewes, and wallows in the mire . . . [and then] Foxe drunke . . . Maudlin drunke . . . Goate drunke, who is in his drunke so lecherous . . . Martin drunke . . . [and] Bat drunke.[29]

Behind these fears of bestial transformation is the myth of Circe. Circe, daughter of Helios and Perse, and sorceress on the island of Aeaea, seduced visitors with wine and transformed them into animals – most famously detaining Odysseus, returning from the Trojan wars, and changing his men to swine.[30] Richard Younge in fact makes this connection with the Circe myth explicit when he notes that drunkards 'suffer themselves to be transformed from *men* into *swine*; as *Elpenor* was transformed by *Circes* into a *hogge*'.[31] There is also a compelling idea in the lists of creatures in *Englands Bane* that drinkers are transformed into beasts who are their *true representations*: drinkers are changed, but in changing, become more genuinely themselves.

---

[25] Younge, *Blemish*, p. 1.
[26] Montaigne, *Essays*, p. 382.
[27] Young, *Bane*, sig. F2v.
[28] *Characters*, sig. E12. Invoking this fear of transformation, but without making particular reference to animals, *Whimzies: or, a New Cast of Characters* (1631) describes 'A wine-soaker' as 'hee [that] is in the Evening, what you shall not finde him in the Morning' (p. 172).
[29] Young, *Bane*, sigs F2v–F3.
[30] See *The Oxford Guide to Classical Mythology in the Arts, 1300–1990s*, ed. Jane Davidson Reid (New York & Oxford: Oxford University Press, 1993), 2 vols, vol. 1, pp. 304–6.
[31] Younge, *Blemish*, p. 4.

The Circe myth also informed discussions of sites of drinking. Karen Britland suggests that Circe's island 'occupies a foreign liminal space within the Homeric text',[32] and denunciations of drink often attacked the withdrawn, disengaged, or (in particular) concealed drinking space. Thus Richard Younge's *The Blemish of Government* is particularly concerned about woods as sites for potential transgressions. A forest is

> a Station of wilde Beasts: and likewise I think the inhabitants of these places, learne their sauage manners, and brutish behauiour, because they conuerse chiefely with Beasts: For they haue no Magistrates, nore they will hire no Ministers, for they goe ten times to an Ale-house, before they goe once to a Church.[33]

Woods are dangerous spaces since they are unpoliced by magistrates, and are home to 'wilde Beasts'. The image of Circe's island as a detached, unregulated and corrupting space is formative, once again.

What alarmed George Gascoigne about the notion of bestial transformation was, in particular, the idea that all men – no matter what rank – were reworked by drink. Not only are 'all common Droonkwards . . . Beasts',

> but even the wysest councellor, the gravest Philosopher, the coonoingest Artificer, the skylfullest wryter, and the most perfect of all sortes and Estates, if they chance at any time to bee infected, and contamynate with this Beastly vice, shall be, (in that dooing) very Beastes also.[34]

Gascoigne's fear was the destruction of social hierarchies, and this is a refrain in many criticisms of drunkenness. Darby's *Bacchanalia* notes how drink leads to an undesirable mingling of social types: around the drinking table men of high and low rank mix.

> One Noble was, yclep'd a Lord, I wis,
> Another did a meaner Title take,
> A Tinker hight: but all's one, that, or this,
> *Lyæan*-Laws no difference do make.
> Cups reconcile Degrees, and Natures too.

New ranks are created, based not around nobility of blood, but the ability to drink.

> He Noblest is, who can in Drink out-do.
> No boast of Blood will here allowed be,
>   But what from tender Grape is prest.

---

[32] Karen Britland, 'Circe's Cup: Wine and Women in Early Modern Drama', p. 114.

[33] Younge, *Blemish*, sig. F.

[34] George Gascoigne, *A Delicate Diet, for daintie mouthde droonkards* (1576, reprinted 1789), p. 6. Noted in Steven Earnshaw, *The Pub in Literature: England's altered state* (Manchester & New York: Manchester University Press, 2000), p. 10.

This drinking order is a parody of the social hierarchy Darby desires: among drinkers, there is 'No talk of Race, or Pedigree, / For Honour here is a meer sudden thing'.[35]

This same mixing of types is described in *The Character of a Tavern* (1675). The site of drinking is

> a *Babel* of Voices, a *Gallimans fry* of *Opinions*, and an *Hodge Podge* of *Nations*, you shall hear one talking very gravely of *Religion*, and another *Ranting*, and swearing *Dammee*, and *Sink mee*, at the same instant, parties of different Sects and perswasions will meet here, and be sociable though not at Church; And below in the Cellar you shall see the *French* and the *Spanish*, with the Natives of the *Rhine* (notwithstanding the present Wars between them) lye quietly alto-gether.[36]

Careful hierarchies and distinctions are blown apart as previously separate worlds mix together. And with hierarchies upset, authority is challenged: 'at these places men learne to contemne *Authority*, as *boies* grown tall and stub-born, contemne the *rod*'.[37]

As part of this challenge to authority, even time is threatened. Drunkenness is often described as a 'losse of time',[38] or an inversion of time – it 'hath some-times the operation to make midday looke with them, like midnight'.[39] But particularly fearful is drink's ability to reject time altogether: to throw off even this last regulatory frame. The drinker who *will never stop* is a resonant figure frequently invoked in accounts of drink. Thus, most vividly, Richard Younge fears those drunkards that

> can disgorge themselves at pleasure, by onely putting their finger to their throat. And they will vomit, as if they were so many live *Whales* spuing up the *Ocean*; which done, they can drink afresh.[40]

This endless drinker finds an institutional equivalent in the tavern that resists any notion of a beginning and an end. Like the drunkard who 'can disgorge . . . [and] drink afresh', the tavern never stops:

> A house of sinne you may call it, but not a house of darknesse, for the Candles are neuer out, and it is like those Countries farre in the North, where it is as cleare at mid-night as at mid-day.[41]

Running through all these discussions of the destructive potential of drink is, paradoxically, an emphasis on the seductive qualities of alcohol. In his

---

[35] Darby, *Bacchanalia*, sig. A2v.
[36] *The Character of a Tavern*, pp. 2–3.
[37] Younge, *Blemish*, p. 7.
[38] Young, *Bane*, sig. D.
[39] Heywood, *Philocothonista*, pp. 29–30.
[40] Younge, *Blemish*, p. 2.
[41] Earle, *Micro-cosmographie* (1628), sig. C10v.

Miscellanea; or, Serious, Useful Considerations, Moral, Historical, Theological (1661), Thomas Goddard describes pleasure as a kind of seductive death. In a description that is Petrarchan in its alignment of delight and suffering, pleasure is defined as that which

> strangles the soul with silken halters, smothers it in a bed of down, throws it from a Tower of Pearl, stabs it with a Golden dagger, kils it with a delicious banquet, and drowns it in a Sea of Wine.[42]

In Goddard's account, pleasure is gendered female, too, and his descriptions are informed by mythological narratives about female enchantresses. Goddard's vivid personification of pleasure

> hath a *Sirens* tongue, wherewith is sings such Melodious Lullabies unto it that at length the heart is laid down by it so fast asleep in the Cradle of security, that nothing but either the thunder of threatning, or the lightning of flaming wrath and scorching anger . . . can awaken it.[43]

Drink is often similarly presented as a delicious poison. Indeed, the seductive power of drunkenness is at the heart of most seventeenth-century denunciations: drink is dangerous precisely because it is so powerfully alluring. Heywood describes 'a sweet sinne, a pleasant poyson, and a bewitching devill';[44] *A looking glasse for drunkards: or, The hunting of drunkennesse* (1627) – a text that cites Biblical passages to prove the danger of drunkenness – employs a similar vocabulary to define 'Drunkennesse . . . [as] a flattering Devill, a sweet poyson, and a pleasing sinne'.[45] And Samuel Clark's *A Warning-piece to All Drunkards and Health-Drinkers* (1682) calls drink an 'infatuation'.[46] Even texts that do not seek to denounce alcohol register this idea of a seductive corruptor. In a discussion of cider, John Taylor's *Drinke and welcome: or The famous historie of the most part of Drinks, in use now in the Kingdomes of Great Brittaine and Ireland* (1637) notes that '*Syder* (whose Anangram is *Desyr*) . . . is thought by some to have beene invented and made by *Eve*, and afterwards practised by *Cain*, who by the making of it in the time of his vagrancy, got a very competent estate.'[47]

---

[42] Thomas Goddard, *Miscellanea; or, Serious, Useful Considerations, Moral, Historical, Theological* (1661), p. 63.

[43] Ibid., p. 62.

[44] Heywood, *Philocothonista*, p. 80.

[45] *A looking glasse for drunkards: or, The hunting of drunkennesse. Wherein drunkards are unmasked to the view of the world. Very conuenient and usefull for all people to ruminate on in this drunken Age* (1627), sig. A2v.

[46] *A Warning-piece to All Drunkards and Health-Drinkers: Faithfully Collected from the Works of English and Foreign Learned Authors of good Esteem, Mr. Samuel Ward and Mr. Samuel Clark, and Others. With Above one Hundred and twenty sad and dreadful Examples of Gods severe Judgements upon notorious Drunkards* (1682), sig. A2v.

[47] John Taylor, *Drinke and welcome: or The famous historie of the most part of Drinks, in use now in the Kingdomes of Great Brittaine and Ireland; with an especial declaration of the potency, vertue,*

But this attempt to condemn drunkenness through expositions of its seductive power creates a problem for these texts. I began this chapter by noting how Darby's poem attempts to introduce some critical distance between narrator and subject: while describing drunkenness, the narrator is at pains to stress his disengagement from a world that is variously described as disordered, bestial, demonic, murderous ('Think, each of you this day has kil'd a Man, / Stabbing, with Murd'rous Hand, / That noble Reason, by which Mortals are / Most like their Maker').[48] Texts that emphasise the seductive power of drink are forced into an even more compromising position. In order to alert readers to the dangers of drunkenness, authors emphasise the ensnaring seductive potential of alcohol, stressing that drink 'is a most bewitching sinne, and being once entred into, hard to forgoe'.[49] But to undertake this convincingly – to assert the real danger of drink – these texts must come close to exhibiting a delight in the subject being denounced. Just as every act of condemnation has to declare the strength and presence of that which is being condemned – and so, by extension, has to *foster* it – anti-drinking texts exhibit a complicating reverence for their subject.[50] George Gascoigne wittily and self-referentially glances at this fear: among the various social types who might be transformed by drink is 'the skylfullest wryter'.[51]

Within texts that describe drink as seductive, particular vituperation is directed towards those who seduce the previously sober, aiming 'to turne others into *beasts*' by drink: such individuals are 'another *Absalom*, who made a feast for *Amnon* whom he meant to kill'.[52] Richard Younge's *The Blemish of Government* (1656) is characteristic in its denunciation of drinkers who recruit potential accomplices in gradual stages, using toasts like 'a *pulley*, or *shooing-horn* to draw men on to drinke more':

> they will winde men in, and draw men on by drinking first a health to such a *man*, then to such a *woman* my *mistris*, then to every ones *mistris*; then to some *Lord* or *Ladie*; their *master*, their *magistrate*, their *Captain, Commander*, &c. and never cease, until their *brains*, their *wits*, their *tongues*, their *eies*, their *feet*, their *sences* & all their *members* fail them: that they will drink until they *vomit up their shame* again, like a *filthie dog*, or *lie wallowing* in their beastlinesse like a *brutish swine*.[53]

---

and operation of our English ALE . . . Compiled first in the high Dutch tongue, by the painefull and industrious Huldricke Van Speagle, a Grammaticall Brewer of Lubeck, and now most Learnedly enlarged, amplified, and Translated into English Prose and Verse (1637), sig. A2v.

[48] Darby, *Bacchanalia*, 'Epilogue', sig. D2v.

[49] Young, *Bane*, sig. Ev.

[50] A comparable notion of the dynamic between authority and rebellion is considered by Stephen Greenblatt in 'Invisible Bullets: Renaissance authority and its subversion, *Henry IV* and *Henry V*', in Jonathan Dollimore and Alan Sinfield (eds), *Political Shakespeare: New Essays in Cultural Materialism* (Manchester: Manchester University Press, 1985), pp. 18–47.

[51] Gascoigne, *Diet*, p. 6.

[52] Younge, *Blemish*, pp. 4–5.

[53] Ibid., p. 4. Philpot, *A prospective-glasse for gamesters* is similarly alarmed at the piecemeal

By depicting drunkenness as 'a most contagious sinne', and by noting that 'commonly, one drunkard infecteth another', Heywood's *Philocothonista* presents a similar warning of the powers of the seducer.[54] *A looking glasse for drunkards* is more forceful still – the person who 'giveth his neighbour drinke, that putteth the bottle to him, maketh him drunken' is worthy of the most complete denunciation:

> oh miserable and deflowered estate of all those accursed wretches that compel others to be the very vassailes of the devill, by forcing them to the most beastly and accursed sinne of drunkennesse. Woe, woe unto them, whosoever they be.[55]

Part of the reason for the vehemence of these denunciations is surely that these texts themselves become – or almost become – forces of seduction: like drunkards who spread corruption by 'draw[ing] men on to drinke more', texts such as *A looking glasse for drunkards* and *The Blemish of Government* portray the charms of drink, and, as a result, become instances of the seduction process being denounced. When the former text condemns the process of seduction that operates through any 'means whatsoever',[56] we might read this as self-implication. These anti-drinks texts exhibit an instability at the heart of their condemnations as they teeter on the edge of celebration. Remember Cotton's anxious, unconvincing plea: 'Mistake me not, it is not my intention to make Gamesters by this Collection, but to inform all in part how to avoid being cheated by them.'[57]

Thus far my discussion has considered texts that denounce drinking: Charles Darby's *Bacchanalia*; Richard Younge's *The Blemish of Government*; Thomas Heywood's *Philocothonista*; and others. But there were, of course, endorsements of drunkenness, too. Mention has been made of the Sons of Ben, and of mid-century royalist poets – two groups that celebrated drunkenness. I would now like to examine one rather different text – a text that aims for the same kind of reader as did many of the condemnations already discussed – to investigate how it constructed drinking and drunkenness as a legitimate pursuit. In the face of the accusations I have described – that drink robs men of language, renders them beasts, disrupts social hierarchies – how did this text

---

seduction of 'many young-men of good education [who] being sent from their parents in severall countries hither to gain a trade or way of living, have by sundry provocations been by little and little drawne to this vice, which having once used, they have found so much sweetnesse in this *dulce venenum*, that they have not left sucking this poysonous bait, till they have thereby brought themselves to much poverty, penury, want and misery, besides the consideration of the unbecommingnesse of so sensuall a vice in such sad and distracted times' (sig. A2–A2v).

54 Heywood, *Philocothonista*, p. 80.
55 *A looking glasse for drunkards*, sig. A7v.
56 Ibid., sig. A8v.
57 Cotton, *Gamester*, sig. A6v.

endorse and even celebrate drinking and drinkers? How did this text write about drunkenness?

John Cotgrave's *Wits Interpreter* (1655, 1662, 1671) is a printed miscellany of poems, dialogues, exemplary letters, proverbs and witticisms. Presenting itself as a socially educative guide book, *Wits Interpreter* claims to offer readers the chance to enjoy the graces that 'compleat our English *Gentry*', and includes sections detailing 'The Art of Reasoning, A New Logick'; 'Accurate Complements'; 'New Experiements and Inventions'; 'Letters A la mode'; and 'Cardinal Richeleiu's Key to his manner of writing of Letters by Cyphers'.[58] It was a widely read, thrice-republished collection, and represents one of the most well-known examples of the increasingly popular printed miscellany form.[59] Within this educative context, Cotgrave's book includes a lengthy discussion of drinking and drinking habits entitled 'Bacchus his Schoole, wherein he teaches the Art of Drinking, by a most learned Method'.[60] Through this discussion, Cotgrave's miscellany attempts to describe a drinking community – a community who might, in Darby's words, 'Celebrate, / In Evening late, / The *Bacchanalian* Solemnity'[61] – but with none of the negative connotations displayed in the texts examined so far.

In *Wits Interpreter*, drinking is not an anarchic pursuit. 'Bacchus his Schoole' presents readers with a studied and complex explanation of 'the art of drinking', or what Cotgrave's text terms 'The eighth liberal Science'. The most striking feature of this exposition is the attention paid to ritual and decorum and the very precise procedures necessary for drinking to occur. Included in the account is a lengthy prose section titled, rather intimidatingly, 'Customes to be observ'd', which proclaims in unequivocal, almost belligerent prose, a litany of drinking etiquettes:

> Not to drink to any man, if a woman be in presence. Not to drink to the Tapster or Drawer, upon pain of drinking twice. To keep the first man, and to know to whom you drink. To have a care to see your selfe pledg'd. . . [To] see the health go round.[62]

And on it goes, with a dizzying list of decorums. The effect of these and similar prescriptions is to construct drinking as arcane and difficult. Rather than bringing any sense of clarity to these modes of consumption, such

---

[58] *Wits Interpreter* (1655), title-page.

[59] For printed miscellanies, see my *Profit and Delight: Printed Miscellanies in England, 1640–1682* (Detroit: Wayne State University Press, 2004).

[60] *Wits Interpreter* (1671), pp. 329–38. Unless otherwise noted, I quote from this third edition. The discussion of drink appears in a slightly altered form in Heywood's *Philocothonista* (1635), pp. 51–65. 'Bacchus his Schoole' is clearly related to texts in the *Trinkliteratur* tradition such as Richard Brathwaite's *A Solemne Ioviall Disputation, Theoreticke and Practicke; briefly shadowing the Law of Drinking* (1617), discussed by Michelle O'Callaghan, above.

[61] Darby, *Bacchanalia*, sig. A2.

[62] *Wits Interpreter*, p. 337.

'explanations' construct drinking as a complex and opaque process, beyond the comprehension of the uninitiated; they suggest endless other, intricate rules, forever unexplained. Thus while denunciations of drink were exercised with the connection between drinking and a loss of reason – drinking 'extinguisheth the memory, opinion and understanding . . . [and the drinker] can neither stand nor speake'[63] – *Wits Interpreter* argues the very opposite: a precise comprehension of complex rules was a necessary condition for drinking to occur. Far from being obscured by drink, reason in fact enabled heavy drinking.[64]

The drinking community constructed in *Wits Interpreter* is a community built around notions of hierarchy. The text abounds with rankings and social ladders, which, the reader is told, must be respected and maintained. The text lists 'Titles proper to the young Schollars of Bacchus', and describes how the physical condition of the drinker indicates the degree of competence in drinking: 'A fat corpulent fellow, [is] a *Master of Arts*. A lean drunkard, a *Bachelour*. He that hath a purple face enchac'd with rubies, a *Bachelour* of *Law*.' The behaviour of drinkers is similarly categorised and ordered: the drinker who 'laughs and talks much' is considered a student of 'Natural Philosophy'; the drinker 'that gives good Counsel' is a student of 'Morality'; 'He that builds Castles in the air, Metaphysics'; 'He that sings in his drink, Music'; 'He that brags of his Travels, Cosmography'; 'He that rimes extempore, or speaks play-speeches[,] Poetry'; 'He that proves his Argument by a Pamphlet, or a Ballad, a Grammarian'; 'He that knocks his head against a post, then looks up to the sky, an Astronomer.'[65] A similar attention to hierarchy characterises discussions of types of drink. Particular kinds of alcohol are linked with particular nations: to study the English tongue, the text reveals, one must drink beer; to study Dutch, ale; Spanish, sack; Italian, Bastard; German, Rhenish; Irish, Usquebagh; Welsh, Metheglin; Latin, Allicant; Greek, Muscadel; and Hebrew, Hypocras. There are even careful hierarchies for drinking vessels: distinctions are drawn between 'The Tankard', 'The black Jack', and 'The quart pot rib'd'.[66]

William Harrison's discussion 'Of Food and Diet of the English', in *The Description of England*, argues that ritualisation is socially stratified. While the nobility and gentry follow careful rules about when, how and what they eat and drink, 'the poorest sort . . . generally dine and sup when they may, so that

---

63 Young, *Bane*, sig. D.
64 This tendency to prescribe precise rituals for consumption is ridiculed in John Grove's *Wine, Beer, Ale, and Tobacco, Contending for Superiority. A Dialogue* (1658), where a personifed Ale describes the various stages in the militarised ritual of smoking: '1 Take you seal. 2 Draw your box. 3 Uncase your pipe. 4 Produce your Rammer. 5 Blow your Pipe. 6 Open your box. 7 Fill your pipe. 8 Ramme your pipe . . . 14 Mouth your pipe. 15 Give fire . . . 17 Puffe your smoke . . . 19 Throw off your loose ashes. 20 Present to your friend. 21 As you were . . .' (sig. C3).
65 *Wits Interpreter*, p. 330.
66 Ibid., p. 329.

to talk of their order of repast it were but a needless matter'.[67] Apparently sharing this assumption of a correlation between ritual and social eminence, Cotgrave's account of drinking seeks legitimacy through its precise litany of etiquettes and orders. Condemnations of drinking describe a world where social hierarchies are destroyed and notions of 'Race, or Pedigree'[68] are obscured. *Wits Interpreter* responds to just these perceptions with its sustained emphasis on rank and order.

In turn, texts attacking drink vehemently objected to the sense of legitimacy generated by discussions of drinking as an ordered, ritualised process. The puritan and parliamentarian Robert Harris (1581–1658), President of Trinity College, Oxford, used his sermon 'The Drunkards Cup' to criticise texts like *Wits Interpreter* for pursuing a false legitimacy through an emphasis on rules and hierarchies. The notion of drinking as an organised, regulated 'Science' or 'Art' proves particularly vexing for Harris:

> There is (they say) an Art of drinking now, and in the World it is become a great procession; there are degrees and titles given under the name of Roaring boyes, damned crew, &c. there are lawes and ceremonies to be observed, both by the firsts and seconds, &c. there is a drinking by the foot, by the yard, &c. on the die, on the knee &c. a drinking by the douzens, by the scores, &c. for the wager, for the victory, man against man, House against House, Town against Town, and how not.[69]

Even here Harris carefully distances himself from his subject, relying on the words of others: '*they say*', he notes, there is 'an Art of drinking now'.

As part of this construction of drinking as an ordered, rule-bound activity, *Wits Interpreter* prescribes the various terms that might be used to describe fellow drinkers. Instead of using the word 'drunkard', a number of alternatives are permitted:

> No man ought to call a good fellow Drunkard. But if any time he sees any defect in his neighbour, he may without a forfeit say, he is fox'd, he is flaw'd, fluster'd, cupshot, cut in the leg or back, he hath seen the French King, he hath swallowed a Hare, or a Tavern token, he hath whipt the Cat, he makes Indentures, he hath bit his Grannam, he is bit by a barn Weesel; with many such like.[70]

In *Philocothonista*, Heywood similarly notes the great number of terms that the English language offers in place of 'drunkard'. In terms of drinking, 'wee [the English] apparently exceede . . . [other nations] in all things', and 'whereas other languages afford but some few wordes' for the drunk, English offers a great litany. The drunkard

---

67 William Harrison, *The Description of England*, ed. Georges Edelen (Washington, DC & New York: The Folger Shakespeare Library and Dover Publications, 1994), p. 144.

68 Darby, *Bacchanalia*, sig. A2v.

69 Harris, 'The Drunkards Cup', p. 284.

70 *Wits Interpreter*, p. 334.

is a good fellow, Or, A boone Companion, A mad Greeke, A true Trojan, A stiffe Blade, One that is steel to the backe, A sound Card, . . . A Low-Countrey Souldier, One that will take his rowse, One that will drinke deepe, though it bee a mile to the bottome, One that knowes how the Cards are dealt, One that will be flush of all foure, One that will be subtile as a Fox, One that will drinke till the ground lookes blew, One that will wynde up his bottome, One that beares up stiffe, One whose nose it durty, One whom the Brewers horse hath bit, One that can relish all waters, One that knowes of which side his bread is butter'd, One that drinkes upse-freeze, One that drinkes supernaculum, . . . One that can up off his Side, &c.[71]

The list, significantly, concludes with an ampersand: an end that suggests no end – like the eternal drinker, 'disgorg[ing] at pleasure'.[72] Heywood notes that the term 'drunkard' is never employed: it is 'so grosse and harsh' a name, while the above list of alternatives – 'A true Trojan'; 'One whom the Brewers horse hath bit' – are 'more mincing and modest'.[73]

Wits Interpreter's insistence on phrases like the magnificent 'bit by a barn Weesel' is in part an attempt to avoid the discrediting connotations that surround the word 'drunkard'. But *Wits Interpreter* is also confronting that fear, articulated in anti-drink texts, that drink leads inexorably to a loss of control over language. In place of the drinker who 'belcheth forth nothing',[74] *Wits Interpreter* presents the drinker with his very own vocabulary. By stressing the many words that are particular to the drunkard's speech, *Wits Interpreter* shows not only that drinking is literally part of English culture, embedded in the language; it also constructs a drunkard's discourse that is lexically rich and, rather than being disordered, subject to very particular rules ('No man ought to call a good fellow Drunkard'). Rather than drink leading to a 'grouelling on the earth speechlesse',[75] drinking and words – precise, regulated words – depend upon each other.

This creation of an alternative drinking discourse, in particular, angered critics. In 'The Drunkards Cup', Robert Harris objects to the variety of terms 'fetched from Hell' used to describe the state of drunkenness:

> one is coloured, another is foxt, a third is gone to the dogs, a fourth is well to live, &c. but none is drunken; that is as odious here, as Adultery in that state wherein no body was chaste.[76]

What angers Harris is that the state of being drunk, through this lexical shuffling, evades its properly shaming name, and escapes a rightful moral condemnation.

---

[71] Heywood, *Philocothonista*, pp. 43–5.
[72] Younge, *Blemish*, p. 2.
[73] Heywood, *Philocothonista*, p. 44.
[74] Younge, *Blemish*, p. 6.
[75] Young, *Bane*, sig. A4v.
[76] Harris, 'The Drunkards Cup', p. 284.

However, just as condemnations of drunkenness are unstable texts, always close to celebrating the subject they denounce, so the effort of *Wits Interpreter* to find a legitimate way of writing about drink is similarly frail and self-subverting. *Wits Interpreter* attempts to present a drinking community by confronting common criticisms of drink – in particular, the associations of drink with a loss of reason and words, and with an absence of social order and hierarchy. Thus the drinking world of *Wits Interpreter* is characterised by careful speech, order, rationality and hierarchy; by social rankings, laws, orders, titles, rituals, vocabularies, regulatory punishments.

But the problem here is the constant threat of collapse into the drinking world *Wits Interpreter* attempts to resist. The careful articulation of rules and rituals draws attention to the potential absence of rules and rituals; the detailed discourse raises the prospect of disordered speech. And in the cracks between artful drinking etiquettes, disorder, bestial transformation and wordlessness can be glimpsed.

This threat of collapse is particularly vivid when *Wits Interpreter* considers its likely audience. As we have seen, the book's culture of drink is predicated on ideas of ritual, difficulty and exclusivity; yet the book offers to transfer this coterie culture to the anonymous popular reader. *Wits Interpreter* does not simply depict an exclusive, ritualised drinking community: it encourages readers to employ the patterns of behaviour on display. As a result, the book is caught between two conflicting modes: on the one hand it depicts an exclusivity built upon rituals, the careful maintenance of hierarchies, and the inclusion of only the initiated; but at the same time it offers this world to anyone who will part with a few pennies. The exclusive is available to everyone. The material form of *Wits Interpreter* betrays this tension: while the text's preface conveys a sense of the arcane and the exclusive, the book is small, cheap, printed, available to all.

This is a tension to which *Wits Interpreter* is alert. As the book's prefaces lurch between celebrating the opening up of the previously secret and denouncing the idea that the non-elite might read its secrets, Cotgrave pours particular scorn on the notion that 'the *Chambermaid* . . . may be easily completed with *offensive* and *defensive terms* of *Language*, so to manage her *Wit* as if she were at a *prize*'.[77] But Cotgrave's angry scorn cannot extricate him from his book's central paradox: *Wits Interpreter* is celebrating a culture of restricted access and hierarchies by flinging open the doors that preserve it. The book's ordered, ritualised drinking community is threatened with collapse by this imminent moment of transfer.

Writing about drink consistently presents difficulties, both for texts that condemn and texts that endorse a culture of drink and drunkenness. Condemnations of drunkenness, in order to prove their seriousness and significance, seek to portray vividly not only the destructive consequences of drunkenness,

---

[77] *Wits Interpreter*, sigs A3v–5.

but also its seductive allure. As a result, these condemnations teeter on the edge of celebration and so illustrate the necessary and destabilising proximity of censure to encomium. *Wits Interpreter* is similarly frail: descriptions of elite, exclusive drinking communities are necessarily dependent on evocations of a chaotic other, and the promised transfer of an ordered and hierarchical community to a popular readership makes this other appear imminent.

A *looking glasse for drunkards* (1627) can stand as a final example of a text perilously close to collapsing into the state it condemns. *A looking glasse* invokes extracts from the Bible in order to expose 'drunkards . . . to the view of the world', and to cause 'all people to ruminate . . . in this drunken Age'.[78] Its arguments are familiar: drunkenness is not only a sin, but a sin that 'maketh a man a beast' – a 'swine [or] . . . a goose'.[79] And, like many condemnations of drink, *A looking glasse* asserts with particular force the perceived link between drunkenness and a loss of control over language: drink 'causeth an ill behaviour in words'; not only 'abominable and fearfull swearing and cursing', but also a general state of lexical anarchy.[80] But when *A looking glasse* draws to a conclusion, the prose – previously precise and regular, and characterised by numbered lists and marginal references – begins to lose control, and unravel.

> Oh that all the revell rout of beastly drunkards, would seriously thinke of this, before they be hurryed by devils into hell, where their bed shall bee a red hot gridyron, legions of damned ghosts your best sights your dyet shall bee griping hunger, and famine intollerable there your drink shall be lakes of fire and brimstone, your musicke shall be howling and weeping, and gnashing of teeth, in the company of devils for evermore.[81]

Punctuation slackens; the rhetoric becomes less controlled; substantiating Biblical citations are dropped; and the careful enumeration of causes and consequences is abandoned. The prose becomes rowdy, fervent, unbalanced. Not quite drunk, perhaps – but certainly intriguingly close to the state of intoxication being condemned.

---

[78] *A looking glasse for drunkards*, title-page.
[79] Ibid., sigs A5, B2v.
[80] Ibid., sig. A5.
[81] Ibid., sig. B4.

INDEX

Studies in Renaissance Literature